P9-DUK-532

5 1404 00818 7798

ANGLICAN
APPROACHES TO
SCRIPTURE

MAY 1 0 2007

ANGLICAN
APPROACHES TO
SCRIPTURE

FROM THE REFORMATION
TO THE PRESENT

ROWAN A. GREER

A Herder & Herder Book
The Crossroad Publishing Company
New York

The Crossroad Publishing Company
16 Penn Plaza – 481 Eighth Avenue, Suite 1550
New York, NY 10001

Copyright © 2006 by Rowan A. Greer

All rights reserved. No part of this book may be reproduced, stored in a retrieval system, or transmitted, in any form or by any means, electronic, mechanical, photocopying, recording, or otherwise, without the written permission of The Crossroad Publishing Company.

Printed in the United States of America

The text of this book is set in 11/15.5 Sabon.
The display face is Goudy Sans.

Library of Congress Cataloging-in-Publication Data

Greer, Rowan A.
    Anglican approaches to Scripture : from the Reformation to the present / Rowan A. Greer.
        p. cm.
    "A Herder & Herder book."
    Includes bibliographical references and index.
    ISBN-10: 0-8245-2368-7 (alk. paper)
    ISBN-13: 978-0-8245-2368-8
    1. Bible – Criticism, interpretation, etc. – History. 2. Anglican Communion – Doctrines.   I. Title.
    BS500.G74 2006
    220.088′283 – dc22
                                                                2006006251

1 2 3 4 5 6 7 8 9 10   12 11 10 09 08 07 06

Contents

Acknowledgments

My first and foremost debt is to the dean and faculty of the General Theological Seminary, who kindly invited me to deliver the Paddock Lectures in October of 2003. I remain grateful to Dean Ward Ewing and Dean Bruce Mullin for their hospitality and to the students of the General Seminary for their courteous attention. This small book is an elaboration of those Paddock Lectures. Marilyn Adams and Stanley Hauerwas read the first draft of the lectures and gave me helpful suggestions. It is to Cynthia Shattuck that I owe the encouragement to turn the lectures into a book. With some diffidence I asked Brevard Childs to read the resulting manuscript, a task he performed with his characteristic kindness and generosity. It was largely because of his support that I decided publication might be possible. Last but not least I am entirely grateful to John Jones of Crossroad, not only for his encouragement regarding this project, but also for his support over many years. The book attempts to underline the complexities and difficulties that attach to understanding scripture and its authority not merely for Anglicans but for all Christians. But it is my hope that it will suggest positive ways forward. The ancient rabbis said that just as the grit in the oyster is what makes the pearls, so the difficulties in scripture are what produce the pearls of exegesis. Attending to them is a way of digging ever more deeply into the mysteries of God's word.

A Foreword Written Afterwards

"Let the jury consider their verdict," the King said, for about the twentieth time that day.

"No, no!" said the Queen. "Sentence first — verdict afterwards."

"Stuff and nonsense!" said Alice loudly. "The idea of having the sentence first!"

"Hold your tongue!" said the Queen, turning purple.

"I won't!" said Alice.

"Off with her head!" the Queen shouted at the top of her voice. Nobody moved.

— *Alice's Adventures in Wonderland*

It may well be that I am agreeing with the queen rather than with Alice by placing in this foreword themes that will become clear only in the essays that follow. But far from chopping heads, my aim is to say something about what the essays seek to do and what they do not pretend to be. The second point may be the more important one. It has been neither within my competence nor within my interest to master the vast literature related to Anglican attitudes toward scripture. Instead my purpose has been to sample some of the more important evidence from the English Reformation to the later years of the twentieth century. Moreover, I have confined my attention not only to England but also to the writings of the leaders and scholars of the Church of England. It is my hope that this will shed some light on more popular attitudes and on the issues as they are and have been posed in this country, as well as on the broader question of the place of the Bible in Christianity as a whole. But that hope by no means represents any claim for what I have sought to do. Moreover, I have largely avoided the controversies that are exercising the imagination of the Episcopal Church and other Christian denominations at this time. My aim has been far more modest and has been limited to trying to describe and assess the samples of evidence I have collected. The only true thesis to emerge from the discussions that follow is a double one. Negatively, there is no single approach to scripture in Anglicanism, just as there is no single understanding of what Anglicans have believed and taught. Positively, however, the Bible has managed to keep a place in Anglicanism, no matter how differently that place has been construed. I should regard this as the capacity of scripture to resist all the attempts made to tame it by making it the mouthpiece for one or another religious and theological party platform. It is in this sense that the Bible, to use Sir Thomas Browne's phrase, is "too hard for the teeth of time."

The Sufficiency of Scripture

Despite this rather limited thesis the discussions that follow do revolve around a number of themes that have to do with the function of scripture and the various tools that have been employed for interpreting it. To speak first of the Bible's function, it has seemed to me that if we allow for a fairly broad interpretation of it, Anglican approaches have tended to honor the Sixth Article of Religion: "Of the Sufficiency of the Holy Scriptures for Salvation." The article states that scripture "containeth all things necessary to salvation: so that whatsoever is not read therein, nor may be proved thereby, is not to be required of any man, that it should be believed as an article of the Faith, or be thought requisite or necessary to salvation." The article continues by listing the canonical books of scripture, and it includes the Old Testament Apocrypha as books the church reads "for example of life and instruction of manners; but yet doth it not apply them to establish any doctrine."[1] Of course, it is not clear that the Thirty-Nine Articles have binding authority. Not all Anglican churches have adopted them, and the 1979 Prayer Book includes them as "Historical Documents" and so leaves their authority ambiguous. Consequently, it might be more cautious to say that Anglican views tend to honor Article Six by at least refusing to dispense with the Christian Bible.

Article Six, however, does imply several points worth noting. The function of scripture to contain all things necessary to salvation must surely mean that its chief purpose is to form Christians and to guide them toward the destiny prepared for them by God and revealed to them through Christ. While it is probably impossible to argue that scripture cannot be used to resolve religious controversy, this would not appear to be its chief purpose. A second implication has to do with matters that are *not* necessary to salvation. In other words, we cannot expect scripture to reveal everything. The Bible is not omni-competent, and a good argument can be made for Hooker's insistence that the English Reformers had no wish to substitute a biblical infal-libility for an ecclesiastical one. To be sure, Hooker regards scripture itself as infallible; but he surely wants to recognize the fallibility of our attempts to understand it. None of this means that the Bible is incapable of speaking to us in matters of indifference, only that as we move away from what is necessary to salvation or away from what will come to be called the "essence" of Christianity and scripture, we must be less confident that we are in fact hearing the voice of the Bible.

Not everyone would grant the points I have just made, and it is obvious that the Bible has been used to resolve controversy and to address issues that do not directly affect what is necessary or es-sential to Christian faith and practice. But this is really a way of showing that the conviction of scripture's sufficiency for revealing what is necessary to salvation papers over a central difficulty. The distinction between what is necessary and what is a matter of indif-ference, made by Luther and accepted by the English Reformers, fails to tell us how we are to ascertain the difference between the two. It would seem true that religious and theological interpretations of scripture always give pride of place to part of the Bible, whether we are to think of particular passages, aspects, themes, or patterns. Not all interpreters would think of this as a quest for what is necessary to salvation or for what is essential. But we obviously encounter quite differing construals of scripture. It does not seem to me necessary to conclude that interpreters simply read their own presuppositions and prejudices into the Bible. Careful interpreters will respect the text, including those passages that present difficulties to them. And they will beware of hearing in scripture no more than the echo of their own voices. Nevertheless, presuppositions and prejudices have a shaping effect upon their approaches.

It is in this way that presuppositions tend to affect what is regarded as necessary or essential. For example, in the sixteenth and early seventeenth centuries the question that dominated religious sensibility was how to attain salvation. In the West the doctrine of the atonement held central importance. Put as simply as possible, Christ's death on the cross established the possibility of the forgiveness of sin and of a reconciliation with God to be perfected in heaven after death. While there were differing ways of articulating this belief, there was no real disagreement between Roman Catholics and Protestants regarding it. The argument revolved around *how* the possibility established by Christ was to be actualized for the believer. The Roman view, of course, saw this as something accomplished by the church and the sacraments, and particularly by the penitential system. Protestants, however, located the actualization of salvation primarily in justification by faith. This created puzzles and problems partly because Luther, Calvin, and the English Reformers kept the church and at least the dominical sacraments in place and partly because there came to be a number of different ways of understanding justification in its relation to God's eternal purposes and to the holy living meant to follow justification. There were questions. What is the relation of infant baptism to justification by grace through faith? Are those justified to be identified as God's predestined saints? Is faith entirely and absolutely the free gift of God's sovereign grace?

The picture can be complicated in another way. If we grant that the key to what is necessary or essential in the Bible is its message of salvation, is it necessary to think of that message in terms of the Western doctrine of the atonement? Michael Ramsey has argued that the period in the Church of England from the publication of *Lux*

Mundi in 1889 to the beginning of the Second World War was an era dominated by an incarnational theology.[2] The equation of the gift of salvation with Christ's death on the cross became problematic for theologians like Maurice, Jowett, and Gore largely because of the popular preaching of the atonement. Though an argument for this preaching from scripture was often made, Maurice and others argued that it was unscriptural. The popular view saw Christ's death as reconciling God to us, whereas St. Paul says that "in Christ God was reconciling the world to himself" (2 Cor 5:19). It also spoke of the forgiveness of sins rather than of "the removal of sin" (Heb 9:26). And, finally, it interpreted Christ as the one who died *instead of us* rather than *on our behalf*, as the New Testament consistently puts it. There were, then, scriptural arguments for the move to an incarnational view of salvation that understood incorporation into Christ's humanity as a participation in the christological union of his humanity with his divinity. The incarnational understanding of salvation also tended to treat Christ's death and resurrection as the climax of his incarnate life. Whereas the atonement treated the story of salvation as the solution by Christ's death of the problem posed by the Fall and original sin, the incarnational view saw in Christ the completion and perfection of creation. The reversal of the fall was no longer an end in itself, but a means toward the fulfillment of God's creative purpose.

> Careful interpreters will respect the text, and they will beware of hearing in scripture no more than the echo of their own voices.

It is possible to discern these two rather different ways of telling the Christian story in the eucharistic prayers of the 1979 Prayer Book. Prayer I comes close to defining salvation as the forgiveness of sins, and it understands the way salvation has been accomplished as focused rather narrowly on Christ's death on the cross. The implied story is one of paradise lost in Adam and restored in Christ's cross. In contrast, Prayer B has a far wider understanding of salvation. In Christ God has "delivered us from evil, and made us worthy to stand before him." This involves not only a passage from "sin into righteousness," but also one "out of error into truth" and "out of death into life." Moreover, if we ask how God has effected salvation in these senses, the answer is not merely by Christ's death, but by the whole of his incarnate life, culminating in his death *and resurrection* — and not only that, but by God's work in creation, in the "calling of Israel," and in his "Word spoken through the prophets." The story, then, treats creation and redemption as two aspects of the same evolutionary process. And it correlates better with the sensibility of the early church before Augustine and with Eastern views to this day than with the Western development.

The point of what I have said is that even if we grant that what is necessary or essential in scripture is its message of salvation, there are differing ways of articulating that message that can be regarded as equally valid. But another consideration comes into play. Whether we think of the story of salvation as the recovery of Eden or as the progress from innocence to experience, what are we to say about the moral demand the story makes upon those who accept it? Granted that the promise of the gospel carries with it a demand, how are we to understand that demand and what is its relation to the promise? Neither of these questions is easy to answer. The Christian churches have specified the demands down through the ages in what can scarcely be called a consistent fashion, and it is obvious that changing social mores have affected judgments about issues such as war, slavery, divorce, and attitudes toward outsiders and especially Jews. It becomes somewhat difficult to discern what forms of behavior are necessary for salvation. Turning to this second question, Anglicans have defined the relation of promise to demand by various understandings of grace. In the sixteenth century an Augustinian understanding of grace as sovereign tended to prevail. Sinners, quite apart from any merit or any capacity to save themselves by responding to God's call, received justifying grace without in any sense deserving it. And it was this sovereign grace, mysteriously selective, that supplied the motive and basis for the holy living that characterized God's demand.

It was largely the antinomian implications of this view that called it into question. If all people were born irrevocably doomed and incapable of good, and if they were obliged to wait for God's inexplicable and selective sovereign act, two reactions were natural — despair or living a life without moral restraints. The emphasis upon holy living in seventeenth-century Anglicanism is surely a response not only to the religious civil warfare that took place but also to these problems, which were pastoral in character. Some divines, like Richard Baxter, introduced holy living as in some degree necessary before justification by modifying the usual Protestant framework and by speaking of the contrast between a covenant of works and a covenant of grace. Because of Adam's Fall works can no longer bring salvation, but through Christ God established the covenant of grace in which justification becomes God's reckoning of our insufficient righteousness as though it were sufficient. God gives sinners the benefit of the doubt, provided they have some measure of righteousness to show and are willing to repent and turn to Christ in faith. The view that gradually dominated the Restoration church, however, tended to abandon the usual Protestant view of grace as sovereign and to treat grace as a gift that depended for its proper effect upon its right use. Moreover, this grace was to be found not primarily in the experience of conversion but ordinarily in baptism and the sacramental life of the church. It is important to add that this repudiation of grace as God's sovereign act on the part of writers like Jeremy Taylor and William Law cannot be construed as a Pelagian denial of grace. Instead, I should argue that it represents a return to the view that dominated the early church apart from Augustine. Grace and the human capacity to choose the good belong together, operating simultaneously at different levels. Grace is really the love of God and represents the larger context in which humans make their choices. And love can never compel.

Shifting attention to the moral choices Christians make leads to yet another way of understanding what scripture contains as necessary to salvation. The latitudinarians of the late seventeenth and eighteenth centuries thought that what was most important in scripture was its republication of natural religion. It would be necessary to qualify the point, but their tendency was to reduce the scriptural message to a set of duties that could also be discerned apart from scripture. Salvation, then, becomes the reward for those who live their lives by these duties; and it even becomes primarily a sanction for those duties. Such a view by no means perished with the eighteenth century and has survived in American evangelical Protestantism in a great many different ways.[3] If for no other reason, the point sticks because the controversies that bedevil the churches in our time all revolve around moral issues. Some of them, like those that involve human sexuality, abortion, and medical ethics, have to do with personal morality; others involve social and economic issues. But it seems reasonable to ask whether this means that scripture must be reduced to its moral meaning and that it is only that meaning that is somehow necessary to salvation, whether in this world or — it may be hoped — in a world to come.

Interpreting Scripture

Granted that scripture contains all things necessary to salvation or, to put the point the other way, contains the essence of Christianity, it is obvious that this can mean a great many different things and can find articulation in a wide range of theological positions. It is equally obvious that this happens only because of differing interpretations of the same Bible. Scripture, then, must be interpreted. Even those who claim that the plain passages in scripture interpret themselves have in fact engaged in an interpretive task by deciding what those plain passages are. The essays that follow will describe a number of interpretive tools that Anglicans have employed in their approach to scripture, but I shall argue that these tools are not used in a single consistent way, nor do they mean the same thing to different writers. Consequently, I shall want to place a large question mark after the common assumption that scripture, reason, and tradition represent the triple cord or the three-legged stool at the heart of Anglicanism. Bishop McAdoo's cautious formulation of the idea is worth citing as a point of departure for my discussion:

> It does not follow from the word "spirit" that what is implied is something indeterminate, an attitude loosely defined, for the spirit of Anglicanism is something real and ponderable expressing itself by a specific theological method. This method, varying its stress according to the demands of different situations, consists in the appeal to Scripture, to antiquity and to reason, and it is not confined to any individuals or groups during the century.[4]

McAdoo's statement is cautious not only because his observation is limited to the seventeenth century, but also because he is speaking of a method rather than of a doctrine, and of a method "varying" in its application.

The value of McAdoo's work is not tied to this idea of a threefold method, nor is that idea employed as a procrustean bed by which to examine seventeenth-century writers. And at least in the cases of Sanderson, Taylor, and Patrick we do see the triple cord at work.[5] Moreover, it is possible to add another rather interesting example. William Laud's conference with Fisher, the Jesuit, took place in 1622, though his *Relation* was not published until 1639. At one point the question arises of how we can know scripture to be the word of God. Laud argues that four arguments are commonly used. Scripture is proved to be scripture from tradition, from scripture itself, from the experienced testimony of the Holy Spirit, and from natural reason. No one of these proofs is demonstrative, and we must appeal to the notion that the first principles of any science cannot be demonstrated but must be assumed a priori. Nevertheless, these four arguments are sufficient because they reinforce one another when we look at them in the context of a person's coming to faith. It is "the authority of the present Church" that persuades him to believe scripture to be the word of God. His study of scripture itself "with the help of ordinary grace and a mind morally induced and reasonably persuaded by the voice of the Church" then enables him to accept scripture for what it claims to be.[6] The church calls attention to scripture, and believers by consulting it through their experience of grace and their use of reason come to understand the church's claim that scripture is the word of God. The "method" involved, however, is not really a theological one so much as one that seeks to understand how scripture functions as a guide to salvation.

My questions about the triple cord begin to appear, and in the first two chapters that follow I shall conclude that the idea is less helpful than might be supposed. I do not want to dismiss it altogether, at least in the careful and limited sense in which McAdoo defines it. Nevertheless, I should want to part company with attempts to generalize the idea and to make it constitutive of Anglicanism. One such attempt is attractive. "Anglicanism may be defined as a way of being Christian that involves *a pastorally and liturgically oriented dialogue between four partners: catholics, evangelicals, and advocates of reason and experience.*"[7] Presumably, the "catholics" speak for tradition; the "evangelicals" for scripture. We now have a quadruple cord or a four-legged stool. But is the implication that all Anglicans will choose one of the four appeals, or that the appeals are to the same sort of authorities?[8] That the differing voices in a dialogue can be treated as authorities has become a common understanding. For example, A. R. Vidler in *Soundings* persuasively argues that the only "unconditional authority" is God himself. "In the long run the authority of the Holy Spirit in the Church is mediated and becomes effective through the interaction of the various elements in its constitution." This means that what is at our disposal is a set of dispersed and secondary authorities, and that their judgments are "to be ascertained from the *consensus fidelium.*" The "elements" involved are scripture, tradition, and reason. "Authority embraces all these elements, and it is through the interaction of them all that the Holy Spirit is guiding the Church into all truth."[9] What might have been the idea that tradition and reason are tools for interpreting scripture has now become not only a method involving the apparent coordination of all three (or four), but also a view of dispersed, secondary, but coordinate principles of authority.

There may be much to be said about voices in a dialogue or dispersed principles of authority, but my concern is with treating reason, tradition, and experience as instruments for interpreting scripture. Here my major difficulty revolves around the many different meanings that have been and can be given to the terms. To take "reason" first, in the following chapters we shall be able to see that it can mean a good many different things. Part of the problem is that writers seldom explain what they mean by reason. Even in the so-called Age of Reason, the eighteenth century, the term is difficult to pin down. In the later seventeenth and early eighteenth centuries writers refer to reason "in adoring terms"; nevertheless, "amidst all this debate and discussion, in which the word 'reason' was never omitted and rarely defined, there were few who questioned its nature, or wondered why so many men, all applying reason to the same problem, found so many different answers."[10] To be sure, the earlier writers such as Hooker, Chillingworth, and Hammond are oriented toward a modified Thomism that includes some view of intuitive knowledge stamped by God on the mind that is not innate but somehow becomes so. At the same time, Chillingworth's emphasis is upon the critical character of reason when making judgments, while Hammond restricts what can be known intuitively by reason to moral issues.

In 1689 John Locke published *An Essay Concerning Human Understanding*. The first book of the *Essay* is a lengthy argument rejecting innate principles of knowledge, both speculative and practical. Book Two treats of ideas, which represent the raw material for the limited knowledge we can have. We receive ideas not only from sense impressions but also from reflection, and we must distinguish simple ideas from complex ones (2.23.37). Locke's argument, of course, is far more detailed, suggestive, and subtle than I am making it seem. After his discussion of "words" in Book Three he turns in the last book to "Knowledge and Opinion." "The knowledge of our own being, we have by intuition. The existence of a God, reason clearly makes known to us, as has been shown. The *knowledge of the existence* of any other thing we can have only by *sensation*" (4.11.1). Demonstrative knowledge, then, seems confined to the knowledge of

God, probably to moral norms, and certainly to mathematics. Other knowledge is probable. Two reactions to Locke's epistemology, one certain and the other possible, are worth mentioning. In 1696 Edward Stillingfleet, the latitudinarian bishop of Worcester and friend of Tillotson, published his *Discourse in Vindication of the Doctrine of the Trinity.* Stillingfleet's primary worry is that Locke has left no room for the Trinity, but he also takes exception to Locke's rejection of innate ideas on the grounds that the argument for God's existence from universal consent would be undermined.[11] It is instructive that latitudinarians such as Stillingfleet, Tillotson, and Burnet insisted upon innate ideas, probably in the form of the Stoic idea of common notions stamped on the blank slate of the mind, notions including belief in God and, as well, the principles of morality. The second case is John Wesley's discussion of reason in *An Earnest Appeal,* to which I shall refer in chapter 3. What Wesley says reflects Locke's argument in part, but his reference to "spiritual" ideas at least drives in the direction of a fideist position.

While the notion that reason represents an intuitive grasp of God's existence and of moral principles is common both to the Thomistic view held in a modified way by Hooker and others and to what I take to be the Stoicizing form it assumes with the latitudinarians, there is a third alternative found in the Cambridge Platonists. Here it is the likeness of the soul to God that determines the meaning of innate ideas or common notions. On the whole, however, an intuitive understanding of reason tends to disappear until its revival in an altered form in the nineteenth century. Coleridge, early in the century, influenced by German idealism, makes a distinction between the understanding and the higher capacity of "reason," which is intuitive in character, while later in the century Charles Gore's idea of faith as "reason in the making" represents a variation on the theme.[12] Much more would need to be said regarding the impact of Kant, Hegel, and German idealism on Anglican understandings of reason in the nineteenth century.[13] But in another sense, if reason tends to become a faculty of judgment in the eighteenth century, with the rise of historical criticism of scripture the judgments involved are a weighing of scripture as evidence for historical reconstructions. My discussion has clearly been only a skimming of the surface and may have even been misleading in part. But my only concern is to argue that "reason" is a very slippery word and scarcely has any simple agreed meaning. Indeed, reason sometimes seems to be no more than common sense, whatever that might be. In any case reason can interpret scripture in many different ways — by making deductions from it, by discerning principles of nature in it, by assessing and judging it as historical evidence. And these may not be the only ways.

"Tradition" is an equally slippery term, but for rather different reasons. In a general way it refers to the faith handed down by the church from generation to generation. In this sense it is possible to appeal to the so-called Vincentian canon — what has been believed by all everywhere and at all times. But this scarcely solves any problems, since there can obviously be no agreement with respect to what should be included in the canon. One approach finds expression in Laud's *Conference with Fisher* and depends upon distinguishing the "apostolic" tradition from the ongoing tradition of the church. Tradition in the second sense has no true authority, but is merely the persuasive force of the community guiding people to the Christian faith. Laud does not say so, but one reason to deny authority to post-apostolic faith would be the recognition that we are obliged to speak of differing churches with differing and even competing understandings of the faith. If we restrict authority to the apostolic faith and argue that it correctly interprets scripture, the problem becomes where do we locate apostolicity. At one extreme it is possible simply to equate the apostolic tradition with scripture itself, though some writers would include as apostolic such practices as infant baptism and features of church order not expressly revealed in scripture. At the other extreme what is "apostolic" would include articulations of the apostles' message represented by the creeds and the decisions of the first four councils. It could be argued that such a view is the implication of the first five Articles of Religion, which appear to accept the dogmas of the Trinity and of Christ's person. This interpretation would not need to be rejected by the assertions of Articles Eight and Twenty-One that restrict the meaning of creeds and councils to what is warranted by scripture. Newman goes still further and is convinced that the entire development of "historical" Christianity is the organic growth of the apostolic faith.

The problem of what tradition means is further complicated by the relationship of the Church of England and Anglicanism to Protestantism and to Roman Catholicism. There can be little doubt that before the Oxford Movement in the early nineteenth century, Anglicans saw themselves as Protestants. Nevertheless, George Herbert's poem "The British Church" describes the "praise and glory" of the Church of England as the golden mean between Geneva and Rome. That is, Anglicans are Protestants but not High Calvinists. It is difficult to ascertain how widespread this idea was, but it is certainly characteristic of the Laudians. On the other hand, many would argue that the Elizabethan church is best described as an episcopal Calvinism and that "Calvinism remained dominant in England throughout the first two decades of the seventeenth century."[14] Yet even those who sought to distance the Church of England from Calvinism saw the middle way as a perspective that treated the church as Protestant, but not Calvinist. The relation of the Church of England to international Protestantism is further complicated by the division between the Reformed and the Lutheran traditions, particularly with respect to their conflicting doctrines of the eucharist. For this reason and others a Protestant "internationale" never found full expression. In Britain the full emergence of the anti-Calvinist Arminians during the reign of Charles I (1625–49) led to the English Revolution (1640–60), but it also set the stage for Restoration Anglicanism.

"Tradition," then, becomes quite complex. There is a real sense in which there are two defining points of departure for Anglicanism, two traditional foundations. An appeal to the sixteenth century and the Elizabethan Settlement yields a tradition that is probably best described as a moderate Calvinism and that is certainly oriented toward justification by faith. On the other hand, appealing to the seventeenth century and to the Restoration settlement of 1662 yields a tradition that underlines the importance of the church, the sacraments, and episcopacy, together with an understanding of grace that usually parts company with the Augustinian tradition. I should want to support this conclusion by pointing out that the evangelical revival of the eighteenth century sought to repristinate the sixteenth-century church, while the Oxford Movement in the nineteenth century quite consciously grounded itself upon the seventeenth century and the assumption that the Caroline divines had remained true to the teaching of the patristic church. Even old-fashioned high church Tories in the early nineteenth century, however, would have regarded their stance as a Protestant one. It was John Henry Newman who subtly changed the picture. In 1837 he published his *Lectures on the Prophetical Office of the Church viewed relatively to Romanism and Popular Protestantism*. In this work he used the term *via media;* but as the title suggests, the middle way is between Rome and Protestantism. The implication is that the Church of England is Catholic, but not Roman Catholic. It is no longer a particular form of Protestantism, but a branch of the Catholic Church.[15] When the Episcopal Church dropped the word "Protestant" from its title, this was a victory for the novel definition of the middle way.

Whether we think of tradition as a tool for interpreting scripture or as a second dispersed but coordinate principle of authority, we are left with the question *whose* tradition, or *what* tradition. The same observation applies to the fourth term often added to the triple cord — experience. It is not even necessary to raise the complicated issues involved in assessing Schleiermacher's thought or his impact on Anglican theology. Some simple considerations will make my point. Are we to think of an individual's experience? Surely this would not suffice, since it would lead to solipsism and at least the possibility that there might be as many human experiences as there are individuals. Presumably, the experience in question must be somehow a shared one. But on some commonly held views there are obvious difficulties. Can we assume that there is a single black experience or a single female experience? Generalizations of this sort are problematic not only because there would be some members of a given collective entity who would be uncomfortable with them and would say, "That is not my experience," but also because the experience of one group does not always cohere with that of another. The risk is that theologies that focus upon a particular segment of the population will become, as it were, collective solipsisms unless they are placed in dialogue with other similar views. Perhaps a way around the difficulty is to argue for the experience of the worshiping community, and we could appeal to the notion that theology seeks to articulate its meaning. Worship implies belief; the *lex orandi* is the *lex credendi*. Yet even here the appeal is really to forms of worship rather than to the experience of the individuals who participate in those forms.

At the beginning of this somewhat extended discussion I noted my unwillingness to dismiss the triple cord altogether. What I shall want to do in my final chapter is to suggest an alternative that has the possibility of incorporating the insights of what we might call the triple or quadruple cord theory. The alternative is a schema suggested by Coleridge which depends upon several developments that can be discerned in the nineteenth century even after Coleridge's death and in the twentieth century. The first of these is a growing awareness that we must distinguish revelation from its instantiation and apprehension in scripture. We find the idea that the more we are able to see the writers of scripture as human, the more we are able to see it as the word of God addressed to those writers. The second development is a denial of the verbal inerrancy of scripture and is really a correlate of the first point. It seems doubtful to me that the early Anglicans understood inspiration as some sort of dictation by God, but such a view became common in Coleridge's time. The third development is an increasing insistence that the Bible is the church's book. Coleridge's basic idea is that we find God's revelation both in scripture and in the church. The work of the Holy Spirit, then, presides over the dialectic between the church and scripture, and also over the "preacher," who attempts to articulate that dialectic. As I shall argue, this structure solves no problems and simply represents a framework in which the meaning of scripture may be considered. Moreover, that consideration has to do primarily with the way in which scripture in dialogue with the church guides and assists Christians in their pilgrimage, not with the resolution of religious controversies. Instead of "tradition" we have the church. And it would be possible to think of particular churches and the traditions they espouse, as well as their understandings of a number of other slippery terms such as "revelation" and "inspiration" and their attitudes toward history and nature. And Coleridge speaks of the Holy Spirit, which could easily mean graced reason and experience that enables the articulation of the dialectic of church and scripture. Such a view does not seem to me entirely to one side of Coleridge's idea of reason as an intuitive and somewhat mysterious faculty. Suffice it to say that it is possible to treat Coleridge's schema as a reworking of the triple cord idea.

Presuppositions and Prejudices

Throughout my discussion of the sufficiency of scripture and of how it should be interpreted, the attentive reader will have noticed certain presuppositions, some of which may well represent prejudices on my part. Since I suppose that the Enlightenment is dead, I find it difficult to believe in such a thing as objectivity. Nevertheless, I should argue that fair-mindedness is still possible, but that such an approach obliges us to discern our own presuppositions and to make them clear to others so that they can make their own judgments about what we say. One of my prejudices, to put it that way, is a bemusement about the controversies that now divide Christians in general and Anglicans in particular. It is hard for me think of any time in history when people have not cried out that the church is in danger, but it does not seem to me that God is in danger. The present controversies have resulted in an unfortunate polarization that makes it difficult to engage in argumentation, passionate or dispassionate. I am obviously thinking of the gay issue and the various forms it takes. Perhaps because academics are supposed to try to see all sides of a question, I have many more questions than answers; and even though I see myself on the "liberal" side, I remain confused. For these reasons I do not regard what I have tried to do in what follows as having any direct bearing upon present controversies save for insisting that we need to be somewhat more cautious in appealing to the "right" view of scripture. Certainly, what I have to say gives no account of the present state of affairs, nor does it suggest anything more than one way of thinking about it.[16] The point of the book is primarily descriptive.

> It is the church that makes Christians and not the other way around.

It would be less than honest, however, not to admit that these descriptions are informed by a number of assumptions and that these assumptions, like those of many old-fashioned Episcopalians, find roots in childhood experiences of the church. The Bible, of course, was part of the Sunday service; but it did not occur to me that it was of primary importance, since the best parts were in the Prayer Book or read as the lessons at Morning Prayer. Consequently, the Bible has been for me an acquired taste. Only gradually by studying it in seminary and afterward and by examining its role in the life of the early church did I begin to see its central importance. This was, I suppose, a failing; but it was a natural one. And, positively, it meant that I saw no need to regard historical criticism as destructive of scripture and that it was always clear to me that the Bible belonged to the church. These convictions obviously inform my discussions.

Several other memories of the parish church in which I grew up have continued to inform my attitudes. Mite boxes in Lent were quite important, and they had pictures of children on them, children who came in all colors and in a variety of exotic costumes. This reminded us that our little church was part of something much bigger scattered throughout the world among people who were not at all like us. Another important event in the life of the parish was what we called "the Feast of Lights." This was a pageant during Epiphany, and we children dressed up so as to represent figures of the Christian past

from Augustine of Canterbury to Philander Chase. We were learning that the church extended in time as well as space, and that we
were merely a small part of a very long procession. A third memory
extended this sensibility. In confirmation class the rector asked us to
open the Prayer Book to the title page, and he called our attention
to that fact that the word "church" appeared twice. The first time
was a reference to the sacraments and other rites and ceremonies "of
the church." The second was the phrase "according to the use of the
Protestant Episcopal Church in the United States of America." The
rector pointed out that it was to the first church that we belonged, as
did our Presbyterian, Methodist, Catholic, and other friends — who,
I am afraid I must admit, were all Christians. We were a smaller
family in that larger church and did things in our own peculiar way
or "use."

What these memories imply is my sense that it is the church that
makes Christians and not the other way around. Launcelot Andrewes
in his *Pattern of Catechistical Doctrine* compares the church to a fire
burning in the fireplace. Baptizing a new Christian is like putting a
new log on the fire; only gradually does it catch fire and burn. The
Christian life, then, becomes a process by which individuals learn to
make the church's faith their own. The faith *that* they believed becomes the growing faith *by which* they believe. This is certainly not
the only way people become Christians; there are numberless "twice-
born" Christians who see their conversion as the important thing. The
two views need not be opposed to one another. Nevertheless, I should
want to think of the church as a society rather than as no more than
an association of like-minded people. If a community is only such an
association, it is fragile because it is at the mercy of those who come
to disagree with it and are no longer of a like mind. In their socio-
logical study of individualism and commitment in America Robert
Bellah and his associates point out that the "freedom, openness, and
pluralism of American religious life" make it hard for Americans to
understand "the traditional pattern" that "assumes a certain priority of the religious community over the individual. The community
exists before the individual is born and will continue after his or her

death."[17] I surely do not want to argue that my commitment to such a traditional understanding is normative and am merely making my own assumption clear.

Growing up in a lawyer's family has left me with another set of sensibilities. It was drummed into us as children that it was not possible to equate the law with perfect justice. In the full sense justice was an ideal beyond human reach, but one toward which all should aspire. Consequently, the true test of the law was not whether it rendered perfect justice, but whether it moved toward justice. Similarly, I have come to see the church as a very human enterprise and to judge its effectiveness by the degree to which it assists people in their journey to God through Christ. This does not mean we are incapable of speaking of God's providence and the grace of the Holy Spirit at work in the church, or in the law for that matter. But it does mean that we cannot assume that the church possesses an infallibility that properly belongs only to God. Being an Episcopalian was an accident of my birth, but justifying remaining one has been my task. And that justification rests in part upon what I take to be an emphasis in Anglicanism upon the fallibility of the church. Even the Thirty-Nine Articles speak of the "sufficiency" of scripture rather than its infallibility; and however much the earlier Anglicans regarded scripture as infallible, they do not seem to have tied this judgment to verbal inerrancy nor did they regard interpretations of scripture as infallible. The first part of Laud's *Conference with Fisher* is a long refutation of the Roman Catholic claim to an infallible church and an insistence that there can be no such thing. And while the aim of the Oxford Movement was to make the Church of England more dogmatic, its net effect was to make it broader.[18] It would be easy to multiply examples.

There is obviously something problematic about prizing fallibility. Anglican churches have great difficulty making up their minds, and this is partly the product of complex authority structures that seldom speak with a clear voice. For example, in 1847 Bishop Phillpotts of Exeter refused to induct George Cornelius Gorham to the living of Brampford Speke on the grounds that his denial of baptismal

regeneration was heretical. Of course, Gorham was a dedicated evangelical, and his was the usual evangelical view at the time. His
appointment to the living took place precisely because he was an
evangelical. Gorham sued the bishop to compel him to induct him,
and the case wound its way to the highest court of appeal, which
was then the judicial committee of the Queen's Privy Council. The
ultimate verdict in 1850 was that it could not be demonstrated that
Mr. Gorham's view contradicted the formularies of the Church of
England. But had Mr. Gorham's view been precisely the opposite
of what it was, the same verdict would have been rendered. Again,
examples could be multiplied; and the Episcopal Church's decision
to ordain women supplies another one. The decision of the General
Convention did not find favor with several bishops, who refused to
implement it and who at least implicitly assumed that episcopal authority was stronger than synodal. Moreover, parochial resistance to
women priests further complicated the issue. The checks and balances
involved in dispersed synodal, episcopal, and congregational authorities led to a partial paralysis from which the Episcopal Church is
only now beginning to recover.

If Anglicanism can be understood as an "ordered freedom," the
freedom is more evident than the order. Consequently, there are several appeals possible to ordering principles; and scripture is one of
them. The Prayer Book, the creeds, and even the Lambeth Quadri-
lateral are other candidates for such appeals. But none of them seem
to be persuasive to all. As a result the controversies continue. There
are surely those who lament this state of affairs, and perhaps they
are right to do so. My own worry has less to do with our failure to resolve controversy than with what looks like a reluctance
to continue the argument. Certainly, in the lawyer's family in which
I grew up what I vividly remember is long and sometimes heated
arguments of a Sunday afternoon when the family gathered. They
were usually about politics, but nobody minded that they never came
to any agreed conclusion. Perhaps an agreement to disagree without abolishing freedom is the best we can hope for at least for the
time being.

In any case my study of the ancient church has convinced me that unity need not be equated with uniformity. A distinction must be made between dogma and doctrine. The only two dogmas found in the early church are those of the Trinity and of Christ's person, and I should argue that both of them leave room for a range of doctrines. It is easier to see this in the Chalcedonian Definition of Christ's person.[19] The Definition primarily ruled out what was regarded as error. No one could deny Christ's divine nature as Arius did, or his human nature as Apollinaris did; nor should one divide the natures as Nestorius did or confuse them as Eutyches did. But these negative rules imply a positive grammar by which to test doctrines; and Chalcedon in fact recognized three very different ones — an Alexandrian, an Antiochene, and a Western christology. While the argument is somewhat more difficult to make with respect to doctrines of the Trinity, both the Cappadocians and Augustine observe the dogma as expressed in the version of the Nicene Creed adopted at the Council of Constantinople in 381, even though their doctrines differ significantly from one another.

To think of doctrinal unity this way would not require a single correct doctrine or system of doctrines. The analogy that occurs to me is that of literary criticism. It would certainly be the case that one could show that certain interpretations of Milton's *Paradise Lost* are incorrect, but it would not follow that we can speak of a single correct interpretation. Rather, we must recognize a range of valid interpretations. The same point applies to scripture; admitting that there may be incorrect interpretations correlates not with the claim that there is a single correct meaning, but with the assumption that there is a range of possibly valid interpretations. The question then becomes by what standard or standards are we to judge validity. We find ourselves back at the question of what are the ordering principles that put limits upon the freedom of interpretation. In the case of literary criticism it is probably argumentation among the critics themselves that settles the question so far as it may be possible to do so. In the case of churches it would seem to be the judgments made by institutional authority structures that in the short run determine what doctrines or interpretations of scripture are acceptable.

Nevertheless, in Anglicanism such institutional decisions are not only difficult to make because of the lack of a clear magisterium, but they are also subject to reversal over time. An instructive example is the debate over slavery in the nineteenth century. Most of the Protestant churches split over the issue because of the abolitionist controversy and did so considerably before the outbreak of the Civil War. Both the northern and the southern churches appealed to scripture, but they made opposing judgments. The Episcopal Church, of course, did not fall apart before the war and even continued for a while to function as a unity after secession and war had created two nations. And after the war the unilateral actions of the Confederate church in electing a bishop and in turning a missionary district into a diocese were ratified by the reunited General Convention. But this reflects no great credit on the Episcopal Church, since its failure to support abolition before the war had more to do with social and economic factors than with a resistance to schism. Explaining what happened in the Episcopal Church and in the other Protestant denominations would require a more considered examination of the evidence, but what does seem clear is that events ultimately overtook the pro-slavery churches in the South, as well as the Episcopal Church's reluctance to oppose slavery in any official way.

My point is not to argue that the institutional church has no obligation to make decisions about doctrine and moral issues, but merely to suggest that these decisions do not always stand the test of time. Consider, for example, the way in which the Episcopal Church has altered the canon dealing with marriage and divorce. The new canon is more realistic and pastoral, but it also seems to me to have removed the harsh stigma on divorce implied by the old canon. However much most of us would welcome the change, it surely reflects changing mores in our society. Granted that the church ought not simply yield to secular mores, it is hard to see how it can be unaffected by them without moving to a purely sectarian stance. Another example is the marriage service in the 1979 Prayer Book. The opening exhortation restores an explanation of the purposes of marriage, but in a curiously revised way from that found in the English Prayer Book tradition. There, from 1549 to 1662, three reasons for marriage appear — the procreation of children, a remedy for fornication, and mutual support. Our Prayer Book abandons the second of these reasons and reverses the order of the other two. Moreover, the procreation of children is a purpose of marriage "when it is God's will." What does this mean? My suggestion is really a simple one. The impact of changing social attitudes toward marriage and divorce is already to be discerned in our canons and our Prayer Book. Perhaps we should adopt Gamaliel's counsel (Acts 5:33–39) and recognize that the final court of appeal is "reception" by that mysterious force, the mind of the church.

And so I confess to two sets of prejudices that will appear in my discussions and particularly in the last chapter, where I shall try to argue for Coleridge's schema as a helpful framework for considering scripture. The first revolves around a deep respect for the past and for locating Anglicanism in the wider ecumenical context of worldwide Christianity. I suppose this amounts to a rather odd mixture of Anglo-Catholic and latitudinarian sensibilities. The second set of prejudices more clearly reflects a latitudinarian stance. By granting the fallibility of the church I should want to argue for drawing a circle within which there can be differing views and differing commitments. And while I should not want the circle to be all-encompassing, my puzzles with respect to how to draw it imply making it larger rather than smaller. In a sense my point of view means that it becomes increasingly difficult to speak of an Anglican identity. This, I confess, does not trouble me; and I am attracted by Paul Avis's judgment that the quest for identity ought not to be our prime concern. He points out that while identity "is important both to individuals and to institutions," it is "neurotic" to be obsessed by defining it. "A distinctive identity does not necessarily bring integrity. Identity can be contrived by dubious means, but there is no short cut to integrity. Preserve integrity and identity will take care of itself."[20]

In looking back at my attempts to describe some of the differing ways Anglicans have approached scripture and in reflecting on my own attitudes, it occurs to me that I could assess my study the way Mark Pattison assessed his study of religious thought in England from 1688 till 1750 in its relation to his own time in 1860:

> Such appears to be the past history of the Theory of Belief in the Church of England. Whoever would take the religious literature of the present day as a whole, and endeavour to make out clearly on what basis Revelation is supposed by it to rest, whether on Authority, on the Inward Light, on Reason, on self-evidencing Scripture, or on the combination of the four, or some of them, and in what proportions, would probably find that he had undertaken a perplexing but not altogether profitless inquiry.[21]

Chapter One

The Bible Moves to Center Stage
1529–1603

John Barth's novel *The Sot-Weed Factor* is an entertaining if somewhat bawdy account of Maryland in its early colonial period. At one point the hero encounters a Jesuit missionary called Thomas Smith, who tells him about one of his Jesuit predecessors. Fr. Joseph FitzMaurice arrived in Maryland on the *Dove,* one of three Jesuit missionaries. His zeal took him beyond the heathen Indians near the landing site, since they "were already half converted by the Virginians, though like as not to some rank heresy.... The true worth of the missionary could be assayed only among the pure and untouched heathen that had ne'er set eyes on white men." And so Fr. FitzMaurice, alone, wanders far up the Choptank River and finds what he supposes to be unharvested fields for his mission. Finding an Indian village, he distributes crucifixes to the inhabitants and tries "to explain, by signs, the Passion of Our Savior." After some delay the Indian chief points to the cross and issues an order to one of the tribe. The man quickly returns "with a small wooden box, at sight of which all the savages fell prostrate on the beach." Fr. FitzMaurice, expecting some heathen idol, finds that the box contains a King James Bible "fronted with a woodcut of the Crucifixion." The Indian king holds the Bible up, "whereon with one accord the assembled Indians sang by rote the Anglican *Te Deum.*"[1] My reason for retailing this fiction is to point out that in earliest Anglicanism, at least from the reign of Edward VI (1547–53), the Bible occupied a central place that no one disputed.

1

The Henrician Reformation:
Scripture in the Wings

It was, however, no foregone conclusion that scripture would occupy center stage during the first scene of the drama of the English Reformation. Henry VIII summoned the Reformation Parliament in 1529 at least partly in the context of his attempt to secure an annulment of his marriage to Catherine of Aragon. It was only by a papal dispensation that he had married Catherine in 1509, the year of his accession to the throne. This was because Catherine had been the wife of Henry's deceased brother, Arthur. For this reason the "great matter" of the king's divorce required that a new pope would be obliged to overturn an earlier papal dispensation. Henry's motives for seeking the divorce seem to have been as complicated as the situation itself. Catherine had succeeded in giving birth to only one living child, Mary; and there were repeated miscarriages and monstrous births. Did Henry regard this as God's judgment upon his incest in marrying his deceased brother's wife and, consequently, a divine condemnation of the papal authority that allowed the marriage? Other factors included his wish for a male heir to the throne and his infatuation with Anne Boleyn.

The one thing that seems clear is Henry's concern to establish the independency of his royal supremacy and of England as a self-sufficient "empire." Therefore, the first years of Henry's reformation revolved primarily around freeing England from papal judicial and financial control. It can also be argued that the king's divorce was only the match that lit the powder keg of various currents pressing for the reform of the church. These forces included a weakening of the papacy and the institutional church, together with the emergence of nationalism. The papacy suffered its "Babylonian captivity" from 1305 till 1378, moving to Avignon and becoming in some degree subservient to neighboring France. In 1378 the return of the pope to Rome merely precipitated the papal schism (1378–1417), which allowed rulers in the West to play one pope off against the other. Even when the papacy began to regain its strength, putting down the conciliar movement as far as possible, the more successful it became in implementing judicial and financial control of the church throughout the West, the more it provoked resistance. As well, the emergence in the late Middle Ages of centers of piety that emphasized the humility and poverty of Christ called into question the power and wealth of the institutional church. For this and other reasons it is possible to discern currents of anti-clericalism. Another force was the new learning expressed by humanists such as Erasmus, John Colet, and Sir Thomas More. Perhaps most important of all was the emergence of a strong monarchy in England after the battle of Bosworth Field in 1485, when Henry VII ended the Wars of the Roses.

However much it may be true that the English Reformation might have taken place in some other way, it cannot be denied that the king's divorce was the precipitating cause. The meeting of the Reformation Parliament in 1529 coincided with the fall of Cardinal Wolsey and the emergence of Thomas Cranmer and Thomas Cromwell as agents of the king. Both were in power by 1533. In that year the papal bulls arrived, enabling Cranmer to be consecrated archbishop of Canterbury. Soon afterward he granted Henry the divorce, and Anne Boleyn was crowned queen. These developments, of course, presupposed that England no longer remained subject to the papacy. As the culmination of parliamentary acts that brought this about, the Act of Supremacy was passed in November of 1534. Henry VIII became officially the "Supreme Head" of the Church of England, and the following July Sir Thomas More was executed for his unwillingness to subscribe to the royal claim. The break with Rome, though clearly an essential aspect of the English Reformation, was from another perspective the precondition of the reform of the church. These steps toward reform included the dissolution of the monasteries in 1536 and 1539, as well as liturgical changes particularly in burial rites and requiems.

It was in 1536 that there appeared the first Henrician attempt to define in theory a basic Protestant religious party platform. The Ten Articles addressed the issues disputed at the time — the sacraments, justification, images, the place of the saints in Christian piety, certain rites and ceremonies, and purgatory. They were a very hesitant

step toward reform, and despite what seems to be "a degree of Lutheran influence" they were largely conservative in character.[2] The
Ten Articles are divided into those "necessary to our salvation" and
those concerning "such things as have been of a long continuance
for decent order and honest policy . . . although they be not expressly
commanded of God, nor necessary to our salvation." The preface
and the whole of the first article at least imply the identity of things
necessary for salvation with the Bible and the three creeds. The Royal
Injunctions, also issued in 1536 to implement the Ten Articles, are primarily concerned with ordering the clergy to observe and to preach
against the usurpation of the bishop of Rome and to confirm the
king's authority as Supreme Head of the Church of England. Among
the other instructions the only direct mention of scripture is the order
that clergy, instead of giving themselves "to drinking or riot, spend-
ing their time idly, by day or by night, at tables or card-playing,
or any other unlawful game," should spend their leisure in reading
or hearing "somewhat of holy Scripture," or should "occupy themselves with some other honest exercise." The Bible begins to make its
appearance, as well as the distinction between things necessary for
salvation and matters of indifference.

In 1537, perhaps partly in reaction to the uprisings against the
royal policy known as the Pilgrimage of Grace, Henry instructed
the bishops to draw up the *Institution of a Christian Man,* known
as the Bishops' Book.[3] The preface puts a stronger emphasis upon
the importance of scripture. The bishops and divines say that they
have responded to the king's command "upon the diligent search
and perusing of holy Scripture" and have "set forth a plain and sincere doctrine, concerning the whole sum of all those things which
appertain unto the profession of a Christian man." The decisive step,
however, is the order in the second Henrician Injunctions of 1538
that by Easter of the next year "you shall provide . . . one book of
the whole Bible of the largest volume, in English, and the same set
up in some convenient place within the said church that you have
cure of." As well, the clergy are to encourage the people to read this
Bible, while at the same time they are to admonish them "to avoid

all contention and altercation therein . . . and refer the explication of obscure places to men of higher judgment in Scripture."[4] This order is further underlined by the provision that the clergy must present to the authorities anyone trying to prevent the reading of God's word in English. Thomas Cromwell was the king's vice-gerent in issuing these injunctions.

The Bible in question was the Great Bible, basically Coverdale's completion of Tyndale's translations; but there was a delay in implementing the injunction because of difficulties in securing a printer. Thus, it was not until the second edition of the Great Bible in 1640 that Cranmer's preface appeared.[5] His argument revolves around finding the golden mean between two sorts of people, those "too slow" and unwilling to read the Bible in English and, at the opposite extreme, those "too quick" and given to "inordinate reading, undiscreet speaking, contentious disputing." Cranmer refutes the slow by citing a long passage from one of John Chrysostom's sermons; the quick, by an excerpt from Gregory Nazianzen's second theological oration. Scripture is "in darkness, light; in hunger, food; in cold, fire." It contains "fruitful instruction and erudition for every man; if any things be necessary to be learned, of the Holy Scripture we may learn it." Here are "the fat pastures of the soul," designed to supply wholesome food for all people — "men, women, young, old, learned, unlearned, rich, poor, priests, laymen, lords, ladies, officers, tenants, and mean men, virgins, wives, widows, lawyers, merchants, artificers, husbandmen, and all manner of persons." There is no doubt that Cranmer and Cromwell wanted to put the Bible at the center of the stage and so commit the Church of England to *sola scriptura* in the sense that scripture alone contains all things necessary to salvation.[6]

The king, however, thwarted this aim. To many people the Act of Six Articles, promulgated in 1539 by Parliament acting under Henry's orders, amounted to a wholesale repudiation of reform. It was "the whip with six strings." Henry had been alarmed by religious disputation and unrest, which in his view threatened civil unity and peace. Reaction continued in the Convocation of Canterbury that met in

1542.[7] The bishops proposed a revision of the Great Bible, which
would have involved banning all other translations, as well as the
proscription of the works of evangelical writers. Cranmer thwarted
this effort by referring the issue to the universities, where the measure
collapsed. Nevertheless, in 1543 Parliament passed an Act for the Advancement of True Religion. This act forbade Tyndale's "crafty, false
and untrue" translation and "all other books . . . teaching or comprising any matters of Christian religion . . . contrary to the doctrine set
forth by the King." It also limited the reading of the Great Bible to
certain classes.[8] In the same year Henry authorized a revision of the
Bishops' Book that became known as the King's Book. In the preface
that he wrote for it Henry mentioned the act of Parliament and said
that it was designed to curb "an inclination to sinister understanding
of Scripture, presumption, arrogancy, carnal liberty, and contention."
Thomas Cromwell became a victim of this reaction and was executed
at its beginning in 1540. Cranmer, however, survived and was able to
implement his view of the centrality of scripture after Henry's death
and the accession of his ten-year-old son as Edward VI.

The Edwardine Reformation:
Scripture Attains Center Stage

The brief reign of Edward VI (1547–53) was not only the high tide
of Protestantism in England, but also supplied the basis in a modified
form for the Elizabethan Settlement of 1559. The Edwardine Injunctions of 1547 largely republished the Henrician Injunctions of 1536
and 1538.[9] This meant the provision of the Great Bible, insistence
upon scriptural preaching, and the prohibition of any attempt to restrict access to scripture in the vernacular. Several new commands
built upon this foundation. Clergy "under the degree of Bachelor
of Divinity" must have the New Testament in English and Latin, together with the Paraphrases of Erasmus (item 20). It was Henry VIII's
last wife, Catherine Parr, who sponsored the English translation of
these explanations of scripture that were designed to inculcate a biblical piety.[10] A second measure was the order that "all parsons, vicars,

and curates shall read in their churches every Sunday one of the homilies which are and shall be set forth for the same purpose" (item 32).
Cranmer had apparently begun to prepare what became the twelve
Edwardine Homilies during the previous reign. Two of them survived
during Mary's reign and were incorporated into her Roman Catholic
book of homilies; and the entire book was reissued by Elizabeth I.[11]
Finally, for private devotion only the Henrician primer is to be used
(item 34). These measures, which amplify the importance given the
Bible in the Henrician Injunctions of 1538, were themselves expanded
by the English Books of Common Prayer in 1549 and 1552 and by
the Forty-Two Articles of Religion in 1553, which were the basis for
the Thirty-Nine Articles in Elizabeth's reign. Article Five is basically
the same as Article Six in the Thirty-Nine Articles: "Holy Scripture
containeth all things necessary to salvation: so that whatsoever is neither read therein, nor may be proved thereby, although it be sometime
received of the faithful, as godly and profitable for an order and come-
liness: yet no man ought to be constrained to believe it or repute it
to the necessity of salvation."[12]

Cranmer designed the English Books of Common Prayer as a
means for inculcating a thoroughly biblical piety. In the preface to the
1549 book several principles underlying the liturgy find expression.[13]
As well as simplicity and uniformity, conformity to scripture is the
rule. Appealing to the church fathers, the preface points out that they
ordered the Bible ("or the greatest part thereof") to be read yearly.
The purpose of this was to rouse the clergy "to godliness themselves,
and be more able to exhort others by wholesome doctrine, and to
confute them that were adversaries to the truth." It was also a means
to help the people through "daily hearing of holy Scripture read in
the Church" to grow and "profit" in "the knowledge of God" and
to be "inflamed with the love of true religion." This explains why
the early Prayer Books had lectionaries with readings that seem to us
excessively long, provision for a fuller reading of the Psalter, and the
omission of "Anthems, Responds, Invitatories, and such like things,
as did break the continual course of the reading of the Scripture." It

also explains why everything must be said in a language understood
by the people.

Scripture, then, is what forms and shapes a Christian people
through their worship. The same idea appears more generally in the
first of the Edwardine Homilies, which Cranmer himself wrote.[14] "A
Fruitful Exhortation to the Reading of Holy Scripture" begins by insisting upon the necessity and profit of the knowledge of scripture,
"forasmuch as in it is contained God's true word, setting forth his
glory and also man's duty." All doctrine necessary for justification
and salvation "is, or may be drawn out of that fountain and well
of truth." Scripture contains not only what Christians must know
and believe, but also what they must do. Belief in the Trinity must
be followed by learning "to know ourselves, how vile and miserable
we be, and also to know God, how good he is of himself, and how
he maketh us and all creatures partakers of his goodness." Cranmer
surely implies that belief in the Trinity and in Christ's redemptive
work must become the lively faith given in justification by faith.[15]
Such a faith is God's free gift enabling Christ's atonement to become
effective for the believer and expressing itself in his growth in holiness
and virtue. This is why the books of scripture "ought to be much in
our hands, in our eyes, in our ears, in our mouths, but most of all in
our hearts." The contrast between human misery and sin, and God's
goodness involves the conviction that God's mercy bridges the gap
by freely justifying the sinner. The same conviction dominates Cranmer's Prayer Books. In the homily he briefly cites John Chrysostom,
and we can remember his extensive citation of Chrysostom's words
in his preface to the Great Bible.

Scripture, then, is not merely instruction; nor is it treated as a way
of resolving religious controversies. Instead, the words of scripture
"have power to convert." Scripture is food and drink; it is light and
wisdom. It is God's instrument of salvation and makes us holy. It
"comforteth, maketh glad, cheereth, and cherisheth our conscience."
Because it does all these things "it is a more excellent jewel or treasure
than any gold or precious stone; it is more sweet than honey or honey-
comb; it is called the *best part,* which Mary did choose, for it hath

in it everlasting comfort." What seems most interesting to me about Cranmer's argument is that, while scripture clearly exposes human helplessness and sinfulness, it does so by revealing the God who in his mercy saves rather than the God who by his justice condemns. God's power to convert, expressed in scripture, not only reconciles sinners, but by giving them a lively faith enables them to bring forth the fruits of justification in a holy life. Most important of all, Cranmer's assessment of scripture includes the exhortation to "search for the well of life in the books of the New and Old Testament, and not to run to the stinking puddles of men's traditions, devised by men's imagination."

In the second part of the homily Cranmer raises the question of the difficulty of scripture and addresses the objections some would make to his argument by pointing out the obscurity of scripture or their own ignorance and incapacity to understand it. The question really has to do with the "perspicuity" of scripture. If the simplest person is able to find God's saving word in the Bible, what are we to make of the obvious difficulties we find? Cranmer's answer involves distinguishing the plain passages of scripture from the obscure ones. There are "low valleys, plain ways, and easy for every man to use and to walk in," as well as the "high hills and mountains" few can climb. It is in the plain and easy passages that we find the necessary and perspicuous message of scripture. The only thing required is a humble and prayerful approach to the Bible. Once we come to it this way, when we encounter one of the "mountains" in scripture, either God will send us "some godly doctor" to enlighten us, just as he sent Philip to the Ethiopian eunuch to explain to him what he was reading, or failing that, "God himself from above will give light unto our minds, and teach us those things which are necessary for us, and wherein we be ignorant."

The Elizabethan Settlement:
What Does "Center Stage" for the Bible Mean?

With the exception of Mary's brief reign (1553–58) the central place accorded scripture in the Edwardine formulas remained secure for more than a century. What I want to argue in what follows in this chapter and in the next is that scripture remains the prime authority even into the period beginning with the Restoration of Charles II in 1660. At the same time it is also apparent that scripture's central position admitted a fairly wide range of understandings. Thus, Cranmer's claims for the Bible proved far more ambiguous and complicated than one might at first suppose. The Elizabethan Settlement did endorse the main lines of the Edwardine reformation. To be sure, the Act of Supremacy designated the queen as "Supreme Governor" rather than "Supreme Head" of the Church of England, and the Act of Uniformity authorized several small but crucial changes in the 1552 Book of Common Prayer. The petition in the Litany for deliverance "from the Bishop of Rome and all his detestable enormities" disappeared, as did the Black Rubric that was designed to persuade the more committed Protestants to receive communion kneeling, on the grounds that doing so did not signify any presence of Christ in the sacramental elements of bread and wine. The words by which the priest or minister administered communion spliced together the more traditional formula of 1549 ("The body of our Lord Jesus Christ, which was given for thee," etc.) with the unambiguous Protestant formula of 1552 ("Take and eat this in remembrance," etc.). These changes represent an attempt to include all reasonable Protestant opinion in the uniform worship of the church. But if comprehension of a range of Protestant beliefs combined with uniformity of public worship characterizes the Elizabethan Settlement, it is important to add that this should by no means be understood as toleration. Indeed, the point of comprehension was to avoid the necessity of toleration; and few at the time would have admitted that religious division was anything but a threat to civil order.

The two acts of Parliament I have mentioned were passed in 1559, the year after Elizabeth's accession to the throne, and were accompanied by the Elizabethan Injunctions.[16] In large measure these simply repeat the Edwardine Injunctions of 1547, and they mandated the setting up of the Great Bible in the churches, as well as Erasmus's Paraphrases. They also ordered the use of the Edwardine Homilies, to which Elizabeth added a second Book of Homilies in 1563 with one final additional homily against rebellion in 1571. The final form of the second Book of Homilies stands in some degree of tension with the first, partly because it includes homilies for Christmas, Good Friday, Easter, and Whitsunday, and partly because it tends to imply that faith is not only God's gift but is somehow in our control. But there is no retreat from the biblical piety that Cranmer and the earlier reformers espoused. At the same time, the Elizabethan Injunctions add a warrant underlining earlier concerns about the misuse of scripture. Item 37 forbids anyone from talking or reasoning of scripture "rashly or contentiously." There is implicitly the recognition that, while all might agree about the centrality of scripture, they might not agree about what that meant.

It is probably impossible to know to what degree the Elizabethan Settlement found acceptance, but it is certain that its enemies included Roman Catholics both outside the Church of England and the "church papists" within it, as well as those within the church who argued that it should be further reformed and purified of "Romish" abuses. The struggle against Rome was a practical one. Though the Northern Rebellion of 1569 failed in its social and religious purposes, it may have contributed to Pope Pius V's decision to excommunicate Elizabeth in 1570, thereby releasing papists from their allegiance to the queen. The plots surrounding Mary Queen of Scots, who was executed in 1587, and the Spanish Armada of 1588 are part of the picture. Moreover, Roman missionaries from William Allen's seminary in Douai as well as others began their work in England, which was designed to overthrow the Protestant regime. A considerable controversial literature emerged on both sides, but it is arguable that while the underlying issue involved whether prime authority should be attributed to the Bible or to the Roman church and the pope, the ambiguities of scriptural authority had no need to be addressed. It was the struggle to maintain the settlement against the Puritans within the church that clearly raised this question. To be sure, the Vestiarian Controversy of 1563 revolved around public worship and

the Puritan demand to be freed from wearing the surplice, from kneeling to receive communion, from the cross in baptism and the ring in
marriage, from organs in the churches, and from most of the holy
days in the church Kalender. In addition, the dispute between Cartwright and Whitgift at Cambridge was caught up in the Admonition
Controversy that began in 1572 and involved a demand for the abolition of episcopacy and the establishment of a presbyterian polity in
supposed accord with scripture.

> The centrality of scripture by no means solves all
> problems; a great many vexed questions begin to
> appear.

Associated with the Admonition Controversy were the "prophesyings" and the "classis" movement. The prophesyings were meetings
of the devout for prayer and preaching, while the "classis" was fundamentally a presbytery designed to establish discipline at a local
level. Elizabeth's second archbishop of Canterbury, Edmund Grindal,
encouraged these developments from 1575 until he was sequestered
two years later. While there is a good deal of room for scholarly debate, these developments need not be seen as of themselves attempts
to undermine the religious settlement. It also seems reasonably clear
that partly because of the return of the Marian exiles from Geneva
and elsewhere, the bishops and divines of the Church of England were
strongly influenced by Calvin. Nevertheless, there emerged a party of
extremists we can call the "High Calvinists," who were associated
with Cartwright, Travers, and John Field and who increasingly used
what might have been harmless and even helpful developments as a
way of undermining what could be called an episcopal Calvinism in
England. At least this is one way of trying to put the pieces of evidence together. What does seem the case is that from the time Whitgift
became archbishop of Canterbury in 1583, most of the Puritan divines became reconciled to the settlement. Nevertheless, it proved

necessary in 1593 for Parliament to pass an act designed to penalize those Puritans who separated themselves from the Church of England. The Puritan threat did not disappear, and it was in 1593 that Richard Hooker published the first four books of his comprehensive refutation of their position.

The "Triple Cord"

Before turning to Hooker's understanding of the centrality of scripture as he opposed it to the Puritan view, let me in a preliminary way make a few observations about what has sometimes been a common way of describing Hooker's view in particular and an Anglican view in general. I have argued that the centrality of scripture by no means solves all problems; a great many vexed questions begin to appear. Are those passages in scripture thought necessary for salvation to be found in the plain passages, so that we can speak of the perspicuity of scripture as its capacity to inform and to inflame the simplest reader by these pleasant valleys in scripture? If the plain passages are those necessary for salvation, what are they? Does scripture at this level interpret itself? How may we distinguish these passages from those that are unnecessary for salvation? On the other hand, if we must interpret scripture, how shall we proceed? If we do so by reason, what do we mean by reason? If we employ as interpretive tools the church and its traditions, how can we distinguish such a view from the Roman one? Should we restrict tradition to apostolicity, and, if so, what is apostolic?

The common way of resolving these questions to which I have alluded is to appeal to the "triple cord" of scripture, tradition, and reason.[17] We could follow Bishop McAdoo and argue that scripture remains the prime authority, but that reason and tradition are tools for interpreting it. The triple cord, then, is more a method than a doctrine, and a method attributed to Hooker and to the mainline development of Anglicanism. Indeed, the triple cord — or the "three-legged stool" — seems to have become something of a shibboleth in

current Anglican thinking. I should not wish to dismiss the idea altogether. Moreover, in this chapter and the next I shall attempt to
examine it by asking how reason and tradition function as interpretive tools in the writings of Hooker, Hall, Chillingworth, Hammond,
and others before the Restoration of 1660. But my suggestion will
be that the idea is less helpful than it appears and that it proves impossible to argue that Hooker's view really illustrates it or that the
Caroline divines after Hooker follow his views.

Let me suggest what I mean in a preliminary way by offering some
remarks about Sir Thomas Browne's *Religio Medici*. Browne first
published his work in 1642 at the time of the first Civil War, and he
clearly wants to articulate his own lay view of religion in the midst
of a controversy in which, to borrow a phrase from Jeremy Taylor,
faith had learned to cut the throat of charity. Browne claims that
"there are two bookes from whence I collect my Divinity; besides
that written one of God, another of his servant Nature, that universall and publik Manuscript, that lies expans'd unto the eyes of all."[18]
Despite this adumbration of the preoccupation of late seventeenth-
and eighteenth-century Anglicanism with the relation of natural and
revealed religion, Browne does give pride of place to the Bible. Here
it looks at first as though he is employing the triple cord. He assents
to the necessary things of scripture, but for "points indifferent" he
employs "the rules of my private reason, or the humor and fashion of
my devotion." He elaborates what he means by arguing that "where
the Scripture is silent, the Church is my Text" and that where both
scripture and the church betray "joynt silence," he follows neither
Geneva nor Rome, "but the dictates of my own reason."[19] We do
not really have the triple cord. In the first place the church and reason come into play only in connection with "points indifferent" in
scripture. Furthermore, it is not entirely clear that the church and reason are tools for interpreting scripture. They may simply be ways of
answering non-essential religious questions scripture cannot resolve.

Browne's major point, however, is to insist upon scripture's sufficiency in teaching what is necessary for salvation. He contrasts the
word of God with "the fallible discourses of man" and concludes that

only scripture "is a Worke too hard for the teeth of time, and cannot perish but in the generall flames, when all things shall confesse their ashes."[20] This suggests to me that the Bible has a way of resisting all human attempts to tame it and make it serve human purposes and prejudices. Or, to put the point another way, we cannot suppose that our interpretations of scripture are easily identified with scripture itself and, still more, that they are in any sense infallible. For this reason scripture functions primarily to guide Christians toward God through Christ and only secondarily as a rule designed to resolve religious controversies. Of course, most of the writings I shall seek to examine appeared in the context of controversy; and this last point can easily be obscured. Perhaps Hooker can be our guide. His *Laws of Ecclesiastical Polity* is surely a work designed to refute Puritan opposition to the Elizabethan Settlement, and by pursuing his footnotes it is possible to enter fully into the controversy. Nevertheless, his genius was to rise above the controversy and to present a positive exposition of Elizabethan Anglicanism from as irenic a point of view as possible.

Richard Hooker (c. 1554–1600)

Born in Exeter, Hooker went up to Corpus Christi College, Oxford, in 1573. There he enjoyed the patronage of John Jewel, the Elizabethan apologist against Rome. His tutor was John Reynolds, who became the leader of the Puritan cause at the Hampton Court Conference in 1604. Hooker became deputy professor of Hebrew at Oxford in 1579, vicar of a country parish in 1584, and finally master of the Temple Church in London from 1585 till 1591. In 1588 he married Joan Churchman, and it seems possible that his father-in-law, together with his friends from Oxford, Edwin Sandys and George Cranmer, persuaded him with the support of Archbishop Whitgift to undertake a comprehensive refutation of the Puritan objections to the religious establishment. At any rate Hooker left the Temple in 1591, and on January 29, 1593, registered eight books of the *Laws of Ecclesiastical Polity*, endorsed by the archbishop. He published the first four books in 1593 and appears to have revised and greatly expanded Book Five, which he published in 1597. Books Six and Eight were not published until 1648; Book Seven, not until 1662. The posthumous books, once regarded as suspect, are now regarded as authentic. In his preface Hooker hopes for the day "when the passions of former enmitie being allaied, we shal with ten times redoubled tokens of our unfaignedlie reconciled love, shewe our selves each towards other the same which Joseph and the brethren of Joseph were at the time of their enterview in Aegypt" (Preface 9.4).[21]

Hooker's professed irenic approach may not have been perceived as such by his opponents, but his attempt to press beyond the particular bones of contention to the deeper issue of authority in religion in the first four books does raise the level of the debates. He clearly wants to accept the prime authority of scripture, but at least in one place he treats that authority in the context of the Christian life rather than in that of controversy. At one point in Book Three Hooker explains how scripture functions as a central path to salvation. He does so by examining the question of how we know scripture to be scripture (III.8.13). Because we maintain that scripture teaches all things necessary to salvation, some people "childishly" ask "what scripture can teach us the sacred authoritie of the scripture, upon the knowledge whereof our whole faith and salvation dependeth." Hooker addresses the question by pointing out that the first principles of any science are either "plaine and manifest in them selves" or proved by the evidence of "former knowledge." The main principle assumed in Christian belief is that "the scriptures are the oracles of God him selfe." But this "in it selfe wee cannot say is evident." There can be no demonstration that scripture is the first principle of Christian belief and practice.

Hooker then turns to the question of how Christians come to accept scripture and argues that "by experience we all know, that the first outward motive leading men so to esteeme of the scripture is the authority of Gods Church." This authority is by no means coercive in character. It is merely persuasive and is in no sense sufficient. Hooker speaks not of the tradition of the church but only of the persuasive role of the Christian community. To live in that community is to be directed toward scripture. Once this has happened, the more we take the trouble to read and hear "the misteries" of scripture, the more we find scripture itself confirming "our received opinion concerning it" (III.8.14). Thus, reading scripture takes us beyond the "inducement" of the church. Clearly we must think of a journey that takes us deeper and deeper into scripture. Elsewhere Hooker says, "Let us not thinke that as long as the world doth indure the wit of man shal be able to sound the bottome of that which may be concluded out of the scripture" (I.14.2).

Hooker continues and concludes his argument in this small portion of Book Three by asking how we should read scripture once the church has induced us to take it up. He points out that the ancient church fathers, who themselves relied upon scripture, tried to maintain its authority against the opposition of unbelievers "by arguments such as unbeleevers them selves must needs thinke reasonable, if they judged thereof as they should." This fact implies that Christians must attend to scripture by using their reason, and Hooker claims to suppose that those who say "that of this principle [scripture] there is no proofe but by the testimony of the spirit" cannot mean by this that reason is utterly excluded. It is true that reason is an insufficient tool for reading scripture "if the special grace of the holy ghost concur not to the inlightning of our minds." On the other hand, there is the further question of how the testimony of the Spirit may be discerned. Since the Spirit's workings in us "are so privy and secret," we "stand on a plainer ground, when we gather by reason from the qualitie of things beleeved or done, that the spirit of God hath directed us in both" (III.8.14–15). Reason by no means displaces the Spirit, but it does test it. There are really three points. The community of the church is an outward inducement for Christians to search the scriptures. Once they do so, they find themselves on a path leading to salvation. Finally, searching the scriptures involves the use of reason, but reason assisted by the Holy Spirit. We could draw out the implication that inspiration attaches as much to the readers of scripture as to its writers. What we find, then, is a pattern that is at least correlative with the triple cord. The church leads to scripture, which is interpreted by reason. At the same time, the church is not quite the same thing as tradition; nor can reason function without the assistance of the Holy Spirit. Moreover, the three strands of the triple cord are ordered by the way they describe the Christian's path.

Let me turn now to the place of scripture in religious controversy and employ the conclusions of Hooker, to whom all Anglican roads lead, as a way of establishing a framework for examining later writers. Of course, Hooker in the *Laws* is concerned with refuting the Puritan attacks on the Elizabethan Settlement found in the Vestiarian and Admonition controversies. We can best understand "Puritan" to refer to anyone who held that the Church of England needed to be further purified from Romish corruptions and abuses, which included the ring in marriage, the cross in baptism, kneeling to receive communion, as well as the Prayer Book and episcopacy. Hooker's comprehensive defense of the Settlement presses beyond the specific issues involved to the question of authority. He repudiates the Puritan claim that scripture necessitates a form of church polity and the ceremonies used in Christian worship. And his central point is that these matters are indifferent and accessory; they are not necessary for salvation. Thus, he accepts the prime, indeed virtually sole, authority of scripture *for its purpose,* namely, to reveal all those things necessary for salvation. But this has the effect of seriously restricting and qualifying the authority of scripture. We must not ask scripture to do what it was not designed to accomplish, and so we must begin by defining the purpose of scripture. Influenced by an Aristotelian and Thomistic framework of thought, Hooker defines law teleologically. That is, a law describes the proper development of something from its potentiality to its full actualization. Of course, God is himself exempt from this understanding. His being is a law to his working; that is, he is *actus purus,* and we can make no distinction between his essence and his existence. All other parts of the divine law, however, describe how all things are meant to find their true being in relation to God. For humans God is the chief good and our happiness. It is our reason that in principle allows us to gain some knowledge of God and so of the duties and works that will enable us to find bliss.

That Hooker's understanding of reason depends upon Thomas is clear from his citation of the *Summa Theologica* in III.9.2: *"Out of the precepts of the lawe of nature, as out of certaine common and undemonstrable principles, mans reason doth necessarily proceede unto certaine more particular determinations."*[22] At the same time, Hooker modifies Thomas in several ways. He prefers to speak of the law of reason rather than of natural law, but it is not entirely clear that he means to make any absolute distinction. Hooker's preference may have to do with the wider meaning of natural law and his own emphasis upon distinctions within the created order. That is, the law of nature for the non-rational creation differs from the law of reason for human beings, who are rational. Moreover, Hooker adds "the law celestial," which governs the angels (I.3.1). A second difference from Thomas is that we find no mention of *synderesis* or *synedesis*. Despite such complications there can be little doubt that Hooker's thought is oriented toward Thomas and Aristotle. Nevertheless, there is one puzzle in his understanding of human reason difficult to resolve. He can cite Romans 2:15 (the Gentiles have a law "written on their hearts") as a reference to "the universall law of mankind, the law of reason, whereby they judge as by a rule which God hath given unto all men for that purpose" (I.16.5). Later he denies that scripture abrogates "the lawe of nature; which is an infallible knowledge imprinted in the mindes of all the children of men, whereby both generall principles for directing of humaine actions are comprehended, and conclusions derived from them." These conclusions represent progress and growth in choosing good and evil "in the daylie affaires of this life" (II.8.6). Passages like this give the impression that Hooker embraces the idea of innate reason, understood in a Platonizing fashion as the participation of the human soul in God. Such a view would be an understanding quite different from those of Thomas and Aristotle, and it would contradict other places where Hooker adopts a *tabula rasa* epistemology.

One way of resolving this difficulty is to argue that what Hooker regards as innate is not so much knowledge of the good as a potential capacity for such knowledge. Even in the last passage I have cited, his emphasis is upon growth in the moral and spiritual life. He does not share the opinion of some who suppose "that nature in working hath before hir certaine exemplary draughts or patternes" that exist in God and that, when discerned, function to guide nature the way "the pole-starre of the world" guides sailors. Yet he embraces "the Oracle of Hippocrates,[23] that *'Each thing both in small and in great fulfilleth the taske which destenie hath set down'* " (I.3.4). Since God is the chief good that represents the goal for human beings, he has created humans with the potential for attaining that goal by actualizing their capacity for knowing the good and so fulfilling the law of their being. "The soule of man" is at first a book with nothing written in it; "yet all thinges may be imprinted." Consequently, we must "search by what steppes and degrees it ryseth unto perfection of knowledge." The growth involved includes "the abilities of reaching higher then unto sensible things." And the chief means by which it takes place are education and instruction, "the one by us, the other by precepts" (I.6.1–5). This may mean that the actualization of our capacity to reason involves not only progress in reasoning, but also attending to the consent of mankind with respect to moral norms. In the final analysis it may not be possible to resolve the tensions in Hooker's view, but to regard "the law written on the heart" as a capacity that must be actualized comes closest to doing so.

It is important to add that Hooker does not suppose that this natural capacity of reason disappears when scripture comes into play. His discussion in III.9 has to do with cases where scripture has not provided any explicit law. In these cases "what is so ... partly scripture and partly reason must teach to discerne." Moreover, we must agree with Augustine not to *"refuse ... the light of nature"* (III.9.1).[24] Nevertheless, human reason is not unassisted. "The light of naturall understanding wit and reason is from God, he it is which thereby doth illuminate every man entering into the world." Hooker's allusion to John 1:9 leads to an appeal to Romans 1:19 and 2:15, and to the conclusion that the laws of the heathens insofar as they derive from "the light of nature" come from God, who was "the writer of them in the tables of their hartes" (III.9.3). Thus, even apart from scripture Hooker can agree with Thomas that grace perfects nature. Presumably, if there had been no Fall, and if humans had not been in some degree affected by Adam's sin and had not inherited his guilt, grace perfecting nature would have sufficed. But the Fall rendered reason, even when graced, insufficient. It is difficult to discern Hooker's understanding of original sin. He clearly does not suppose that our natural capacities have disappeared or become completely disabled, and so he is far from espousing any notion of total depravity. Nevertheless, it is not easy to describe how badly wounded we have been by the Fall.

It is in this context, however, that Hooker defines God's gift of scripture (I.11.5–6), and he begins by arguing that "our naturall meanes…unto blessednes are our workes." Original sin, however, renders these means impotent. No one can be saved this way because "all flesh is guiltie" and, consequently, incapable of "performing exactly the duties and workes of righteousnes." Excluded from salvation and bliss this way, "behold how the wisdome of God hath revealed a way mysticall and supernaturall." This second way, "prepared before all worldes," is scripture, designed to supply a redemptive way to bliss and a remedy for what nature now lacks because of the fall. Scripture, then, is God's supernatural remedy for the Fall and has a special place in the divine law. As we have seen, this does not mean that scripture merely replaces the natural law. Indeed, it includes the natural law, teaching us "how that which is desired naturally must now supernaturally be attained" and clarifying for us "such naturall duties as coulde not by light of nature easilie have bene knowne" (I.12.3). Scripture is "fraught even with lawes of nature"; and Hooker cautions us that when we extol "the complete sufficiencie" of scripture, we must understand "that the benefite of natures light be not thought excluded as unnecessarie, because the necessitie of a diviner light is magnifyed."[25]

If Hooker parts company with his opponents by denying that the light of scripture extinguishes that of nature, he also disagrees by insisting upon a distinction between what is necessary for salvation and what is merely accessory or indifferent. As we have seen, this distinction is important for the Anglican formularies of Hooker's time. The idea that there are *adiaphora* correlates with Hooker's distinction between the divine law in all its aspects and positive laws. Positive laws may be imposed by individuals, public societies, all nations, or even by God. They can be either permanent or changeable, but in any case they are mutable and, presumably, fallible (I.15.1). Citing Whitaker, Hooker draws the same conclusion about ecclesiastical laws and customs (I.14.5). Granted that the apostles instituted "rites and customes" to regulate the church without committing all of them to writing, apostolic rites and customs, whether written or unwritten, have "the nature of things changeable" and can be altered. While Hooker can admit that scripture includes general principles to be followed in ordering the church, he is quite clear that "matters of fayth, and in generall matters necessarie unto salvation, are of a different nature from Ceremonies, order, and the kinde of Church-governement" (III.2.2).[26] The "accessory" points can be altered, since there is no difference in changing a path by covering it with grass, gravel, or stone. While they need not find a place in scripture, we can remember that scripture is a "storehouse abounding with inestimable treasures of wisdome and knowledge in many kindes, over and above thinges in this one kinde barely necessary." Even "matters of Ecclesiasticall politie are not therein omitted, but taught also, albeit not so taught as those other thinges [principles of church order] before mentioned" (III.11.16). With respect to episcopacy, then, Hooker's view is complex. In principle, its authority rests upon that of the monarch acting through Parliament. Nevertheless, it can be grounded in scripture, though not as something necessary for salvation or immutable.

It is somewhat more difficult to discern what Hooker includes as points necessary for salvation. In his *Learned Discourse* he is concerned with arguing that Rome has preserved the "foundacion of faith," however much she has corrupted it. Part of his reason for this conclusion is his wish not to excommunicate the "thowsandes of our fathers lyving in popishe supersticions."[27] In explaining what he means by the foundation of faith he draws a distinction between the mystical church "whereof Christe is the onely hed" and the visible church "the *foundacion* whereof is the doctryne *of the prophettes and Apostles* profeste" (Eph 2:20). Hooker clearly means scripture, but in going on to define the foundation included in scripture he cites the first verse of Mark's Gospel:[28] By "gospel" Mark means the teaching of salvation, and he adds "of Jesus Christ, the Son of God" because salvation is by him. This Jesus was conceived by the Holy Ghost, embraced by Simeon, condemned by Pilate, crucified by the Jews, and preached by the apostles. The Savior is the foundation on which "the frame of the gospell is erected." As Paul says (1 Cor 3:11): "other foundation can no man lay." At least we can conclude that the chief point necessary for salvation is accepting Christ as the only Savior.

If we begin here, it is arguable that Hooker's best account of the points necessary for salvation is his lengthy discussion in Book Five of the *Laws* (V.50–67). The aim of his discussion is to treat the sacraments, but he starts it a long way off. Since the sacraments are "the powerfull instrumentes of God to eternall life," and since this means "the union of the soule with God," we must posit Christ as the mediator and "must first consider how God is in Christ, then how Christ is in us, and how the sacramentes doe serve to make us partakers of Christ" (V.50.3). Hooker opens his argument with the doctrine of the Trinity, claiming that it insists upon Christ's consubstantial divinity, which in the incarnation is united with human nature. We who "are born children of wrath" can be adopted as children of God "through grace" only because "the naturall sonne of God" is the mediator between God and us (V.51.3). Human beings can neither understand nor explain "how this was brought to passe" (V.52.1). But Hooker adopts what is usually called a neo-Chalcedonian understanding of Christ's person, an understanding fully formulated in the East by John Damascene and in the West by Thomas Aquinas. This Christology argues that the terms "substance" and "nature" are generic and that a nature always expresses itself in concrete "subsistences" (*hypostaseis*). Thus, the divine nature expresses itself in the three divine subsistences or persons of the

Trinity, while ordinarily human nature expresses itself in the subsistences of individual human beings. But in the case of Christ human nature finds concrete expression in the divine subsistence of the Son of God. Hooker, then, concludes that "in Christ there is no personall subsistence but one, and that from everlastinge." This is because "the Sonne of God tooke not to him selfe a mans person but the nature only of a man" (V.52.3). Christ has a full human nature, but there is no individual man Jesus.

Hooker would not have been obliged to adopt this Christology, which seems to us so very strange. He employs it simply because he supposes it to be the usual and accepted understanding. His major conclusion at this point is that Christ is by three degrees a receiver: by his eternal generation from the Father he is the Son of God; by his incarnation he receives union between God and humanity; and he also receives the grace of unction, which establishes the possibility for humans to be drawn into that union (V.54). Next we must conclude that Christ's body can have only a local presence, and yet because of the conjunction of the divine and human natures Christ's humanity can "after a sorte" be present everywhere, drawn along by the ubiquity of the Son of God (V.55). At this point Hooker has established the possibility of Christ's presence. His next step is to consider how we may participate in that presence. Of course, in a general way all things participate in Christ, since the divine nature is, to use our words, the ground of all being. But saving participation is something else (V.56.6).

Hooker begins his discussion of saving participation in Christ by speaking of those who "were in God eternallie by theire intended admission to life" and who "have by vocation or adoption God actuallie now in them." God's predestination of the elect becomes effective by his triune operation — from the Father, by the Son, and through the Spirit (2 Cor 13:13); and this is what St. Peter means by "the participation of divine nature" (2 Pet 1:4). The emphasis is upon the working out of God's eternal decrees of election. "Our beinge in Christ by eternall foreknowledge saveth us not without our actuall and reall adoption into the fellowship of his Sainctes in this present world." Hooker's view is almost certainly meant to be an interpretation of Article Seventeen of the Thirty-Nine Articles with its emphasis upon predestination to salvation and upon the mysterious character of the doctrine. Despite complexities, it is reasonably clear that Hooker repudiates any notion of a limited atonement and that he treats God's eternal decrees of election as the cause of salvation, but his eternal decrees of reprobation as based upon foreseen sin.[29] Nevertheless, what seems to be crucial is our incorporation into the fellowship of God's saints and into the church. "As therefore wee are reallie partakers of the bodie of synne and death receaved from Adam, so except wee be trulie partakers of Christ, and as reallie possessed of his Spirit, all wee speake of eternall life is but a dreame" (V.56.7).

Our actual participation in Christ requires us to recognize that "Christ imparteth plainelie him selfe by degrees" (V.56.10). It is easy to overlook the next step in Hooker's argument, but before he turns his attention to the sacraments he argues that "wee participate Christ partelie by imputation...partlie by habituall and reall infusion" (V.56.11). These references are to justification by faith and to sanctification. Elsewhere Hooker succinctly defines the terms by saying: "That whereby here we are justefied is perfecte, but not inherente, that whereby we are sanctified, inherent but not perfecte."[30] What he means is that the righteousness we receive in justification is not our own ("inherent"), but is Christ's perfect righteousness imputed to us, while the righteousness we receive in sanctification is our own, but is never perfected in this life. Underlying Hooker's complex and technical exposition is the simple idea that Christ brings us God's forgiveness when we neither deserve it nor have done anything to elicit it. That forgiveness then expresses itself in holy living; it is "faith working through love" (Gal 5:6). Hooker remains true to the Protestant doctrines that dominate the Articles of Religion, and the only reason he does not say more at this point in Book Five is because the topic he is addressing is the meaning of the sacraments.

Hooker, then, continues by considering what sacraments are. They do not merely instruct us, but are "marks" enabling us to know "when God doth impart the vital or saving grace of Christ unto all that are capable thereof," as well as "means conditional" that God requires of those who receive his grace (V.57.1–2). They are necessary not because they are efficacious in themselves, but because they are "*morall instrumentes* of salvation. . . . For all receyve not the grace of God which receive the sacramentes of his grace." What Hooker means is that it lies in God's will how he will make the sacraments instruments of his grace. The "use" of these instruments is "in our handes," but "the effect in his." Yet the sacraments "reallie give what they promise, and are what they signifie" (V.57.4–5). Baptism represents the beginning of the Christian life and is given once for all. Its purpose is to incorporate people into Christ so that by his merits they may "obteine as well that savinge grace of imputation which taketh away all former guiltines, as also that infused divine vertue of the holie Ghost which giveth to the powers of the soule theire first disposition towardes future newness of life" (V.60.2). The grace we have by the eucharist "doth not begin but continue life" (V.67.1). Baptism, then, correlates with justification by faith ("imputation") and the first beginning of sanctification ("infusion"), while the eucharist functions in the context of sanctification.

Hooker, of course, says much more about the sacraments; and he addresses a number of different questions — the necessity of baptism, the fate of unbaptized children, baptism by women, godparents, the cross in baptism, confirmation, transubstantiation, and consubstantiation. With respect to the eucharist he argues that everyone agrees that the sacrament is a means of effecting Christ's presence in the heart of the worthy receiver and that we need not inquire whether this involves any change in the elements of bread and wine. "The reall presence of Christs most blessed bodie and bloode is not therefore to be sought for in the sacrament, but in the worthie receiver of the sacrament" (V.67.6). And it is arguable that "the worthy receiver" is, at least in the first instance, the one who has been justified by faith. While Hooker does reject both transubstantiation and consubstantiation, he simply remains agnostic with respect to some sort of spiritual presence of Christ in the elements of bread and wine.

My point in this rather long discussion of Hooker's argument in Book Five has been to suggest that it supplies a fairly extended account of what he regards as necessary for salvation. Of course, he does not say this in so many words, but his exposition is a reasonably full statement of how he understands the Christian life. And surely he supposes his account to derive from scripture. In a sense, he simply elaborates what it means to affirm Christ as the Savior. What seems most interesting to me is his correlation of justification and sanctification with the two dominical sacraments. He appears concerned to bind together the Protestant doctrines and their individualistic implications with an equal insistence upon the corporate significance of the church and its sacraments. What Hooker sought to join together began to fall apart after his death. Even though it is obvious that reformers such as Luther and Calvin had no wish to dispense with the church and the sacramental life, the logic of Protestantism tended toward arguing that access to the saving work of Christ was not primarily through the church. A "conversion" understanding of Christianity, then, stands in some tension with an "ecclesiastical" understanding. During the early Stuart period and the English Revolution the High Calvinists tended to emphasize the Protestant doctrines and their "conversion" implications, whereas the Arminians sought to underline the church and the sacraments.

> For Hooker, tradition is at best a negative criterion that obliges us to search scripture for warrants related to the ordering of the church.

To return to Hooker, implicit in his understanding of the purpose and function of scripture and of the necessary points it reveals for salvation is the question of its interpretation. And it is to that issue that I wish to turn. He raises the problem of the sense in which scripture "contains" all things necessary. Does this mean an "expresse setting downe in plaine tearmes," or are we to think of scripture as "*comprehending* in such sort that by reason we may from thence conclude all things which are necessary"? He points out that the Trinity, "the dutie of baptizing infants," and "such other principal points, the necessitie whereof is by none denied, are notwithstanding in scripture no where to be found by expresse literall mention, only deduced they are out of scripture by collection" (I.14.2). In the first three books Hooker creates the impression that, generally speaking, we are obliged to make deductions from scripture. This appears to restrict the number of "plain passages." But in tension with this he later argues (V.22.14) that the plain passages are sufficient for revealing what is necessary for salvation. The simplest Christian after the publication of the gospel has now "a key unto knowlidge which the Eunuch in the Actes did want." Even children can understand what is "plaine and easie" without an interpreter. "Scripture therefore is not *so harde* but that the *onlie readinge* thereof may give life unto willinge hearers." Perhaps reason is necessary in some sense as a tool enabling the reader to discern the plain passages. But it is certainly clear that when we are obliged to make deductions from scripture, reason *is* a tool rather than an authority. Since the word of God with respect to the end God ordained for it is "perfect, exact, and absolute in it selfe," reason is not meant to supply any "maime or defect" in scripture. Instead, it is "a necessary instrument, without which we could not reape by the scriptures perfection, that fruite and benefit which it yieldeth" (III.8.10). Hooker, as I have noted, wants to add that reason requires the assistance of the Holy Spirit. But he also argues that the idea works both ways. He says that "nature hath need of grace, whereunto I hope, we are not opposite, by holding that grace hath use of nature" (III.8.6). Reason is more than that faculty of judgment by which we make deductions; it is a power by which God enables us, at least imperfectly, to discern the divine law. God himself, who is "that light which none can approch unto, hath sent out these lights whereof we are capable, even as so many sparkls resembling the bright fountain from which they rise" (III.8.9). He also appeals to Romans 2:14 and the Apostle's idea that the Gentiles who do the law by nature are a law to themselves (I.8.3). The major conclusion to be drawn is that we must distinguish between scripture itself and our interpretations of it, the deductions we make by employing our reason. Moreover, we must place reason in a public rather than a private context. These ideas add to his understanding of reason as a natural capacity, but they do not contradict it. Finally, the infallibility of scripture does not necessarily attach to our interpretations.

It is rather more difficult to argue that Hooker treats tradition as another instrument besides reason for interpreting scripture. To be sure, we have already seen that the church has a preliminary and persuasive authority in directing people to scripture. And he says that while scripture is "the ground of our beliefe" in what concerns "salvation by Christ," "yet the authoritie of man is, if we marke it, the key which openeth the dore of entrance into the knowledge of the scripture" (II.7.3). But it is one thing to regard the church and its tradition as what persuades people to consult scripture and quite another to understand tradition as a tool for interpretation. Obviously, Hooker opposes the "traditions urged by the Church of *Rome*" (I.13.2). But he also treats apostolic ordinances as mutable. Indeed, he responds to the accusation that "we have departed from the auncient simplicitie of Christ and his Apostles" by arguing that such an apostolic canon is "either uncertaine or at least wise insufficient, if not both" (IV.2.1). On the other hand, he says that what "the Church hath received and held so long for good" carries with it the presumption that it is "meete and convenient" (IV.4.2). Antiquity, then, becomes a negative criterion for the ordering of the church and its rites and ceremonies. We should not condemn what "long experience of all ages hath confirmed and made profitable" simply "because wee sometimes knowe not the cause and reason of them" (IV.1.3). Thus, the ancient traditions of the church have the benefit of the doubt. And for this reason it is possible to find justification for them in scripture, as in the case of episcopacy. Nevertheless, Hooker is not thinking of what is necessary for salvation. Tradition is at best a negative criterion that obliges us to search scripture for warrants related to the ordering of the church. If my conclusions are correct, it is difficult to see that Hooker employs the triple cord as a theological method for resolving controversies.

What we have is God's divine law for salvation revealed in scripture and interpreted by our fallible reason. The Church of England stands in the middle ground between Rome's belief in the insufficiency of scripture and the Puritan view of its omnicompetence. Hooker has no wish to supplant an ecclesiastical infallibility with a biblicism that would make our interpretations of scripture infallible.

Hooker's thought is far more difficult to interpret than it seems, and it becomes obvious that it is not entirely systematic. Indeed, there seem to be a number of possible Hookers. Is he another Thomas Aquinas? a follower of Calvin? a precursor of Locke? a writer who anticipates the incarnational theology and sacramental piety of William Temple? There is some truth in each of these suggestions. But we must not forget that Hooker was an Elizabethan Protestant, committed not only to the church and its sacraments and to the Tudor understanding of a godly commonwealth, but also to the Protestant doctrines of the Articles of Religion — predestination, original sin, and justification. No matter how we assess Hooker, scripture occupies the central position in his thought; and it is sufficient to reveal all things necessary for salvation. Thus, its prime function is to guide people to holiness and to the blessedness of salvation. This does not require it to reveal accessory matters and arrangements that are capable of change, such as ecclesiastical polity. Scripture overlaps in complicated ways with the law of reason and the law of nature. It does not always explain itself and so must be interpreted. Our interpretations can never exhaust the meaning of scripture, and they are fallible as it is not. Two central problems remain unresolved. First, how are we to distinguish in scripture between what is necessary for salvation and what is a matter of indifference, between the plain and the obscure passages? Second, what are the tools we must use to interpret scripture, and how are we to define them? I am doubtful that anyone has ever given satisfactory answers to these questions. In our time Bultmann has argued that it is not possible to interpret scripture without presuppositions, and it seems likely enough that these presuppositions have a way of dictating what we suppose to be necessary or essential, as well as the tools we use for interpretation. The great risk, if this is so, is that scripture may become a mouthpiece for our prejudices and ideologies.

I surely do not want to conclude on the basis of these considerations that Hooker's position is to be rejected out of hand. He would himself admit that all human attempts to come to terms with scripture fall short of their purpose and that scripture is, indeed, "too hard for the teeth of time." In the next chapter I want to turn to the seventeenth century and to examine several of the Caroline divines important in their time. Two points will inform my discussion. First, the same problems that can be discovered in Hooker's thought re-appear in one way or another. Second, and perhaps more important, while the influence of Hooker is by no means absent, it is difficult to see that these divines follow his lead in a coherent way. Many people would regard Hooker as normative, at least for early Anglicanism. But, as I shall hope to show in the next chapter, this conclusion must be seriously qualified, if not dismissed altogether.

Chapter Two

The Lively Oracles of God
1603–1660

The Elizabethan Settlement proved to be not the end of the Reformation but only the completion of the first act of the drama. The second act began with its gradual collapse during the reigns of James I (1603–25) and his son, Charles I (1625–49), reached its climax in the English Revolution (1640–60), and its denouement in the Glorious Revolution of 1688, which abandoned the attempt of the Cavalier Parliament and Charles II to impose too narrow a religious settlement. There are various ways of assessing the seventeenth century in England, and more broadly in all of Britain, now that the crowns of Scotland and England were united. Some would emphasize the emergence of a constitutional monarchy and the eclipse of the monarch's prerogative powers, that is, those that were in no way bound by Parliament or the common law. Others see the period in social and economic terms as the rise of a mercantile economy and of capitalism. From another point of view the Act of Toleration (1689) marks the beginning of toleration, which did not extend to full civil toleration of dissenters from the Church of England until the nineteenth century. Nevertheless, these differing interpretations all revolve around the transition toward a modern secular society.

The Bible kept its central place at least for the first half of the century, but much of the controversy that characterized the period reflected disagreement as to how this should be understood. In April of 1603 while he was traveling to London, James I received the Millenary Petition, which requested reform of the Prayer Book along the lines of the familiar Puritan objections, together with the removal of other abuses that "we are able to show not to be agreeable to the

Scriptures."[1] James responded by summoning the Hampton Court Conference in 1604, a conference that dashed all the Puritan hopes and made no changes except to set in motion the project that led to the publication of the King James Bible in 1611. The prefatory material attached to the translation insists upon the fullness and perfection of scripture.[2] It is an armor, medicine, meat, and "a shower of heavenly bread," "a panary of wholesome food against fenowed [i.e., mouldy, musty] traditions," a treasure, and a fountain.[3] The aim of the translation is not to repudiate earlier ones, "but to make a good one better, or out of many good ones, one principal good one."[4]

It is clear that the translators in their preface are concerned with meeting possible objections. They recognize that they will "be traduced by popish persons" and "maligned by self-conceited brethren." The latter are obviously the Puritans. Yet even they at the Hampton Court Conference claimed that they could not "subscribe to the Communion book, since it maintained the Bible as it was there translated, which was, as they said, a most corrupted translation."[5] This observation implies the Puritan commitment to the Geneva Bible of 1560 with its Calvinist marginal notes. The preface of the King James Bible, then, reflects the strength of Puritan objections to the establishment. These objections were made with increasing force after 1611, and they clearly involved more than scripture. There is no need to repeat the story of the next half century. Suffice it to say that the policies of James and Charles seemed popish to many, that the rise of Arminianism threatened to undermine the moderate Calvinism of the Church of England, that during the English Revolution episcopacy and the Prayer Book were proscribed, and that the Restoration Settlement of 1662 seems to have established a moderate Arminianism rather than a moderate Calvinism. The so-called Arminians need not be fully identified with the followers of Arminius in Holland; but they certainly opposed Calvinism and, as well, set the stage for Restoration Anglicanism with its emphasis upon the church, the sacraments, episcopacy, and holy living.

Through all these changes the differing parties all appealed to scripture in one way or another, but the conclusions they drew differed widely. Many of the Independents could agree with the Calvinists of the Westminster Assembly, which began to meet in 1643; but they differed in refusing a presbyterian polity and in insisting upon a purely congregational one. Within Independency and the more radical sects that began to appear during the Commonwealth there were both Calvinists and "Arminians" or anti-Calvinists. The authority of the Bible could mean a great many things. In what follows I want to restrict attention to Anglican understandings of scripture and to focus upon Hall, Chillingworth, and Hammond. All three supported episcopacy and the Prayer Book, yet their interpretations of scripture and its authority not only represent three differing views, but also fail to repeat in any clear fashion the party platform established by Hooker.

Joseph Hall (1574–1656)

It was at the age of fifteen, only five years after Emmanuel College, Cambridge, received its charter, that Hall entered the college that became the seminary for Puritan leadership in the Church of England during the late sixteenth and early seventeenth centuries. His education prepared him to be one of those moderate Calvinists who supported episcopacy and the Prayer Book and who were typical of the Elizabethan church. Hall not only took his degrees at Emmanuel College, but also became a fellow. He received the living of Halsted in Suffolk in 1601 and moved to Waltham Abbey north of London in 1608. He came to the attention of the court and became one of Prince Henry's chaplains, then dean of Worcester in 1616 and bishop of Exeter in 1621. He accompanied King James to Scotland in 1617, but was more sympathetic to the Scottish presbyterians than was politic. Despite this and the fact that he was one of the English delegates to the Synod of Dort in 1618, Laud was instrumental in his appointment to the see of Exeter. While the two men were obviously not of the same mind, Laud found no reason to complain about Hall's administration of the diocese. At the end of 1641, shortly after King Charles had appointed him bishop of Norwich, Hall was one of the twelve bishops impeached for treason and sent to the Tower by Parliament. Released in May of 1642, he moved to Norwich; but a year later the parliamentary commissioners ejected him from his see. Hall spent the last thirteen years of his life in a nearby village, where he continued to write.

Hall's earliest works are his satirical poems, but his most characteristic ones are meditative and spiritual writings. Nevertheless, he was constantly involved in controversy — with Rome, with separatists, and with the quarrel over the five articles of Dort. His best-known work, *Episcopacy by Divine Right Asserted,* published in 1640, provoked the *Humble Remonstrance* of "Smectymnuus"[6] and a pamphlet warfare into which John Milton entered. What Hall has to say about scripture certainly appears in his controversial works, but on my reading of him he is more concerned with treating the Bible as what forms the Christian life than as a rule by which to resolve religious controversies. Like Hooker he accords scripture a central place. In one of his letters, published in 1610, he calls "the necessary grounds of Christian faith" the foundation, and identifies that foundation with scripture.[7] In a much later work he shifts the metaphor: scripture is like the sun, while the church is like the clock that tells the time indicated by the sun. Clearly we must "believe the sun against the clock, not the clock against the sun." And "so we cannot but justly tax the incredulity of those, who will rather trust to the Church than to the Scripture."[8] Whether as the foundation or the sun, scripture, contains all things necessary for salvation. All "these fundamental verities . . . are clearly laid before us, in the sacred monuments of Divine Scriptures. In them, is the full and easy direction of a Christian's both belief and practice."[9]

Unlike Hooker, however, Hall insists upon the plain passages in scripture as revealing what is necessary for salvation. The perspicuity of scripture has to do with the fact that these passages explain themselves. "Did God envy unto mankind the full revelation of his will, in the perpetual monuments of his written word? Or, did he not think it expedient to lay up all necessary doctrines in the common store-house of truths?"[10] Borrowing a passage from Gregory the

Great, Hall does acknowledge that there are shallows and deeps in scripture — shallows where even lambs can wade and deeps where only elephants can swim. The idea carries with it the caution that people must be careful of the deeps and even that we must beware of interpreting scripture "according to our private conceit."[11] Reading and hearing scripture require a spirit of holy reverence and an elevation of our hearts to God. Even David prays God to open his eyes (Ps 119:18), since he "can see nothing, without a new act of apertion: letters he might see, but wonders he could not see; till God did unclose his eyes, and enlighten them." For this reason we must work at understanding; but where we cannot understand, we "must admire silently." The "plain truths" of scripture may be enjoyed by all Christians, but the "deep mysteries" require special interpreters. "Those shallow fords, that are in it, may be waded by every passenger; but there are deeps, wherein he, that cannot swim, may drown."[12] Hall's caution against private interpretation, then, appears to refer to the hard passages in scripture which not everyone can understand by adducing the clear passages.[13] The ordinary Christian should be satisfied with the plain and necessary truths of scripture. "What a disease in our appetite, when we have wholesome provision laid before us, to nauseate all good dishes; and to long for mushrooms, whereof some are venomous, all unwholesome!"[14]

Even if we grant that the plain passages in scripture interpret themselves, Hall is obliged to admit that interpretation is in some sense necessary. Presumably, to explain the obscure passages by the plain ones is an exercise of reason. And it is the case that Hall can follow Hooker in saying that reason has a role to play in religious controversies. But I can find no clear place where he treats reason as an instrument for "reaping the fruits of scripture." The first thirteen chapters of *The Old Religion,* which Hall published in 1627, refute a rather long list of Romish errors by appealing to scripture and to reason. But these are two different if complementary appeals and do not treat reason in its relation to scripture, nor does he explain what he means by reason.[15] Perhaps one explanation for this peculiarity is that Hall seems to have become increasingly mistrustful of reason. In

Satan's Fiery Darts Quenched, published in 1647, he addresses the tempter by admitting his doom "if I had no better guide to follow, than that which thou callest Reason." But though he is a man by nature and obliged to use "the dim and weak rush-candle-light of carnal reason," he is regenerate and "the grace of regeneration shows me the bright torch-light, yea, the sun of divine illumination." Satan bids him "to follow the light of reason," but God bids him "to follow the light of faith."[16] Hall qualifies this view by going on to say that even though it can nowhere be found "in the original purity," reason "is the great gift of my Creator." And it is his regenerate reason that "will teach me to subscribe to all those truths, which the unerring Spirit of the Holy God hath revealed in his Sacred Word, however contrary to the ratiocination of flesh and blood." Hall agrees with Hooker in defining reason as fallen and so requiring the assistance of grace. But the conclusions he draws are pessimistic, whereas Hooker's are optimistic and positive.

Hall's appeal to tradition, or better to antiquity, poses an ambiguity difficult to resolve. Positively, he cites with approval King James's declaration that "whatsoever is contained either in the Sacred Scriptures, or the Three Famous Creeds, or the Four First General Councils, that, he embraces with both arms; that he proclaims for his faith."[17] Moreover, in several places he makes it clear that he accepts the authority of the creeds, especially the Apostles' Creed, which is "the common cognizance of our faith."[18] At the same time he asks whether there is "any thing in the substance of that Creed, which we cannot fetch from the Apostles." And he answers his question by appealing to Augustine's opinion that the several clauses of the creed are "scattered here and there in the Scriptures, penned by the Apostles, gathered up and reduced into this sum."[19] The authority of the creeds is reduced to that of scripture, and he nowhere treats the creeds as hermeneutical tools for discerning the necessary points of scripture.

In Hall's polemical works against Rome he does frequently appeal to antiquity. But these appeals are always designed to respond to "those idle demands of some smattering questionists: Where our Church hath thus long hid itself: What year and day it came to

light."[20] By appealing to the Church of England's conformity with
antiquity the charge of novelty made against it by the papists finds a
refutation. Indeed, the charge recoils against the papists themselves.
"I compare the judgment of the ancient Church with yours: see, therefore, and be ashamed of your novelty."[21] Hall's arguments need not
reflect according full authority to the ancient church. In one of his
letters, published in 1608, he makes his position clear. He points out
that "our adversaries," the apologists for Rome, claim to be judged
in "the Court of the Fathers." This apparent courage stems from their
knowledge that they will be defeated at the bar of scripture. Does this
mean that antiquity is "our enemy, their advocate"? This is obviously
not the case, since truth cannot be novel. The implication is that the
antiquity of truth is to be found primarily in scripture.[22] Antiquity,
then, bears witness to the necessary truths found in scripture; but it
has no independent authority. Nor can there be any appeal to unwritten tradition. Indeed, nothing is "more common with the holy
Fathers of the Church, than the magnifying the complete perfection
of Scripture, in all things needful, either to be believed or done."[23] If
we turn from what is necessary to matters of church order, there can
be no secure appeal to antiquity. The church's rites are her apparel,
clothing that "hath her fashions" and is "variable, according to ages
and places. To reduce us to the same observations which were in
apostolical use, were no better than to tie us to the sandals of the disciples, or seamless coat of our Saviour. . . . God meant us no bondage
in their example."[24]

At first Hall's treatise on episcopacy would appear to contradict
the argument I am making. After his dedication to King Charles,
Hall turns to the occasion for the work, the renunciation of episcopal orders by the bishop of Orkney at the assembly in Edinburgh.
This act cannot be thought analogous to the loss of episcopacy by
the Continental Protestants, since they can plead their necessity. It is
one thing to lighten a ship in a storm by throwing cargo overboard,
quite another to do so in a fair and calm sea.[25] Hall's argument after
this introduction is a defense of episcopacy on the grounds that Christ

and his apostles instituted this form of polity and that there are scriptural warrants for it. Does this mean that Hall appeals to the double authority of apostolicity and scripture? Any affirmative answer requires serious qualification. First, Hall makes it quite clear that he is not speaking of a point necessary for salvation. He cites the opinion that the only things that can claim to be apostolic are things recorded in the writings of the apostles. Hall doubts this opinion. He recognizes its truth as applied to "doctrine necessary for salvation," but regards it as excessively rigid if applied to "ritual observation."[26] Not only episcopacy but also the observance of the Lord's day, the baptism of infants, churches, texts for sermons, and public prayers are matters accepted because of apostolic practice, even though they have no express warrant in scripture.

The appeal to apostolicity, then, is in the context of what Hooker called the accessories of the Christian religion. Here, indeed, we do find an authority, at least in certain practices; and Hall clearly takes a positive view of apostolicity in this context. He notes that "the universal practice of the Church immediately succeeding the Apostles, is the best commentary upon the practice of the Apostles." Moreover, what has always and everywhere been practiced in the church is "the best guide and direction for our carriages and forms of Administration." But this is "next unto God's Word."[27] Hall speaks of guidance and direction rather than authority, and he makes it clear that he is speaking of church order and forms of administration. Moreover, the appeal to antiquity and even to what looks very much like the Vincentian canon is subordinated to the authority of God's word. With these qualifications Hall does not hesitate to say that "the first ages were the purest," like the waters that flow first from the spring. Moreover, the church fathers "wrote . . . according to their unanimous apprehension of the true meaning of the Scriptures; and according to the certain knowledge of the Apostolic Ordinances, derived to them by the undoubted successions of their known predecessors."[28] While Hall by no means underlines the mutability of church order, he does not really differ from Hooker's placement of polity under the rubric of accessories.

The same sort of qualification attaches to Hall's grounding of episcopacy in scripture. He says that "our defence" has to do not with
points of faith but is concerned with "matter of fact." Consequently,
"neither do we hold it needful there should be so full a sway of assent to the testimony of the Church's practice herein, as there ever
ought to be in the direct sentence of the Sacred Scripture."[29] What he
means is that the absence of any clear passages in scripture requiring
episcopacy is unimportant for the simple reason we are not speaking of a fundamental point of faith. Nevertheless, he does want to
say that it is possible to deduce arguments from scripture in support of episcopacy.[30] In contrast he argues that "the Presbyterian
Government . . . hath no true footing, either in Scripture, or the practice of the Church, in all ages, from Christ's time to the present."[31]
The Presbyterians, of course, require that the debate be conducted on
scriptural grounds. If, for the sake of argument, scripture alone can
decide the question and no other evidence can be introduced, then in
the controversy "the clearer Scriptures must carry it, and give light
to the more obscure."[32] In part two of the treatise Hall makes his
argument from scripture.

What he wants to show is that a careful reading of the New Testament, particularly of the Pastoral Epistles of St. Paul, allows us to
deduce that Christ and the apostles established a church polity that
required "a settled imparity, and a perpetuity of jurisdiction."[33] Hall's
discussion makes full use of the biblical texts, but it really supplies a
narrative of the divine origin of episcopacy. Christ's own distinction
between the Twelve and the Seventy first established the imparity of
ministers, while his promise to give judgment to the Twelve (Matt
19:28) indicates perpetual jurisdiction.[34] He points out that the various titles — prophet, evangelist, apostle, bishop, presbyter, deacon —
"in Scripture, are so promiscuously used, that a Preacher is more
than once termed a Prophet; an Evangelist, an Apostle; an Apostle, a
Bishop; an Apostle, a Presbyter; a Presbyter, an Apostle, as Romans
xvi.7; a Presbyter; a Bishop; and, lastly, an Evangelist and Bishop, a
Deacon or Minister."[35] Needless to say, this is quite confusing and
presumably explains why scripture gives no clear mandate for church

polity. Specifically, Hall must argue that the obvious identification of bishop and presbyter in the Pastoral Epistles simply reflects this confusion but that it is nevertheless obvious that Timothy is not "an equal Presbyter with the rest" and has jurisdiction over them. Titus, of course, actually ordains presbyters (Titus 1:5). This means that we can infer that the Apostles appointed bishops, presbyters, and deacons "according to the familiarity and indifferency of their former usage therein" and that "the offices grew fully distinct, even in the Apostles' days, and under their own hands; although, sometimes, the names, after the former use, were confounded."[36]

Hall concludes his argument by making it clear that his lengthy treatment of scripture is required by the exigency of the debate with the Presbyterians. To argue for episcopacy on the basis of the church's long-standing practice would be vain and unconvincing to them. Their prejudice against both bishops and tradition has carried them away to the conclusion that the silence of scripture regarding "the universal practice of the whole Church of God" proves the falsity of that practice. Their "unjust jealousy" stands in contrast to "our" view that "when Christ and his Apostles give us the text, well may the Apostolical and Universal Church yield us the commentary."[37] The real argument for the divine right of episcopacy revolves around its dominical and apostolic origin. But it is also clear that "Episcopal Imparity [is] countenanced by the Written Word." The scriptures alone, and even its clear passages, are the foundation for all necessary beliefs and duties. But in matters of church order it is possible to appeal to an apostolic and even a dominical warrant that is coherent with scripture, even though not mandated by it. We do not find the triple cord in Hall's writings. Certainly tradition has no standing apart from scripture; scripture may supply a warrant for tradition, but not tradition for scripture. And even reason fades in importance by tending to be necessary only in seeking to make sense of the obscure passages. In sum, Hall is convinced that the clear passages of scripture teach everyone the moderate Calvinism to which he is committed with its emphasis upon God's free and saving grace in Christ.

William Chillingworth (1602–1644)

Chillingworth's early career opened him to the charge of being unstable and vacillating. He was a native of Oxford, and his education at Trinity College led to his becoming a fellow of his college in 1628. Late in that year or early in the next the Jesuit missionary Fisher persuaded him to become a Roman Catholic and to leave England, presumably for the Jesuit seminary at Douai in the Spanish Netherlands. After a short time he returned to London, where he was given a temporary home by Lady Falkland, a Roman Catholic herself. But Chillingworth's return seems to have been prompted in part by letters from Laud, who was his godfather, and was a return not only to England, but also to the Church of England. Obliged to leave Lady Falkland's household, in 1634 he moved to Great Tew, the country estate of her son, Lucius Cary, where he became tutor to Cary's two sons. Thus, he was part of the circle of friends that met at Great Tew and that included not only people who later became latitudinarians or high churchmen, but also some of the Cambridge Platonists. It was at Great Tew that Chillingworth wrote his major work, *The Religion of Protestants, a Safe Way of Salvation,* which he published in 1638. When civil war began in August of 1642, Chillingworth embraced the royalist cause. Two years later he was at Arundel Castle when it fell to the parliamentary forces; soon after he died of an illness in Chichester, where he was buried. The minister who conducted his funeral, according to John Aubrey, "threw his booke into the grave with him, saying, *Rott with the rotten; let the dead bury the dead.*"[38]

While the discontinuities of Chillingworth's religious pilgrimage are obvious, it is possible to argue that, like John Donne, he recognized that "On a huge hill, / Cragged, and steep, Truth stands, and he that will / Reach her, about must, and about must go."[39] The search for truth, then, led Chillingworth to the fundamental conclusion that our apprehensions of truth, while sufficient, are by no means infallible.[40] It was in this context as well as in that of controversy that Chillingworth wrote *The Religion of Protestants.* In 1630 Edward Knott, a Jesuit, published *Charity Mistaken, With the Want Whereof*

Catholickes Are Unjustly Charged, a work refuted in 1633 by the Anglican Christopher Potter in *Want of Charity Justly Charged*. The next year Knott replied with *Mercy and Truth, or Charity Maintayned by Catholykes*. Chillingworth tackles all this controversial literature, and this explains the difficulty afforded the reader who seeks to unearth a clear view of the author's position. The motto for his book is a citation from a letter written to Cardinal Perron by Isaac Causabon in the name of James I.[41] The king believes that religious concord depends upon separating out necessary points "in order to obtain a proper agreement." Doing so carries with it the obligation to secure "to everyone the enjoyment of his Christian liberty in those which are not absolutely necessary." By what is necessary the king means "either those things which the Word of God expressly commands to be believed or performed, or those which the primitive church has by necessary consequence deduced from the holy scripture."

If Causabon is correct, the king's view correlates with Article Six of the Thirty-Nine Articles and with Hooker's view. At the same time, what are we to make of the claim that the "primitive church" makes the deductions from scripture? Does Chillingworth fully agree with the motto he has chosen? My argument will be that what attracts him to it is its emphasis upon concord and liberty, and that these two rather strange bedfellows explain both Chillingworth's position and certain confusions in it. But first let me focus upon his attitude toward the double claim that things necessary for salvation can be deduced from scripture and that the primitive church has performed this task. To begin with, Chillingworth appears to accept these conclusions. In his preface (Pref. 28, p. 28) he claims that the canonical books accepted by the Church of England are "the infallible word of God" and that "all things evidently contained in them . . . or even probably deduced from them" are necessary for salvation. He continues by identifying these points with what has always been held "by the catholic church of all ages, or by the consent of the Fathers." His appeal is to the Vincentian canon that Christians must believe what is held by all, everywhere, and at all times. And this leads him to include what is held necessary "either by the Catholic Church of this age, or by the consent of Protestants, or even by the Church of England."

Yet elsewhere Chillingworth appears to contradict himself. Shortly after the passage I have just cited he says that his entire argument is "naturally deducible" from the single principle that "all things necessary to salvation are evidently contained in Scripture" (Pref. 30, p. 29). Scripture is a perfect rule of faith; as such it is complete because it "needs no addition" and so evident that "it needs no interpretation" (2.5, pp. 88–89). To be sure, Protestants do not mean that scripture as a rule of faith proves everything. For example, it cannot prove the existence of God or that it is itself scripture. But "to them which pre-suppose it Divine and a rule of faith" it contains "all the material objects of faith" and is "a complete and total, and not only an imperfect and a partial rule" (2.8, p. 91). Moreover, the sufficient perfection of scripture means that it is "sufficiently intelligible in things necessary, to all that have understanding, whether they be learned or unlearned ... because nothing is necessary to be believed but what is plainly revealed" (2.104, p. 149). God is not like Pharaoh, who refused to give the Hebrews the straw with which to make their bricks. Of course, the tradition of the church has a persuasive authority that enables people to "pre-suppose" scripture as the sole rule of faith and duty; but only reason can make this assent (2.114, p. 157).[42] Chillingworth, then, seems to argue against his motto by insisting that we need not worry about deductions from scripture. The plain passages suffice, and there is no need to appeal to the primitive church in order to discover what is necessary for salvation.

Is there any way of resolving the contradiction I have noted? One possibility has to do with Chillingworth's assessment of the Apostles' Creed. He grants that the creed is certain, "that it was from the apostles, and contains the principles of faith." And he is willing to ground it "not upon Scripture, and yet not upon the infallibility of any present (much less of your) church, but upon the authority of the ancient church, and written tradition, which ... gave this constant testimony unto it" (4.16, p. 282). Can we not argue that this is a concession to the requirements of the polemic against Rome? Chillingworth is himself willing to take antiquity seriously. One note of an uncorrupted church, he says, is "conformity with antiquity; I mean, the most ancient church of all, that is, the primitive and apostolic." But he goes on to ask, "How is it possible any man should examine your church by this note?" (2.113, p. 155). The Church of England conforms to antiquity better than the church of Rome. But Chillingworth is unwilling to conclude that this argument gives any independent authority to antiquity or to the creed. After all, points necessary for salvation include "practice and obedience" as well as "simple belief." The creed may be "a sufficient summary of articles of mere faith," but it scarcely includes "rules of obedience" (4.13–14, pp. 280–81). Moreover, it could be true that the creed includes all necessary points of belief; but it does not necessarily follow that all points in the creed are necessary (4.23, p. 290).[43]

If my suggestion that Chillingworth distinguishes his own acceptance of the creed from his insistence upon restricting authority for what is necessary for belief and practice to scripture has merit, then I should wish to argue that his reason lies in the function he wants to give to the idea of things necessary to salvation. Even if we grant that the creed contains "the fundamentals of simple belief," the admission "plainly renders the whole dispute touching the Creed unnecessary." This is because if all things necessary for belief and practice are "clearly contained" in scripture, it makes no difference that the points of belief are contained in the creed (Pref. 33, p. 30). We do not need the creed or antiquity to find our way to salvation, however much some of us may find them helpful. The divine truths "plainly delivered in Scripture" are the foundations. If what we build upon them as "superstructures" are "consequent and coherent with them," Chillingworth is confident that "peace would be restored, and truth maintained against you, though the Apostles' Creed were not in the world" (4.84, p. 325). Chillingworth's minimalist understanding of what is necessary for salvation functions in the interest of concord and liberty. He is willing to concede the importance of tradition, but his underlying view is really that scripture alone suffices. Its plain passages tell us what is necessary for salvation and so can secure religious concord. Liberty of interpretation must be granted in attempts to understand the hard and obscure passages.

The real threat to the peace of the churches and to Christian freedom revolves around truths that are not fundamental and rest merely upon the obscure places in scripture. These truths are at best incidental to the safe way to salvation, and it is pointless to seek any resolution of the controversies that surround them. There is no necessity "that God should assist his church, any farther than to bring her to salvation, neither will there be any necessity at all of any infallible guide, either to consign unwritten traditions, or to declare the obscurities of the faith" (Pref. 32, p. 30). The plain passages in scripture require no interpreter. The obscure and difficult places have an uncertain meaning, but we need not worry. "There is no necessity we should be certain; for if God's will had been we should have understood him more certainly, he would have spoken more plainly" (2.84, pp. 134–35). Moreover, provided we do not interpret the obscure places out of negligence, pride, obstinacy, or worldly fear and hope, we cannot be held guilty by God. If it is only through human infirmity we fall into error, "that error cannot be damnable" (3.52, p. 232). On the whole, religious controversies depend upon trying to resolve questions that cannot and need not be resolved. What this involves is the "presumptuous imposing of the senses of men upon the words of God." It is an attempt to bind consciences "under the special penalty of death and damnation" and vainly to suppose that we can speak of God better than scripture. The sole source of schism in the church is "this deifying our own interpretations, and tyrannous enforcing them upon others, this restraining of the word of God from that latitude and generality, and the understandings of men from that liberty, wherein Christ and the apostles left them." By removing "these walls of separation" and by taking away tyranny, "all will be quickly one" (4.17, p. 283). If only all people would believe scripture without "prejudice and passion," would try "to find the true sense of it," would "live according to it," and would "require no more of others but to do so," then it would follow that there would necessarily "be among all men, in all things necessary, unity of opinion" (3.81, pp. 267–68).

Chillingworth's restriction of unity of opinion to things necessary is crucial, because he fully understands that it is impossible to suppose that all controversies will disappear. Only someone authorized by God as a judge to interpret the rule of scripture could effect such a resolution; and "it hath not been the pleasure of God to give to any man, or society of men, any such authority." However much we may wish that controversy and sin would cease, "there is little hope of the one or the other till the world be ended." We must be content with "an unity of charity and mutual toleration; seeing God hath authorized no man to force all men to unity of opinion" (2.85, p. 135). Granted, however, that unity of opinion can prevail at the level of what is necessary, we can ask what the necessary points are and how we can find them. At this point Chillingworth introduces a confusion into his thought. He can argue that controversy has a positive function because it is a way of struggling to find necessary truth.[44] Liberty seems to have intruded itself into the area where we ought to be able easily to find concord. If what is necessary for salvation is clear in the plain passages of scripture, why do we need the liberty of controversy to discern them?

At any rate, Chillingworth refuses to supply a catalogue of the necessary points of scripture. His Jesuit opponent cannot give any such catalogue for his beliefs, so why should he (Pref. 27, p. 59)? There is, however, a deeper reason for his refusal. If we grant that what is fundamental is believing in Christ and in the forgiveness and salvation he grants to those who perform "the conditions he requires," it follows that all this may be revealed differently to different people. "Consequently, that may be fundamental and necessary to one, which to another is not so. Which variety of circumstances makes it impossible to set down an exact catalogue of fundamentals" (3.13, p. 200). This could mean two rather different things. On the one hand, it might be that since only liberty in controversy can discover what is necessary, and since it is unlikely that absolute agreement can ever be reached, concord becomes an agreement to disagree, though within certain limits defined by the conviction that Christ is the Savior. On the other hand, we might suppose that concord does attach to the necessary points of scripture, but that scripture accommodates those points according to the diverse circumstances of individuals.

Chillingworth employs two metaphors to make his case. We can imagine a traveler to London who knows two roads. He meets someone who persuades him to go by what he regards as the worse road lest the one he supposes to be better prove to be leaving "the true and the only way" (3.56, p. 242) The second metaphor complicates the issue somewhat. A physician prescribes to a sick man a medicine made up of twenty ingredients, and the doctors are themselves disagreed as to which ingredients are necessary and which merely profitable or superfluous. Nevertheless, the sick man takes the entire medicine, since any wise man would recognize that the physicians agreed in general that the medicine would effect the cure. The Protestant doctors, who disagree with one another, all agree that "the Scripture evidently contains all things necessary to salvation both for matter of faith and practice." Since this is so, "what matters it for the direction of men to salvation, though they differ in opinion touching what points are absolutely necessary, and what not?" (3.52, p. 234). While the Bible reveals the safe way to salvation, it apparently includes a range of different ways that different teachers interpret differently and that are suitable to the various people who are seeking such a safe way. Both metaphors seem intended to argue that people do have access to the fundamental points revealed in scripture. But the metaphor of the two travelers implies that the liberty of controversy is what leads to their discernment, while the metaphor of the physician's medicine implies that the concord attaching to the necessary points of scripture accommodates itself to different patients in different ways and that it is not necessary to discern that concord with any precision. There is a rather uncomfortable juxtaposition of liberty and concord, and Chillingworth is on a slippery slope that will so emphasize liberty as to make concord impossible. Moreover, the distinction between what is necessary for salvation and what is indifferent becomes difficult if not impossible to draw.

Another question to be raised is how we should interpret scripture. It seems clear that antiquity does not supply a sufficient tool. And we have also found that there is a sense in which the plain and necessary parts of scripture require no interpretation and explain themselves. Nevertheless, Chillingworth thinks that reason is what enables people to discern the fundamentals. In controversies, of course, when the meaning of scripture is the issue, only "natural reason" can make a determination, since it is "the only principle, beside Scripture, which is common to Christians" (2.3; p. 88). Here Chillingworth appears to allude to a natural law or even a Thomistic understanding of reason. God has constituted our reason so that we can discern in common the laws of nature. This means that "common notions" are stamped on our minds and that reason in the common sense lies behind our efforts to discern what is necessary for salvation. On the other hand, even in the "necessary points of religion" which are "plain and easy" each individual is "to be a competent judge for himself, because it concerns himself to judge right as much as eternal happiness is worth; and if, through his own default, he judge amiss, he alone shall suffer for it" (2.16, p. 98). Here reason has become the individual's critical power of judgment, and its discernment is in some sense tantamount to faith. Faith is "the understanding's assent," and as such it is a response. Faith "doth, and must, originally proceed from Scripture, as the effect from its proper cause." Scripture is, as it were, the light; "the eye of the soul, that is, the understanding, or the faculty of assenting" is like the bodily eye; assenting or believing is like the act of seeing" (2.48, p. 114). Chillingworth wants to add that reason as the exercise of critical judgment is "a public and certain thing" because it is "exposed to all men's trial and examination" (2.110, p. 154). In this way he wants to emphasize the corporate context in which controversy takes place, the positive function of criticism, and the conclusion that critical reason need not be solipsistic. At the same time, the tension between his natural law understanding of reason and his insistence upon reason as a critical faculty of judgment reflects the uneasiness of his attempt to bind together concord and liberty.[45]

Let me conclude this part of the discussion with Chillingworth's well-known eulogy of the Bible. He speaks of different Roman teachers, all of whom recognize the doctrine of the Council of Trent. On the other side, there are many Protestant teachers, but only one religion of Protestants (6.56, pp. 460–61):

> The BIBLE, I say, the BIBLE only, is the religion of Protestants. Whatsoever else they believe besides it, and the plain, irrefragable, indubitable consequences of it, well may they hold it as a matter of opinion; but as matter of faith and religion, neither can they, with coherence to their own grounds, believe it themselves, nor require the belief of it of others, without most high and most schismatical presumption.... I cannot find any rest for the sole of my foot but upon this rock only.... In a word, there is no sufficient certainty but of Scripture only for any considering man to build upon.... In other things, I will take no man's liberty of judgment from him, neither shall any man take mine from me.... I am fully assured that God does not, and, therefore, that men ought not to, require any more of any man than this, — to believe the Scripture to be God's word, to endeavour to find the true sense of it, and to live according to it.

There are two sides to this preliminary peroration. First, the explicit theme of liberty and the implicit theme of concord point toward latitudinarianism, if not to full religious toleration. On the other hand, Chillingworth's concern is also to let God and his word have their way. To the degree that the churches, at least the Protestant ones, can learn to avoid interfering with God's purpose, to that degree they will find the Bible a safe way to salvation.

Henry Hammond (1605–1660)

Hammond's father was one of Prince Henry's physicians, and he gave his son the prince's name. At the age of thirteen Henry Hammond went up to Magdalen College, Oxford, where he took his bachelor's degree in 1622. He was ordained in 1629 and in 1633 became rector of Penshurst in Kent. Ten years later, after the beginning of civil war, he was obliged to leave Penshurst and eventually returned to Oxford, which was then safely in royalist hands. In 1645 he became a canon of Christ Church, public orator of Oxford, and one of King Charles's chaplains. The king fled Oxford the following spring, and after his capture Hammond and Gilbert Sheldon accompanied him as his chaplains until they were compelled by the parliamentary forces to leave during the king's imprisonment on the Isle of Wight. Hammond was forced to leave Oxford as well, and by 1650 he settled as chaplain to the household of Sir John and Lady Dorothy Pakington at Westwood in Worcestershire. It was from this circle that there emanated *The Whole Duty of Man*, which was published anonymously in 1658 and which became for more than a century a central book of devotion for Anglicans who gave pride of place to the church and the sacraments.

Hammond's writings and correspondence during the interregnum planted the seeds of Restoration Anglicanism with its emphasis upon episcopacy, the Prayer Book, and holy living.[46] From another perspective, however, it can be argued that Hammond places scripture at the center of all these concerns. In 1653 he published *A Paraphrase and Annotations Upon All the Books of the New Testament, Briefly Explaining All the Difficult Places Thereof.*[47] Six years later he published a similar work on the Psalms and began his work on Proverbs, which remained unfinished at his death but was published posthumously in 1683. While there can be no doubt concerning the importance Hammond accords scripture, the real problem in assessing his thought is to decide whether he treats the apostolic tradition, and specifically the Apostles' Creed as an instrument for interpreting scripture or as an independent and coordinate authority. The conclusion I wish to draw is that his view parallels that of William Laud in his *Conference with Fisher* (1639). At one point Laud distinguishes the apostolic tradition from the ongoing tradition of the church and says that "all the points of the Apostles' Creed ... are fundamental."

He continues by affirming that "the belief of Scripture to be the word of God and infallible, is an equal, or rather a preceding, prime principle of faith, with or to the whole body of the Creed." It is almost as though Laud corrects himself, retreating from the implication that the creed has equal authority with scripture. His conclusion gives priority to scripture "upon which the Creed itself in every part is grounded."[48]

> Jeremy Taylor makes the same point in his *Liberty of Prophesying* (1647). The Apostles' Creed derives from scripture, but it also separates for us what is "necessary or not necessary" in scripture.

Nevertheless, at least if I am correct in concluding that Hammond has no wish to cast scripture from its throne, his view differs in a crucial way from Chillingworth's. The creed and apostolic tradition assume a far more important place for Hammond. He disagrees with Chillingworth's assumption that the creed is no more than a helpful but unnecessary guide to the necessary points of scripture. Instead, the creed and the apostolic tradition are the essential instruments that enable us to discern what is necessary. Jeremy Taylor makes the same point — the Apostles' Creed derives from scripture, but it also separates for us what is "necessary or not necessary" in scripture. By way of digression, let me suggest that Taylor is a sort of halfway house between Chillingworth and Hammond, who appears to have been unhappy with those aspects of Taylor's argument that reflect Chillingworth's point of view and that imply the toleration of sects that do not disturb the civil order.[49] Let me attempt to test this conclusion by examining some of Hammond's writings.

Hammond's great concern, like Taylor's, is with holy living. In 1644 he published his *Practical Catechism*. The work is a dialogue between the catechist and the scholar, and it begins by repeating Clement of Alexandria's claim that "the end of Christian philosophy is to make men better, not more learned, to edify, not to instruct." The scholar's question is "what kind of doctrines, and what parts of Scripture, will be likely to have the most present influence on my heart, or contribute most to a Christian practice." This brief dialogue introduces the structure of the work as a whole. Book 1 treats the two covenants of works and grace, the names and offices of Christ, the three virtues (faith, hope, and charity), and justification and sanctification.[50] The following books begin with the Sermon on the Mount and imply a logical structure that treats the creed as faith, the Ten Commandments as the practice of that faith, and the Lord's Prayer as the grace necessary for assisting that practice. Hammond makes constant reference to scripture throughout the work. Central to Hammond's argument is his account of justification by faith. He denies that faith is, properly speaking, the "efficient cause of justification." Rather, that cause is to be found in God because of Christ's "satisfaction," the atonement. Moreover, justification means not only that God does not impute our sins to us, but also that he accepts "our persons and our weak performances." While receiving Christ "is clearly the act of man," this is quite distinct from justification, which is God's act.[51] Hammond adopts a federal or covenantal understanding of justification. Because of the covenant of grace God accounts our insufficient righteousness as sufficient, provided we turn to him in faith and repentance. The holy living emphasis is also clear because faith must be made perfect by works (James 2:22) and because there is "no promise of pardon in Scripture to a bare death-bed sorrow."[52]

Hammond not only grounds his discussions in scripture, he also can treat it as the rule of faith. He opposes faith to sight and argues that the object of faith is "either God Himself, or the word of God." The word of God, then, is "the rule of that faith, or matter to be believed." When it is "entirely considered," it signifies "whatsoever I am, or may ever be, convinced to come from Him." It is the whole of scripture that constitutes this rule of faith, and Hammond distinguishes its various parts as affirmations (including historical narration or doctrine), promises of God, commands of God (found in the natural law of the Ten Commandments and its "higher pitch" in the

Sermon on the Mount, and also found in the sacraments), and finally, the threats of the Gospel.[53] While "whatever is affirmed by [God] is infallibly true," nevertheless, there are truths "which have special marks set upon them in Scripture to signify them to be of more weight than others." Presumably, these are what we must recognize as things necessary to salvation. They include belief in the existence of God, in Christ as "the Messias of the world," in life eternal, in the Trinity "into which all are commanded to be baptized"; and we must add "those other fundamentals of faith, which all men were instructed in anciently before they were permitted to be baptized, contrived briefly into the compass of the Apostles' creed, a summary of Christian faith or doctrine necessary to be believed."[54] An obvious question is whether the creed is thought to be a summary of necessary points found in scripture or is the apostolic teaching that has an authority independent of the Bible. Hammond seems uninterested in the question, and he can certainly discuss the creed without reference to its relation to scripture. But it is fairly certain that he answers the question the first way. Book 5 is his discussion of the creed, and there he tells the scholar that "in your conversing with holy writings, especially those of the Apostles in their epistles, you observe how the articles of our creed are seldom or never mentioned but as obligations and pledges of our amendment of life." Hammond's point is that faith has two parts, "a speculative and a practical . . . the one in the brain, the other in the heart."[55] But when he refers to "conversing with holy writings," he implies his assumption that the creed is grounded in scripture.

My argument is that Hammond treats the creed and antiquity as instruments for the interpretation of scripture and does not go so far as to give them an independent authority. In commending meekness of understanding to his scholar Hammond makes several points:

1. That where, in any matter of doctrine, the plain word of God interposes itself, there we must most readily yield, without demur or resistance. But 2. If it be matter neither defined, nor pretended to be defined in Scripture, then with each particular

man among us, the definitions of the Church wherein we live must carry it... [or if there is controversy] the tradition of the universal, or opinion of the primitive Church is to prevail... [or if there is "no light to be fetched from thence"] then that which they shall of themselves... agree upon to be most convenient shall be of force.... But 3. if Scripture be pretended for one party in the debate, and the question be concerning the interpretation of that Scripture, and no light from the Scripture itself ... be to be had for the clearing it, then again the judgment of the universal, or my particular Church, is to be of great weight with me.[56]

Tradition enters the picture in a way significantly different from its persuasive and negative force in Hooker's theology and from its virtual exclusion by Chillingworth, who thinks of reason as the only important tool of interpretation and does not see why controversies such as Hammond envisages need any resolution. Hammond continues his discussion by asking what we should do if we become convinced that our particular church has "departed from the Catholic and Apostolic Church." We must prefer the greater authority, since "next the Scripture the Catholic Church of the first and purest times... is the greatest authority." At the same time this need not require us to find another church, even if our own church excommunicates us. We may "join even with erroneous Churches so far as they are not erroneous."[57]

That Hammond treats the creed and antiquity primarily as instruments for interpreting scripture finds confirmation in some of his other writings. Indeed, tradition sometimes seems to be the only instrument we have. In his *Paraenesis,* published in 1656, Hammond says that the only way we can judge the canon of scripture or "any book, or chapter, or period contained in it" is by the "affirmation and authority" of the witnesses in "the first ages of the Church, either by their writings or by the unquestioned relations of others, brought down and made known to us." What he chiefly means is that we have no way of judging or accepting unwritten tradition. But we can trust the written and "undoubted affirmation of the ancients, — who are presumable by their antiquity to know the truth."[58] Hammond appeals more generally to the Vincentian canon of universality, antiquity, and consent. But he understands this to mean continuity with antiquity in fundamentals. He cites Vincent's caution that the "ancient consent of the holy fathers is not to be sought and followed in all the little questions of the divine law, but only, sure principally, in the rule of faith, those which the Apostles thought necessary to be believed, and so taught them universally."[59] Thus, the Vincentian canon becomes an appeal to continuity with the ancient church, which means for Hammond an appeal to the creed and the first four councils.[60] Indeed, "the inerrableness of general councils" is "a theological verity, which may piously be believed."[61] Nevertheless, all these authorities take us back to scripture. The Nicene fathers grounded their term "of one substance" in scripture; "they fetched their definitions regularly from Scripture, and that sense thereof which the several Churches had received down from the Apostles."[62]

The same general pattern discloses itself in *Of Fundamentals,* published in 1654. Hammond begins with a discussion of the metaphor of his title. A foundation presupposes a house built upon it. Scripture tells us that "house" can mean either heaven or the church, the first identified with bliss and the second with obedience. Since obedience must precede bliss, so the church must precede heaven. Therefore, the church built upon the foundation must be a place where we learn obedience and holy living. With these points in mind Hammond turns to a definition of the foundation in general terms. The fundamentals "must in all reason be taken from the practice of the Apostles, as the interpreter of God's appointment and judgment in this matter."[63] He explains what this apostolic practice is by citing scripture and describing "their first sermons in all their travels." The apostolic fundamentals, while necessary to "the superstructing of Christian practice, must not so be understood, that the hearing and believing of each of them be thought absolutely necessary in every single Jew or heathen."[64] That is, the fundamentals are the foundation of the church and its mission even though different individuals may find different aspects of that foundation suitable for them. In chapter 3 Hammond turns from this general interpretation to "a more particular view of this foundation." It is "compendiously set down in Scripture.... or else more largely and explicitly in the creeds or confessions of the universal Church."[65] "Compendious," of course, can mean several different things, but Hammond must be contrasting the larger, fuller, and more explicit account of the foundation found in the creeds, fathers, and councils with the more concise and implicit account given in scripture. Even though "apostolic" is the general rubric he uses, it is unlikely that Hammond wants to put antiquity on the same level with scripture. Instead, antiquity makes fuller and explicit what we find in scripture. It is scripture that enables us to discern "that this one corner-stone, Jesus Christ, is a most competent, ample foundation, on which to superstruct the largest pile of building, to erect a Church of pious livers, and to bring all rational men within the compass of it."[66] The creeds explain more fully the person and work of this cornerstone. I am obliged to admit, however, that tradition looms so large in Hammond's writings that one does begin to wonder whether the tail does not begin to wag the dog and whether tradition may not begin to eclipse scripture.

Though they are somewhat transformed, we have found Hammond employing the familiar themes of what is necessary for salvation and of tradition. I need to turn, finally, to his assessment of reason. In 1650 he published *The Reasonableness of Christianity* in which he first considers "the grounds of Christianity in the gross, or bulk, all of it together" in order "in some measure [to] justify the reasonableness of them." In Book 2 he turns "to the survey and vindication of those particular branches of Christianity which appear to men at this time to be least supported with reason."[67] His argument in the first part revolves around testimony. Only God's testimony can be infallible, since it is his "nature to be veracious."[68] God's testimony "that Christ was sent from Him to declare His will to us... upon which, being once supposed, the truth of all Christian religion truly so called, is immediately and infallibly founded, — hath more than one way been authentically interposed."[69] As examples, all taken from scripture, Hammond cites the Old Testament prophets, the angel of the annunciations to Mary and Elizabeth, the wise men's star, Christ's miracles and his resurrection, and the voices of God recorded in the New Testament such as the *bath qol* at Christ's baptism. What Hammond needs to prove is that we have access to God's infallible testimony. He sums up his argument by saying that for truths that could not otherwise be known God has been pleased "personally to interpose His own power and authority, and to speak from heaven." Once God has done so, "then are there sufficient human means to convey the truth or history of this fact to other men, viz., the testimony of those who saw or heard it."[70] The writers of scripture, then, are eye and ear witnesses of God's infallible testimony; and it is as reasonable to accept their testimony as it is to accept testimony about Alexander the Great, Caesar, or William the Conqueror. Moreover, while it is not reasonable to expect the continuance of miracles, these ear and eye witnesses backed their testimony by miracles and proofs from prophecy.[71] Their willingness to endure suffering and to risk death is another argument for the truth of their testimony.[72] These ideas will have a long life as the "evidences" of Christianity, and it is important to note that Hammond here treats reason as a faculty of judgment by which we can distinguish true from false testimony.

The second part of Hammond's treatise really deals with the place of reason in deciding controversies, and here he tends to treat reason in the context of a natural law theory that allows it to discern natural and moral truths, but not supernatural ones. He argues that the human power of knowing and judging must be measured by human participation in God and that we can judge only by the attributes that God communicates to us. All controversies concern either goodness or truth. Reason does function as a judge with respect to goodness, unless it is "corrupted by some prepossession, or habitual vice, or some present prevailing temptation."[73] Right reason, then, can judge "of all merely moral objects" and of "natural objects" and of the possibility that what we see done can be done again. But reason cannot judge of supernatural truths save by recognizing that something is possible with God though not with us, that God has affirmed such a truth, and that it comes to us by authority.[74] Hammond applies these conclusions to scripture. We can observe that when scripture gives us supernatural truths, the only proof it gives is God's authority. The only concessions made to human reason are to recognize that it is reasonable "to believe God without any other motive or topic of proof" and to employ "what helps so ever a reasonable man's prudence and diligence can suggest, or furnish him with" in searching for "that word of God which contains these revelations."[75] Hammond does not eliminate reason altogether; it is of use in judging that scripture's testimony is trustworthy and even in locating the places in scripture where the testimony is to supernatural truths. But he restricts its role so severely that it scarcely counts any longer as an instrument for reaping the fruits of scripture in Hooker's sense.

Conclusion

The basic point for which I have argued is that all three of the figures examined agree with Hooker both in claiming the central place for scripture and in insisting that this must be understood in terms of the conviction that scripture is sufficient for its purpose, namely, to reveal what is necessary for salvation. Nevertheless, there is no single view either concerning how scripture reveals these necessary points or what they are. Hall and Chillingworth tend to assume that the plain passages serve scripture's purpose and that, in this sense, scripture somehow interprets itself. But they disagree, partly because Chillingworth takes a minimalist approach to what is necessary for salvation and refuses to identify this with Hall's moderate Calvinism or, indeed, with any single Protestant view. Thus, though neither of them clarify what the plain passages are, they obviously interpret them quite differently. Hammond, at least at a doctrinal level, appears to identify what is necessary for salvation with the apostolic witness of scripture that is more clearly expressed in the Apostles' Creed. The three writers also disagree with respect to the role of reason and tradition in interpreting scripture. Reason can mean a number of different things; and even though all three writers betray some awareness of a natural law or even Thomistic understanding of the term, it is by no means clear that they try to explain or even consistently employ this understanding. For Hall reason has been so wounded by the Fall that it is suspect. For Chillingworth it is more important that reason is a critical faculty of judgment with a role to play not only in matters of indifference but even in the discernment of what is necessary for salvation. Hammond combines the idea of natural reason as capable of discerning truths about natural and moral issues, but treats it as a faculty of judgment in discovering reliable witnesses to supernatural truth. With respect to tradition it is difficult to see that apostolicity has central importance for anyone but Hammond. For Chillingworth it is unnecessary, and for Hall it has an importance only outside what is necessary for salvation.

In any case, despite my attempt to use in part the triple cord as an organizing principle for discussion, it seems doubtful that the idea has been very helpful. It is certainly not a theme that binds the three writers either to one another or to Hooker. Though I recognize how anachronistic the thought is, it has occurred to me that we have a "low church" view in Hall, a "broad church" one in Chillingworth, and a "high church" one in Hammond. Scripture, then, yields three very different theological platforms. Yet despite these quite different understandings of the meaning of scripture, there are two points of underlying agreement. First, all would insist upon the fallibility of our use of scripture and would repudiate any view of the omnicompetence of scripture. Second, even though much of what the three writers have to say about the Bible appears in the context of religious controversy and so must treat scripture in terms of what it can and cannot do to resolve these disputes, at a deeper level they all think of scripture as what guides and forms the Christian life in the corporate setting of the church. George Herbert's second poem on the Holy Scriptures sums up what seems to me the most important point to make about these early Anglican views of scripture. The poem appears in the context of the collection that has the title *The Temple,* and Herbert presupposes that the church has guided him to scripture, which he then consults:

Oh that I knew how all thy lights combine,
    And the configurations of their glory!
    Seeing not only how each verse doth shine,
But all the constellations of the story.

This verse marks that, and both do make a motion
    Unto a third, that ten leaves off doth lie:
    Then as dispersed herbs do watch a potion,
These three make up some Christian's destiny:

Such are thy secrets, which my life makes good,
    And comments on thee: for in ev'ry thing
    Thy words do find me out, and parallels bring,
And in another make me understood.

Stars are poor books, and oftentimes do miss:
This book of stars lights to eternal bliss.

Chapter Three

The Ambiguous Alliance
of Scripture and Nature

At one point in Bertolt Brecht's *Galileo* the major figure in the drama finds himself interrogated by the Vatican. Cardinal Barberini asks him whether God did not sufficiently study astronomy before he fashioned holy scripture, and Cardinal Bellarmine points out to him that the creator knows more about what he made than creatures do. Galileo argues that people can as easily misunderstand the Bible as the motions of the stars.[1] The question whether scripture and the new astronomy are coherent is, of course, a side issue. But the dialectical meaning of the play depends upon the ambiguity of its conclusion. Andrea Sarti succeeds in smuggling Galileo's *Discourses* out of Rome, and we could rightly presume that truth has prevailed and science been preserved. On the other hand, Brecht wrote the play as the atom was being smashed; and he observed that the conclusion could also be regarded as the original sin of science. The ambiguity, then, is whether science is a friend or a foe. The same ambiguity attaches to the developments in England from the Restoration, or at least the Glorious Revolution, through the eighteenth and nineteenth centuries. Are nature and history friends of the Bible or foes? Of course, arguments from nature and history have always been in one way or another connected with the place of the Bible. Nevertheless, some sense is made by regarding nature as the preoccupation of the eighteenth and history as that of the nineteenth century. Let me turn to the first of these alliances in this chapter and to the second in the next.

Nature as an Ally of Scripture

In the late seventeenth and eighteenth centuries nature, whether as human nature, that is, reason, or as a Newtonian account of the physical universe, begins to occupy a central place in assessments of what scripture means and how it has authority. The increasing emphasis upon reason as the light of nature and upon nature itself has multiple explanations, but there are two that stand out. First, the religious wars of the seventeenth century persuaded many that the various banners proclaiming different ways to salvation abolished charity, needlessly spilled a great deal of blood, and did not lead the way to truth.[2] Why should we worry about mysteries that lie beyond our capacity instead of using our God-given reason in order to ascertain our duties in this life? Moreover, the Church of England began to lose its hold on the nation. When the narrow religious settlement of the Restoration proved impossible to maintain and the Toleration Act gave religious freedom to most Protestants, the net effect seems to have been a decline in church attendance and the growth of secularism.[3] The second explanation I should underline revolves around the scientific revolution, and in England we can think of the foundation of the Royal Society in 1662. There was a growing optimism about our capacity to understand human nature and the world around us. We can remember Alexander Pope's couplet: "Nature and Nature's laws lay hid in night; God said, *Let Newton be!* And all was *Light.*"

Perhaps optimism is not quite the right word. There were members of the Royal Society who saw more clearly how much of our world remained unexplained, no matter how they supported efforts to uncover the mysteries of nature. In 1661 Joseph Glanvill (1636–80) published *The Vanity of Dogmatizing.* He was then a young man, educated at Exeter and Lincoln Colleges, Oxford, newly ordained in the Church of England, disaffected from Aristotle, and attracted to Descartes and philosophy. He became a fellow of the Royal Society in 1664 and the same year dedicated a revision of his book to the Society. His prefatory address commends the members for meeting in times when "people of weak Heads on the one hand, and vile affections on the other, have made a divorce between being Wise and Good." The first will have nothing to do with philosophy; the second hold a "secret scorn of religion," though the implication of what he says is that religion is primarily to be understood in moral terms.[4] Glanvill's assumption is that the study of nature and the pursuit of philosophy by no means lead to "irreligion." Indeed, he dares to say that "next after the *divine Word*, it's one of the best friends to *Piety.*"[5] While his emphasis is upon the various ways our senses betray us, and his major conclusion is skeptical, he does insist upon "the certainty of truths either *Mathematical* or *Divine.*"[6] In these and in other ways Glanvill anticipates Locke's theory of knowledge. Moreover, though we may not be able to understand the world presented to our sense in a complete fashion, Plutarch was correct to argue that the harmony of nature induces us to believe in a God. "And a greater then he affirms, that the visible things of the Creation declare him that made them."[7] The argument from design makes its appearance, and it is based on an appeal to St. Paul. Much earlier in the work Glanvill, though he makes no direct appeal to scripture, attributes the uncertainty of the knowledge we gain from sense perception to the Fall. "[A]ll the powers and faculties of Adam," "this meddal of God," were perfect. His soul was not "clogg'd" or "hindered in its actings" by the passions. Even the senses, "the Soul's windows, were without any spot or opacity." "*Adam* needed no spectacles," and he saw "much of the Coelestial magnificence without a *Galileo*'s tube."[8] It would be wrongheaded to draw the implication that natural philosophy and science supply a remedy for the Fall, but such an idea might well have been easier to entertain in 1661 than at present.

Despite Glanvill's reference to scripture ("the *divine Word*"), it is not entirely clear that he sees the correlation of philosophy and religion as more than that between philosophy and natural religion. But there were clearly those who supposed that nature was proving a friend and a servant of the Bible. I think first of two writings of the seventeenth century that had a wide and enduring impact upon religious people throughout the eighteenth century and even beyond. John Pearson's *An Exposition of the Creed* had its origin in sermons he had preached at St. Clement's, Eastcheap, "upon such texts of Scripture as were on purpose selected in relation to the Creed."[9] The work first appeared in 1659, and its fifth edition in 1683 was the last before Pearson's death three years later. He had become bishop of Chester in 1673. Pearson's *On the Creed* remained a standard textbook for theological students well into the nineteenth century.[10] Pearson expounds the creed in a painstaking and systematic way, but he places much of his great learning in a separate volume of notes. He is careful to ground his discussion in scripture. The creed is "a brief comprehension of the objects of our Christian faith, and is generally taken to contain all things necessary to be believed." But he makes it clear that "I have laid the foundation upon the written word of God."[11] He distinguishes between the immediate revelation of God made to prophets and apostles and the mediated revelation we find in their writings. These writings include everything that can be called "matters of divine Faith." And Pearson cites Ephesians 2:20: "the household of God is built upon the foundation of the Apostles and Prophets." Our only access to them is by their writings, and by accepting their testimony we find "the truths which they received from God."[12] In general Pearson's view is coherent with that of Hammond, and scripture remains upon its throne. Nevertheless, nature is part of the picture. The creed comprehends "the principles of our religion" both "as it is a religion" and "as it is ours." As a religion "it delivereth such principles as are to be acknowledged in natural theology, such as no man which worshippeth a god can deny."[13]

The other writing that reflects the idea of nature in the sense of reason as an ally of scripture is *The Whole Duty of Man,* published anonymously in 1658. Henry Hammond's letter to the bookseller recommending it to the public reflects his approval but probably precludes his authorship. For more than a century this book of devotion occupied an honored place in many households beside the Prayer Book and the Bible. It supplies seventeen Sunday devotions with exercises and prayers; read three times over it covers all the Sundays of the year. As well, there are extensive private devotions, including forms for prayers in the morning and evening. The preface

explains the book's purpose. "The only intent of this ensuing treatise, is to be a short and plain direction to the very meanest readers,
to behave themselves so in this world, that they may be happy for
ever in the next."[14] As the title suggests, the emphasis is upon the
Christian's moral duties; but there is also attention to the sacrament
of the Lord's Supper and to worship and prayer. The focus of the
Restoration church upon the sacraments and holy living is apparent.

In a number of places this devotional manual calls attention to
reason and nature. To amend the carelessness of the soul is by no
means an extraordinary task. "The simplest man living (that is not
a natural fool) hath understanding enough for it, if he will but act
in this by the same rules of common reason, whereby he proceeds
in his worldly business."[15] Sunday 7 treats "Of the Duty of Man
by the Light of Nature, By the Light of Scripture." Sunday 1 argues
that some of the things God requires "God hath so stamped upon our
souls, that we naturally know them . . . though we had never been told
so by the Scripture." The idea appears to be the old Stoic view that
"common notions" are imprinted on the blank slate of the mind at
our birth, and that these notions include not only an understanding
of right and wrong but also a recognition of God. *The Whole Duty
of Man* goes on by appealing to Paul's reference to the law written
on the hearts of the Gentiles (Rom 2:14–15). Christ's "greater light"
by no means extinguishes this "natural light," but Christ "added
much both to the law implanted in us by Nature and that of the Old
Testament."[16] Natural religion may supply an introduction to and a
support of the Christian life. But it is scripture that brings completion
and sufficiency.

The themes I have been discussing also appear in a third piece of
evidence that can be regarded as reflecting fundamental assumptions
of Restoration Anglicanism. In 1682 John Dryden (1631–1700), who
had become Poet Laureate in 1668, published his own apology for
the religious establishment in his poem *Religio Laici*. Dryden received
his education at Westminster School and Trinity College, Cambridge.
He became a civil servant during the Protectorate, and one of his
early poems is an encomium of Cromwell after his death. At the

Restoration Dryden embraced the new regime and became a member of the Royal Society in 1662, the year of its founding. Perhaps because of his loyalty to James II, who was obliged to leave his throne in 1688 because he was a Roman Catholic, Dryden converted to the king's religion in 1687 and explained himself in his poem "The Hind and the Panther." His prose introduction to *Religio Laici*, however, makes it clear that the poem is a defense of the establishment that has employed "helps... many of them taken from the works of our own reverend divines of the Church of England."[17] He also says that he has composed the poem for "an ingenious young gentleman, my friend, upon his translation of the *Critical History of the Old Testament*, composed by the learned Father Simon."[18]

Since the book in question challenged the accuracy of the Hebrew Bible, one of Dryden's concerns is to argue that despite such difficulties the foundation laid down for us means "that the scripture is a rule, that in all things needful to salvation it is clear, sufficient, and ordained by God Almighty for that purpose." The distinction between what is necessary and what is a matter of indifference, however, leads him to say, "I have left myself no right to interpret obscure places, such as concern the possibility of eternal happiness to heathens." The allusion is to his discomfort with the Athanasian Creed and its clauses that condemn all who fail to accept "the Catholic Faith." Dryden recognizes that "by asserting the scriptures to be the canon of our faith" he has made two enemies. The papists refuse his view because they "have reserved to themselves a right of interpreting what they [the scriptures] have delivered under the pretence of infallibility." At the opposite extreme "the fanatics" will oppose him "because they have assumed what amounts to an infallibility in the private spirit." By doing so they have twisted scripture "to the damnable uses of sedition, disturbance, and destruction of the civil government."[19]

Dryden's introduction alerts the reader to two central issues treated in the poem itself, the first of which is the relation of reason to religion. His verses begin with a contrast between "the borrowed beams of moon and stars" at night, and the rising of the sun that extinguishes those lesser lights. "So pale grows reason at religion's sight; /

So does, and so dissolves in supernatural light" (ll. 10–11). It is true that "Some few... have been led / From cause to cause, to nature's secret head" (ll. 12–13). But they have not discovered what or who that first principle is; and though the "Deist thinks he stands on firmer ground," he fails to recognize that "Revealed religion first informed thy sight, / And reason saw not, till faith sprung the light" (ll. 42, 68–69). By religion Dryden means scripture, and by scripture he primarily means the revelation of "heaven's will." The Bible outweighs all other revelations of God's will (ll. 121–25). Nevertheless, a tension begins to emerge between this view of scripture and Dryden's reluctance to condemn those who have never encountered the Bible, a reluctance reflected in his doubts about the Athanasian Creed (ll. 212–23). The implication of his concern for the salvation of the heathen suggests that scripture, from this perspective, is dispensable, since "what is taught agrees with nature's laws" (l. 151). If God is merciful and if sinners who know scripture "may pity claim," how much "more may strangers who ne'er heard his name" (ll. 190–91). Dryden appeals to Romans 2:14–16, where Paul argues that the Gentiles, who do not know the law but follow it by nature, will be saved (ll. 198–211). Two views collide. On the one hand, Dryden affirms scripture's full sufficiency for its purpose; but, on the other hand, since natural religion reveals the moral demands included in scripture, together with the moral means of securing divine forgiveness, it suffices for those who have no access to scripture.

The second issue Dryden raises revolves around the complexities raised by his friend's translation of Fr. Simon's book. What are we to say "If Scripture, though derived from heavenly birth, / Has been but carelessly preserved on earth"? (ll. 258–59). The obvious answer is the Roman appeal to tradition as "an unerring guide" (l. 277). We could wish for "an omniscient church," but it is obvious that "her infallibility" could not extend to the restoration of "the blessed original" of scripture (ll. 282–94). Instead, we must be content to affirm that the scriptures "Are uncorrupt, sufficient, clear, entire, / In all things which our needful faith require" (ll. 299–300). This obliges the learned to study scripture in order to teach "which doctrine, this or that, does best agree / With the whole tenor of the work divine, / And plainliest points to heaven's revealed design" (ll. 329–31). We cannot merely pick and choose our favorite proof texts, but must conform our teaching to the entire scope of scripture. Moreover, in doing so tradition is not entirely useless. The church fathers and their interpretations of scripture can help us, since "the nearer to the spring we go, / More limpid, more unsoiled the waters flow" (ll. 340–41). By tradition we must mean written tradition; and we must understand it not as an independent authority, but as what "commends" the authority of scripture (ll. 350–51). The poem ends with a repudiation of Dryden's two foes. The Roman Catholics substitute the priest's word for God's Word (ll. 356–97). At the other extreme, "The common rule was made the common prey, / And at the mercy of the rabble lay" (ll. 402–3). Because of this "private spirit" crowds of the unlearned "About the sacred viands buzz and swarm, / The fly-blown text creates a crawling brood, / And turns to maggots what was meant for food" (ll. 418–20). Faith, then, finds the middle way, since "The things we must believe are few and plain" (l. 432). And in "doubtful questions" it is safest to follow the "unsuspected ancients." It is unlikely "we should higher soar / In search of heaven, than all the church before" (ll. 435–38).

The Latitudinarians

Dryden's conclusions about scripture are basically coherent with those of Hammond and Restoration Anglicanism. Nevertheless, his recognition of the importance of natural religion for those unacquainted with scripture introduces a theme that will become all important for the latitudinarians and will also lead to deism and Anglican attempts to counter it. It is possible to argue that the gradual divergence of high church Anglicans and latitudinarians correlates with the origin of political parties in Britain during the so-called Exclusion Controversy, that is, the debate as to whether to exclude James, the duke of York, from the throne. In 1669 James announced his conversion to Roman Catholicism; and since he was Charles II's heir apparent, the possibility that a Roman Catholic would become Supreme Governor of a Protestant church alarmed those who began to be called Whigs. The duke of York, supported by the Tories, did succeed to the throne in 1685. The high church was largely Tory; the latitudinarians, Whigs. The seven high church bishops who were put on trial for refusing to have James II's Declaration of Indulgence read in the parish churches, and who were acquitted, triggered the Glorious Revolution of 1688. But they refused to take the oath to William and Mary. They and a large number of priests who agreed with them constituted the non-juring schism and deprived the Church of England of many of its high church leaders. With the exception of the reign of Queen Anne (1702–14) the latitudinarians dominated the church in the eighteenth century. During the Pax Walpoliana the Whigs retained control of the central government, partly by conceding much local control to the Tories. The same thing tended to happen in the church. The house of bishops was largely Whig and latitudinarian, while the country clergy were commonly Tory and high church.

It is against this background that I want to focus upon two of the earlier latitudinarians, Tillotson and Burnet. But let me begin by saying something about the Cambridge Platonists. In crucial respects they differed from divines like Tillotson. Yet their emphasis upon the moral meaning of Christianity and upon their own version of natural theology, as well as their qualified interest in Descartes and the new philosophy, set the stage for latitudinarianism. Their central idea played upon the two Platonizing axioms that "like is known by like" and "to know the good is to do it." Human reason is "the candle of the Lord" (Prov 20:27) in the Platonic sense that the soul is akin to God in its nature and is, as it were, the God within. Human reason, then, has the capacity to know God and to find contemplative union with him. But this knowledge translates into moral virtue and holy living. Sometimes this mysticism of reason unveils the true meaning of scripture. Henry More (1614–87) wrote a letter to Descartes in 1648, expressing his admiration but also his differences. He hopes that, though they have traveled two somewhat different paths, they may "meet together ... at the same *Goale,* namely at the Entrance of the holy Bible."[20] Benjamin Whichcote (1609–83) treats scripture as "God's superadded Instrument," which contains God's revelation but which is also the means by which "the natural *Notices* of God, are awaken'd and inliven'd."[21] He also argues that all things necessary to salvation are plainly delivered in scripture even to "the Faith that results from the dark Mists of the ignorant."[22] He wishes that more "were *capable* of the Use of *private Judgment,*" which is "a Fundamental Right belonging to Intellectual Natures."[23] God has given us two lights, that of reason and that of scripture. "Let us make use of these two lights; and suffer neither to be put out."[24] One begins to suspect, however, that the two lights are not entirely equal. Whichcote goes so far as to say "Nothing *without* Reason is to be *proposed;* nothing *against* Reason is to be *believed:* Scripture is to be taken in a rational sense."[25] Reason, of course, does not mean so much a faculty of judgment as an intuitive capacity for the contemplation of God. Ralph Cudworth (1617–88) makes Whichcote's point by arguing that the "excellent truths" found in scripture will be "but unknown Characters to us, untill we have a *Living spirit* within us." Only this can "decypher" scripture. The same Spirit that inspired scripture must comment on scripture "by secret Whispers in our hearts."[26] The mysticism of reason becomes so necessary as the tool for bringing life and meaning to scripture that it is difficult not to wonder whether it has displaced scripture.

The light of nature, however, means something quite different to writers like Tillotson and Burnet than it did to the Cambridge Platonists. While neither writer elaborates a full epistemology, both of them hold that there are common conceptions innate to the human mind that are placed there from nature. The law of nature is the law that Paul speaks of as written on the heart (Rom 2:15). At the same time they agree that reason must be an ally, a friend of scripture, even though this friend sometimes seems to be gaining the upper hand and so displacing scripture. John Tillotson (1630–94) became archbishop of Canterbury in 1691 in place of Sancroft, who had refused to take the oath of allegiance to William and Mary in 1689.

Tillotson was a popular preacher, and his sermons supply full evidence for his views. He did, however, write a treatise entitled *The Rule of Faith or An Answer to the Treatise of Mr. J. S[ergeant] Entitled Sure-Footing in Christianity.* Sergeant, a Roman Catholic, had written a work arguing that oral tradition is the rule of faith rather than scripture. Tillotson's response insists upon scripture as the rule of faith, and he explains what he means in terms very like those that had been used by Chillingworth. The authority of scripture is that of a self-evident principle and cannot be demonstrated. Scripture is sufficiently plain "as to all things necessary to be believed and practised." Indeed, "that the Scripture doth sufficiently interpret itself, that is, is plain to all capacities, in things necessary to be believed and practised" is a basic principle. The church fathers agree with this principle, and their comments on obscure or doubtful texts may be a good help "but no certain rule of interpretation." Tillotson appeals specifically to Chillingworth for his refusal to give a catalogue of the necessary points of scripture.[27] The Bible, then, remains a safe way to salvation, and we need not look to the ancient church for any key to its meaning. Its necessary points appear to be few in number, and Christian concord would prove possible if controversies concerning indifferent points would cease.

Tillotson, however, goes beyond Chillingworth in what he says about reason and nature. In taking Sergeant to task for his failure to provide a sufficient definition of a rule of faith, he defines an "intellectual" rule as "the measure according to which we judge whether a thing be true or false." He identifies the general rule as "common notions, and the acknowledged principles of reason." Every science, then, has its particular rules "according to which we judge whether things in that science be true or false."[28] He recognizes that "reason has a blind side, and is uncertain in some things." But this cannot mean that reason is universally blind, nor can it lead us to doubt the truth of "those common principles of reason . . . which mankind are generally agreed in."[29] Reason is the only way a person can choose to accept a religious claim. We may imagine "a heathen . . . desirous to inform himself of the Christian faith" and obliged to choose between those who hold the oral tradition authoritative and those who stand upon scripture. The heathen can make his choice only "by his own private reason examining and weighing the arguments and pretences of both sides."[30] In this sense the light of nature becomes the foundation for the individual's commitment to Christianity. Elsewhere Tillotson goes further. All religion is either natural or revealed, the book of nature and the book of scripture. Yet "all revealed religion does suppose and take for granted the clear and undoubted principles and precepts of natural religion, and builds upon them." Natural religion means "obedience to the natural law" and fulfilling the duties we learn from "natural light" without any "supernatural revelation." These are moral duties and are eternally obligatory. They "are the foundation of revealed and instituted religion, and all revealed religion does suppose them and build upon them. . . . The great design of the Christian religion is to restore and reinforce the practice of the natural law, or which is all one, of moral duties."[31]

> Tillotson and Burnet agree that reason must be an ally, a friend of scripture, even though this friend sometimes seems to be gaining the upper hand and so displacing scripture.

Scripture, then, builds upon natural religion by restoring and reinforcing it. Part of what this means is that while the gospel teaches us "the very same things which nature dictated to men before," it reveals them more clearly, making what was "doubtful and obscure before . . . certain and plain." The duties taught by scripture are the same as those urged by natural religion, but the gospel "offers us more powerful arguments, and a greater assistance to the performance of those duties."[32] Scripture, then, does have functions that in some sense preserve its special place for Christians. Nevertheless, "[a]ll reasonings about Divine revelations must necessarily be governed by the principles of natural religion; that is by those apprehensions which men naturally have of the Divine perfection, and the clear notions of good and evil which are imprinted upon our natures." Moreover, "by these principles, likewise, we are to interpret what God hath revealed."[33]

In the sermon I am citing Tillotson goes on to add that, granted a revelation does not contradict natural religion, "miracles are owned by all mankind to be a sufficient testimony to any person, or doctrine, that they are from God." Thus, "all assent is grounded upon evidence."[34] He can also add the argument from design. "In this visible frame of the world, which we behold with our eyes, which way soever we look, we are encountered with ocular demonstrations of the wisdom of God."[35] Despite the unsystematic character of Tillotson's arguments, two conclusions suggest themselves. First, he has no wish to demote scripture and wants to see natural religion as its ally. But, second, he so tends to reduce scripture to its moral meaning that one begins to wonder whether it is really necessary. Does the ally become a treacherous one?

The same sort of conclusion is possible regarding Gilbert Burnet's *An Exposition of the Thirty-Nine Articles*, published in 1699. Burnet (1643–1715) was a strong supporter of William of Orange, who named him bishop of Salisbury in 1689 after the Glorious Revolution. His discussion of the Articles of Religion is supposed to be dispassionate, and he speaks of himself as more "an historian and a collector of what others have writ, than an author myself."[36] Nevertheless, his latitudinarian stance betrays itself in his understanding of the Articles as ones of "union and peace," meant to be read in "a literal and grammatical sense."[37] For example, he points out that there are three different senses of the Third Article concerning Christ's descent to hell and notes that if people would only understand all the other Articles "in the same largeness," there would be no need for "censure" and controversy. The fact that the Articles are drawn up "in large and general words" indicates that "the church does not intend to tie men up too severely to particular opinions, but that she leaves all to such liberty as is agreeable with the purity of the faith."[38] This conclusion is correlative with his distinction between "articles of faith and articles of doctrine." The first "are held necessary to salvation," the second, believed true provided they are "revealed in the scriptures, which is a sufficient ground for esteeming them true." Moreover, it is articles of faith that bestow "a foederal right to the covenant of grace."[39]

Burnet's treatment of Article Six, "Of the Sufficiency of the Holy Scriptures for Salvation," follows the main lines of Chillingworth's argument. He emphasizes "the negative consequence" of the article, namely, that no doctrine that may not be read in scripture or proved by it "is to be required to be believed as an article of faith, or to be thought necessary to salvation."[40] With this proviso "the scriptures are a complete *rule of faith*." There can be no appeal to oral tradition; and the ancient written tradition of the church, while it deserves respect, is at best a help to us in understanding scripture.[41] Indeed, it is doubtful that the apostles wrote the creed attributed to them.[42] Burnet's emphasis is upon the plain passages in scripture, though he recognizes the objection that "we cannot understand the true sense of the scripture" because "the scriptures are dark" and require an interpreter. He dismisses this objection by arguing that no such view obtained in antiquity and that if the books of the New Testament were clear to the ancients, "they may likewise be clear to us." To be sure, we can make mistakes both in understanding scripture and in seeking to fulfill our duties. But God accepts "our sincere endeavours." In any case, we can easily read scripture, and much of it is quite clear. If someone "prays to God to direct him, and follows sincerely what he apprehends to be true, and practises diligently those duties that do unquestionably appear to be bound upon him" by scripture, he will save his soul. Any "mistakes" he makes will either be rectified "by some happy providence" or forgiven him by a merciful God who knows "his sincerity and diligence."[43] Burnet defends private judgment but wants to argue that common deliberation will keep it from being divisive provided people "seek for truth more than for victory."[44] In his treatment of inspiration he comes very close to denying the verbal inerrancy of scripture. Inspiration leaves the biblical writers "to the use of their faculties."[45]

Thus far Burnet's perspective is quite congenial with Chilling-worth's, and it certainly leaves room for scripture as the great authority for Christian faith. But like Tillotson Burnet has a place for natural religion. His discussion of Article Eighteen, "Of Obtaining Eternal Salvation Only by the Name of Christ," worries about its apparent meaning. He begins by rejecting the relativistic approach to religions he finds in paganism and Islam, but goes on to make a distinction between being saved *by* a law or sect and being saved *in* one. "The former is only condemned by this article, which affirms nothing concerning the other."[46] A second distinction is between "a foederal certainty of salvation" possible only for Christians and the condition of those others "to whom the tidings of it were never brought." St. Paul speaks of the Gentiles who are "a law unto themselves" and have "the law written in their hearts" (Rom 2:14–15). These people cannot be saved *by* their religion, but we cannot assume that they will not be saved *in* their religion. We must honor "the secrets of God as mysteries too far above us to examine," and those mysteries include "God's uncovenanted mercies." We need not ask "whether any that are only in a state of nature, live fully up to its light," but we cannot deny the possibility that those who have received only natural religion and have never heard of the covenant of grace may be saved.[47]

Natural theology, then, affords the possibility of salvation; but more strikingly it also must be treated as the foundation for belief not only in God but also in scripture. Before we can accept the passages in scripture that "affirm there is a God" we must believe the propositions that there is a God, that all his words are true, and that these are his words. These propositions cannot be proved by scripture. Consequently, it is "a strange assertion, to say, that the being of God cannot be proved by the light of nature, but must be proved by the scriptures, since our being assured that there is a God is the first principle upon which the authority of the scriptures depends."[48] Burnet may not be as explicit as Tillotson, but it is arguable that both writers make natural religion the foundation of the revealed religion of scripture. Of course, they both assume that scripture and the Christian religion will be built upon this foundation and so regard nature as their friend. But the slippery slope toward deism is evident in their latitudinarian views.

Deism

The same judgment can be made regarding John Locke's *The Reasonableness of Christianity as Delivered in the Scriptures,* published in 1695. That is, it seems unlikely that we should judge Locke a deist, however much his ideas came to be construed that way and even though John Toland in his *Christianity Not Mysterious,* published the year after Locke's treatise, builds the case for deism upon what he regards as the foundation supplied by Locke.[49] In his preface Locke indicates his frustration with the different "Systems of Divinity," all of which claim to be based upon scripture. He sets himself the task of engaging in "the sole Reading of the Scripture," and his treatise is the product of his "attentive and unbiassed search." He offers it as his private judgment, but one that stands open to correction by his readers.[50] While Locke rejects original sin and argues that it is mortality alone that we inherit from Adam, he clearly adopts the common contrast between the covenant of works and that of faith. Appealing to Romans 2:14 he argues that "under the Law of Works is comprehended also the Law of Nature, knowable by Reason."[51] Christians, however, are privileged also to be under the law of faith, "which is that Law whereby God Justifies a man for Believing, though by his Works . . . he came short of Perfect Obedience to the Law of Works." In this way God counts "Faith for Righteousness," that is, "for a compleat performance of the Law."[52]

From one perspective Locke's reading of scripture yields a common Protestant view, not unlike that of Richard Baxter. While the only consequence of the Fall is mortality, Locke does assume that this explains why we cannot fulfill the law of works. Justification by faith, then, means that God accounts our insufficient righteousness as though it were sufficient, and so leads us toward salvation. At the same time, Locke understands faith as an assent to Jesus' authority as the Messiah, to the precepts he enjoins and to repentance as well as obedience. Revealed religion, then, tends to become a set of duties, and presumably those duties to be found in natural religion. Scripture, however, not only clarifies these natural duties, but it also gives a clear revelation of that future state which is a sanction for those duties by the rewards and punishments that will attend it. Moreover, God's revelation in scripture assists reason to discover what lies above but not contrary to reason, and it supplies some kind of assistance to us in our dutiful endeavors. But it is "idle to ask in what manner the Spirit of God shall work upon us."[53]

The slippery slope toward deism begins to appear, and Locke's attempt to deal with the problem of those who have not known scripture underlines the point. There are many who never received "the Promise of the *Messiah*" and so were quite unable either to accept or reject it. Nevertheless, "by the Light of Reason," which all possess, God revealed himself as "Good and Merciful," at least to those willing to make use of that light. Moreover, the "same spark of the Divine Nature and Knowledge in Man, which making him a Man; Shewed him also the way of Attoning the merciful, kind, compassionate Author and Father of him and his Being, when he had transgressed" the law of nature. The "candle of the Lord" in principle enables people who have never known scripture to discern their duties and "to find also the way to Reconciliation and Forgiveness" when they fail to act upon that discernment.[54] In *An Essay Concerning Human Understanding* (1690) Locke had taken the point considerably further. He points out that the immense number of differing interpretations of the New Testament prove that, however infallible we suppose the text, "the reader may be, nay cannot choose but to be very fallible in the understanding of it." We should not be surprised at this, since even God's Son, "whilst clothed in flesh, was subject to all the frailties and inconveniences of human nature, sin excepted."

With these limitations in mind we ought to "magnify" God's goodness, "that he hath spread before all the world, such legible characters of his works and providence, and given all mankind so sufficient a light of reason" that even those unacquainted with scripture need not doubt God's existence and "the obedience due to Him." Locke's conclusion is that "the precepts of natural religion" are so "plain, and...intelligible to all mankind" that they seldom cause controversy the way scripture does. So, "methinks it would become us to be more careful and diligent in observing the former [natural precepts], and less magisterial, positive, and imperious, in imposing our own sense and interpretations of the latter [revealed truths in books and languages]."[55]

No one doubted, however, that Toland's book, which I have mentioned, promoted deism. The other work that was regarded the same way was Matthew Tindal's *Christianity as Old as Creation, or the Gospel a Republication of the Religion of Nature* (1730). Deism, of course, took many forms; but in Britain it did not tend to assume an openly hostile approach to institutional Christianity as was the case in France. Perhaps this was partly because the latitudinarians were open to many of the conclusions of some of the deists. It is not always easy to distinguish the two sets of opinions, but one touchstone by which to identify deism is to define it as any view that dispenses with scripture either by regarding the Bible as unnecessary or by treating it as hostile to natural religion. Samuel Clarke (1675–1729) published his Boyle lectures demonstrating the being and attributes of God in 1704–6. Someone has observed that no one thought to doubt the existence of God till Dr. Clarke sought to prove it. Clarke identifies four classes of deists — those who accept God as the first creator of the universe and no more, those who add the idea of natural providence, those who go on to add moral providence, and, finally, those who accept all this, believe in an afterlife, but reject revealed religion. It is, of course, the last of the groups in Clarke's typology of deism that comes closest to the latitudinarian position. And it may be observed that the two major opponents of deism were both latitudinarians and appear to have been most concerned with the refutation of views closest to their own.[56]

Two Responses to Deism

Joseph Butler (1692–1752) grew up in a Presbyterian family, but in 1715 he conformed to the Church of England and entered Oriel College, Oxford. Three years later he received his degree and was ordained, becoming the preacher at the Rolls Chapel. He remained in this post until 1726, the year that his *Fifteen Sermons Preached at the Rolls Chapel* was published. The sermons are, in fact, a full articulation of his moral philosophy, which focuses upon the conscience, insists that conscience and self-interest coincide in principle, and argues that probability is the guide of life. By the nineteenth century Butler's writings were central to the theological curriculum at Oxford and Cambridge. In 1738 he was appointed bishop of Bristol, and in 1747 is said to have declined the archiepiscopal see of Canterbury on the grounds that it was too late to support a falling church. In Bristol he met John Wesley, and in his diary he condemned "the pretending to extraordinary revelations and gifts of the Holy Spirit" as "a horrid thing — a very horrid thing." He was appointed bishop of Durham in 1750, two years before his death. This melancholy saint epitomizes the description of the eighteenth-century Anglican clergy given by the historian L. P. Curtis: "Poised, kind, likely to excuse faults, hopeful, benevolent, empirical, and reverent — they appear to have understood the horror under which man must live."

It was in 1736 that Butler published his response to deism in *The Analogy of Religion.*[57] In his "Advertisement" to the work he says:

It is come, I know not how, to be taken for granted, by many persons, that Christianity is not so much a subject for enquiry but that it is, now at length, discovered to be fictitious. And accordingly they treat it as if in the present age this were an agreed point among all people of discernment, and nothing remained, but to set it up as a principal subject of mirth and ridicule, as it were by way of reprisals, for its having so long interrupted the pleasures of the world.

Butler indicates the structure of his work by citing Origen's "sagacious" observation that "he who believes the Scripture to have proceeded from him who is the Author of nature, may well expect to find the same sort of difficulties in it, as are found in the constitution of nature."[58] Part one deals with natural religion under the headings of a future life, God's government by rewards and punishments, God's moral government, this world as a state of probation involving difficulties and dangers and intended for moral discipline and improvement, and of natural religion as a scheme or constitution imperfectly comprehended. Throughout Butler assumes that the deists accept not only the existence of God and his providence, but also the notion of an afterlife. Part two shifts attention to revealed religion, largely identified with scripture. In other words, God has written two books, one of nature and the other of scripture. We find in both books puzzles and difficulties; consequently, revealed religion cannot be "a subject of ridicule, unless that of nature be so too."[59] This rather odd argument leads Butler to the conclusion that "no revelation would have been given, had the light of nature been sufficient in such a sense, as to render one not wanting or useless."[60] Revealed religion is, first, "a republication, and external institution, of natural or essential religion" and, secondly, "an account of things not discoverable by reason."

At the same time, "natural religion is the foundation and principal part of Christianity" even though it is not "the whole of it."[61] Not only is natural religion the foundation; it also judges revelation. Any passage in scripture that seems to be contrary to natural religion obliges us to recognize that we have not found the true meaning. On the other hand, this does not mean we must reject interpretations of "a doctrine, which the light of nature cannot discover, or a precept, which the law of nature does not oblige to."[62] Scripture, then, does have a role to play. It supplies a warrant for institutionalizing and republishing natural religion, and it does reveal truths like the Trinity that the light of nature could not discover. Yet even the revelation of scripture remains qualified. We are no more competent to judge revealed religion than we are to judge natural religion. We are not "competent judges" of scripture the way we are of "common books." Scripture contains "many truths as yet undiscovered."[63] The miracles and prophecies "recorded in Scripture" are testimony to the truth of revelation both as "an authoritative publication of natural religion" and as "a particular dispensation of Providence."[64] Butler devotes chapter 2 of the second part of the *Analogy* to a refutation of a presumption against miracles. His argument hinges upon our imperfect understanding of nature and the idea that miracles would prove natural were our understanding enlarged.[65] Scripture, then, however uncertain and difficult it proves to be, is a better guide than natural religion, which is no less uncertain and difficult. It gives us a probable revelation that can be regarded as morally certain.[66]

The second figure I wish to examine is William Paley (1743–1805). He was born at Peterborough, where his father was a minor canon of the cathedral. In 1759 he went up to Christ's College, Cambridge, where he spent the next sixteen years, becoming a fellow of his college in 1766. In 1775 he took a cure in the diocese of Carlisle and became the archdeacon of the diocese in 1782. In 1785 he published his *Principles of Moral and Political Philosophy*; in 1790, *Horae Paulinae*. George III is said to have objected to some of Paley's arguments in the first of these books, disapproved of his ideas about the sabbath and toleration, and took offense at his comparison of the divine right of kings with the divine right of constables.[67] In 1794 Paley published *A View of the Evidences of Christianity*, and the next year became subdean of Lincoln Cathedral and rector of Bishop Wearmouth in Durham, where he spent the last years of his life. His last work, published in 1802, was *Natural Theology*, an extended argument from design for the existence and character of God.

Paley begins *Natural Theology* with an analogy. If he were to find a stone on his path while walking across a heath, he would not think much of it. But were he to find a watch, he would be fascinated by its design and would be led to the conclusion that there could be no "design without a designer; contrivance without a contriver; order without choice;...subservience and relation to a purpose, without that which could intend a purpose."[68] This in turn implies that we are to think of "the presence of intelligence and mind." Even were we to suppose that watches somehow reproduce themselves, no matter how long a chain of cause and effect we posit, the same conclusions would follow. Most of the book simply elaborates this basic perspective by appealing to the natural world and, particularly, to the human body. In his last chapters, however, Paley seeks to demonstrate central ways in which to describe the intelligent designer he believes he has found. This contriver must be a "person" with consciousness and thought, with the purpose and means to contrive the world. Therefore, even though this personal God remains unseen and mysterious, he must be "a Being infinite in essence and power."[69] God must be characterized by "omnipotence, omniscience, omnipresence, eternity, self-existence, necessary existence, spirituality."[70] Moreover, God's unity can be proved by "the *uniformity* of plan discernable in the universe."[71]

God's goodness requires a somewhat more complicated demonstration. There are two basic arguments. First, in most cases in nature "the design of the contrivance is *beneficial*." Second, there may be seen the superaddition of "*pleasure* to animal sensations, beyond what is necessary for any other purpose."[72] I cannot resist citing part of Paley's lengthy and lyrical elaboration of the second point:

> It is a happy world after all. The air, the earth, the water, teem with delightful existence. In a spring noon, or a summer evening, on whichever side I turn my eyes, myriads of happy beings crowd upon my view. "The insect youth are on the wing." Swarms of new-born *flies* are trying their pinions in the air. Their sportive motions, their wanton mazes, their gratuitous activity, their continual change of place without use or purpose, testify their joy, and the exultation which they feel in their lately discovered faculties.[73]

Despite his optimism Paley does recognize the obstacle presented to his view by the problem of evil.[74] He suggests that the difficulty may be overcome in part by restricting our consideration to "those effects alone which are accompanied with proofs of intentions" and by recognizing the preponderance of "benevolence of design."[75] To this may be added the idea that the world is a place of probation.[76]

In at least two places Paley insists that his account of natural religion is a prolegomenon to revealed religion. He points out that one of the advantages of "the revelations which we acknowledge" — presumably scripture — is that "they afford a condescension to the state of our faculties." These accommodations of scripture as revealed religion "are well founded in point of authority, (for all depends on that)."[77] In his conclusion Paley argues that what he has demonstrated about the "existence and character of the Deity" is of special interest, since "it facilitates the belief of the fundamental articles of *Revelation*." Natural theology will whet the appetite of the inquirer for "further instruction."[78] In this way Paley seeks to insist upon nature as a friend of scripture in such a way as to prevent the friend from becoming a foe. His defense of revealed religion is to be found in *A View of the Evidences of Christianity*.

He is obliged to refute David Hume's repudiation of miracles, and he does so by insisting upon the reliability of the biblical testimony.[79] Part of Paley's argument revolves around arguing that the institution of the Christian religion by the evidences of miracles and prophecy no more violates the laws of nature than does its progress. God committed the progress of Christianity "to the natural means of communication, and to the influence of those causes by which human conduct and human affairs are governed." Since miracles are confined to scripture and no longer occur, the only problem has to do with refusing to admit that the biblical miracles violate nature. The "seed" and "leaven" of Christianity depend upon God's providence, which is partly concealed from our view. Paley places the argument from design in this rather odd context. Reasoning from our observation of contrivance and design in nature to God includes the realization that the "great powers of nature are all invisible." "Gravitation, electricity, magnetism" are always present "exerting their influence." But they are "totally concealed from our senses." The same thing is true of God, who cannot be seen.[80] Both God's natural and his moral providence are to some degree inscrutable. Consequently, we need not regard the evidences of Christianity as unnatural and can accept them on the basis of the biblical testimony, which is reliable because it is in part that of "eye-witnesses of the facts, ear-witnesses of the discourses [of Christ]."[81]

In combining the argument from design with an insistence upon the inscrutability of providence Paley's argument resembles Butler's. But his interest lies in the proofs for Christianity rather than in the content of either natural or revealed religion. He does want to enlist nature as a friend to scripture, and he also opens himself to the treachery of that friend. But at a deeper level his appeal is to history, albeit to history understood in what will soon be regarded as an extremely naïve and uncritical sense. Paley's proof of Christianity really depends upon a narrative. Certain persons "in the reign of Tiberius Caesar" began to establish a new religion. They "voluntarily encountered great dangers, undertook great labours, sustained great sufferings, all for a miraculous story." They proclaimed this story everywhere they went, and central to it was "the resurrection of a dead man, whom, during his life, they had followed and accompanied."[82] Their success is to be attributed to the miracles and the prophecies that proved their story. Paley makes a comparison with the Christian mission in India. Its small success by comparison with the mission of Christ and his apostles finds an explanation in the fact that Christ and his immediate followers "possessed means of conviction, which we have not; that they had proofs to appeal to, which we want."[83] Miracles and prophecy are confined to scripture.

Paley has little to say about the content of the Christian message, its doctrines and precepts. His concern is to prove the truth of Christianity; and while the transformation of human lives is part of that proof, we gain no very clear idea of what that transformation amounts to. To be sure, Christian precepts enjoin a conduct that is pure, benevolent, and disinterested. And "this purity and benevolence are extended to the very thoughts and affections."[84] Indeed, "the teaching of morality was not the primary design of the mission." Morality need not be discovered, presumably because we understand it by nature. Paley concludes:

If I were to describe in a very few words the scope of Christianity as a revelation, I should say, that it was to influence the conduct of human life, by establishing the proof of a future state of reward and punishment.... The direct object, therefore, of the design is, to supply motives, and not rules; sanctions, and not precepts.[85]

It begins to look as though the moral dimension of Christianity can be drawn from nature and that the most scripture can do is to supply a sanction for morality. Moreover, Paley explicitly says that he has taken care "to preserve the separation between evidences and doctrines as inviolable as I could."[86] His reason is his wish to appeal to Christians no matter what doctrines they espouse and so to dismiss doctrinal controversy from his argument. He takes the same approach to inspiration. "The doctrine itself is by no means necessary to the belief of Christianity, which must, in the first instance at least, depend upon the ordinary maxims of historical credibility."[87]

It is, then, the historicity of the miracles and prophecies that represents the real evidence for the truth of Christianity. While Paley clearly makes use of scripture, he also employs pagan and early Christian texts to describe the spread of Christianity in the ancient world. He cites this evidence more often than not without weighing it in any real fashion. Scripture looks like no more than a small part of a much larger body of historical evidence. In his conclusion to part 3 he repeats the "leading facts" of apostolic Christianity and concludes by making an astonishing statement. It was a "Jewish peasant" who "changed the religion of the world, and that, without force, without power, without support; without one natural source or circumstance of attraction, influence, or success." His companions after his death "asserted his supernatural character, founded upon his supernatural operations." They voluntarily entered into "toil and hardship" in order to proclaim his resurrection and preach his religion. "These three facts, I think, are certain, and would have been nearly so, if the Gospels had never been written."[88] Paley's rhetoric takes him further than he must have intended. But though he clearly regards nature and history as friends to scripture, it is hard to deny that they are treacherous ones.

Several observations about Paley's argument are in order. By the early nineteenth century it will cease to be convincing to most people. Part of the reason for this lies in a return of interest in the inner meaning of Christianity rather than in external proofs that really say nothing about that meaning. We can think not only of theological writers but also of poets and philosophers like Wordsworth and Coleridge. A second explanation has to do with far more sophisticated understandings of historiography from the perspective of which Paley is hopelessly naïve. The gradual impact of German thought is clearly part of the picture, and I think both of the idealists and of the historians. A third reason is that geological advances in the early nineteenth century cast doubt upon the scriptural accounts of creation and of Noah's flood. With respect to nature as friend or foe, I am tempted to conclude that in the eighteenth century scripture ran the risk of somehow being made the servant of nature. Looking ahead, perhaps in the nineteenth century, at least with the *Lux Mundi* school, nature tended to become the servant of the scriptural revelation. Christ becomes the crown and consummation of nature, obliging us to see nature in relation to him.

An Evangelical Return to Scripture Alone

The evangelical revival began fairly early in the eighteenth century by what seems to have been a kind of spontaneous combustion. There are specific connections between it and Pietism in Germany and the Great Awakening in the American colonies. Explaining the revival involves taking account of it both as a reaction against the dominant mood of the century and as a response to social and economic forces that were only partially connected with the industrial revolution. The aspect of the movement that is of interest with respect to scripture is the appeal of the evangelicals in Britain to the party platform of sixteenth-century Anglicanism in general and to the sole authority of scripture in particular. It will suffice for my purpose to limit attention

to the writings of John Wesley (1703–91). In 1729 John, his brother
Charles, George Whitefield, and one other formed a small society at
Oxford devoted to the study of scripture and to good works and holy
living. This beginning for John Wesley led to the gradual formation of
his religious views and to his emergence as the great organizer of the
Methodist societies, which remained within the Church of England
till after Wesley's death.[89]

The Oxford "Holy Club," strongly influenced by the writings of
Jeremy Taylor and William Law, put the strongest possible emphasis
on holy living. In 1735 John and Charles Wesley set out for the newly
founded colony of Georgia and ministered in Savannah. Two experiences shaped John's developing understanding of Christianity — his
encounters with the Moravian missionaries sent from Herrnhut in
Saxony under the patronage of Count von Zinzendorf, and the hostile
reaction of his flock in Savannah to his rigid and moralizing pastoral
stance. Obliged to flee Georgia, Wesley returned to London, where
in 1738 at the Moravian chapel in Aldersgate Street he felt his "heart
strangely warmed" and began to discover the importance of God's
grace and its converting power. His disenchantment with the high
church and holy living Anglicanism of his upbringing was followed
by an increasing dissatisfaction with the Moravians, and it is arguable
that his reading of the two books of Homilies gave him a way of in-
tegrating what he found persuasive in the two religious platforms he
came to reject. His reworking of the Reformation teaching of justification and sanctification included two idiosyncratic doctrines. By
arguing for the universality of prevenient grace and of its identification with the conscience he took what was essentially an Arminian
rather than a Calvinist view. And by regarding "entire sanctification"
as the Christian perfection the believer should expect in this life he
left room for an emphasis upon holy living that did not interfere with
an insistence upon the gratuitous character of God's saving work in
Christ and in the heart of the justified sinner. By 1739 Wesley was
an evangelical field preacher, and as early as 1744 he instituted an
annual conference of the Methodist societies he founded.

Obviously the story would need to be told at much greater length, but my concern is to say something about Wesley's attitude toward scripture. In 1765 he wrote a letter to John Newton, a fellow evangelical and the author of "Amazing Grace," in which he claims that "[i]n 1730 I began to be *homo unius libri* [a man of one book], to study (comparatively) no book but the Bible."[90] He had learned that the one thing needful (cf. Luke 10:42) was "the faith that worketh by love" (Gal 5:6). Wesley's "comparatively" may indicate that his memory has misled him, but many years later he makes the same claim. His sermon "On God's Vineyard" was published in 1788, but probably first preached the preceding year. The vineyard (Isa 5:4) may mean "the body of people commonly called Methodists." And Wesley traces its origin to the society begun at Oxford in 1729. At that beginning "four young men united together, each of them was *homo unius libri* — 'a man of one book.' " Determined to be "Bible-Christians," they were derided as "Bible-bigots" and "Bible-moths." Moreover, the "book which, next to the Holy Scriptures, was of the greatest use to them in settling their judgment as to the grand point of justification by faith was the book of Homilies." No one ordained can oppose them because clergy have subscribed to the Thirty-Nine Articles, and Articles Eleven and Thirty-Five refer to the Homilies.[91]

In looking back Wesley has either misremembered or exaggerated. From 1732 until his first year in Georgia three years later Wesley found himself persuaded by a group of non-juring high churchmen in Manchester.[92] He alludes to this in a lengthy entry in his diary, written on January 25, 1738, on the ship carrying him back to England. He says that "Providence brought me to those who showed me a sure rule of interpreting Scripture." The rule is a version of the Vincentian canon. What has been believed by all, everywhere, and always supplies the key to the meaning of scripture. By the time he writes this, however, Wesley has repented the error of his ways. He had "bent the bow" and gone astray "1. By making antiquity a co-ordinate rather than subordinate rule with Scripture. 2. By admitting several doubtful writings as undoubted evidences of antiquity." He acknowledges several other errors. He had mistakenly regarded antiquity as extending into the fourth century, had assumed more uniformity of practice than was the case, and had failed to understand the limitations of synods, particularly the way their decisions were tied to specific times and places. The passage in the diary continues by describing another change of heart. He has learned to repudiate the mystics. "May I praise him who hath snatched me out of this fire likewise, by warning all others that it is set on fire of hell."[93]

Once Wesley firmly commits himself to scripture as "the one book" he must consult, he seeks to square his reading of scripture with his own experience. Part of what this involves is the refusal to see scripture as a warrant for mysticism, while another crucial part has to do with his repudiation of the Moravian view that justification or the conversion experience happens suddenly and at once. Wesley came to believe that the Moravian tendency to reject the use of all means of grace before this experience was wrongheaded, and that their account of justification failed to account for growth and development after as well as before conversion. One place to discern Wesley's mature view of scripture is in his *Cautions and Directions Given to the Greatest Professors in the Methodist Societies*, published in 1761. This small treatise warns against pride and its "daughter" enthusiasm, as well as against antinomianism, sins of omission, and schism. In the section cautioning against enthusiasm Wesley advises his readers to try everything "by the written Word." "You are in danger of enthusiasm every hour if you depart ever so little from Scripture — yea, or from the plain literal meaning of any text taken in connection with the context." Christians must not expect any blessing "without hearing the Word of God at every opportunity." They make a mistake if they take the fresh "application of any . . . Scriptures to the heart" to be a new gift. That is, the reading of scripture must respect the progressive character of the Christian life.[94]

Wesley employs his Bible Christianity in a work addressed both to deists and to nominal members of the Church of England. *An Earnest Appeal*, published in 1743, led to *A Further Appeal* two years later. Let me restrict attention to the first of these works. Wesley's apologetic concern is complex. He wishes to refute not only deism and nominal Christianity, but also a number of charges brought against the Methodist societies. But he also says what he hopes will enable his opponents to see the light. His own commitment is to "the straight way to the religion of love, even by faith."[95] The allusion is to Galatians 5:6 ("faith working through love"), and the love involved is surely that of God and neighbor. The entire treatise is saturated with scriptural citations and allusions, and Wesley assumes that the nominal Christians he castigates do accept scripture in principle. He urges those who are licentious and lead profligate lives: "Either cast off the Bible or your sins."[96] Those who lead honorable lives and have "an unspotted reputation," but spend their time in idle amusements, are harmless, but "useless" as Indians "sitting in a row on the side of a river."[97] These people cannot possibly think they were made for the life they lead if they did not "tread the Bible under foot."[98] Wesley has clearly profited by reading William Law's *A Serious Call to a Devout and Holy Life*.

> Once Wesley firmly commits himself to scripture as "the one book" he must consult, he seeks to square his reading of scripture with his own experience.

The sections of *An Earnest Appeal* that address those who in no sense accept scripture are the most interesting for my purpose in this chapter, since they deal with religion and reason.[99] The opponents are clearly deists, for they are assumed to believe in God, in the difference between moral good and evil, and in conscience. Wesley places most of his argument in the context of a discussion he claims to have had with an impoverished man lying on his sick bed, friendless, and having attempted to end his miserable life. He tells Wesley not to speak of "your Bible, for I do not believe one word of it." He does, however, know that there is a God; but he thinks of God as the *anima mundi*, the world soul.[100] Wesley begins his response by claiming that the religion he preaches is reasonable. It is reasonable to love God and reasonable to love our neighbor.[101] But Wesley's scriptural Christianity is clearly more than this and involves the faith that is the wellspring for this double love. If by reason the sick man means "the nature of God and the nature of man, together with their mutual relations," then scriptural Christianity gives a full account of all this. But perhaps, says Wesley, "you mean the faculty of reasoning, of inferring one thing from another."[102] To be sure, there are Christians, especially "mystic divines," who "condemn all reasoning concerning the things of God as utterly destructive of true religion." But Wesley and his followers not only allow but also encourage "all who seek after true religion to use all the reason which God hath given them."[103]

Wesley's argument continues by defining what he means by reasoning. Right reasoning "presupposes true judgments already formed whereon to ground your argumentation." That is, argumentation depends upon true premises, and Wesley appears to think that it rests at least in part upon an Aristotelian syllogistic logic. A true judgment or premise, in turn, depends upon "ideas," which are not "innate, but must all originally come from our sense." Our ideas, then, are the raw material from which we form judgments by which to reason. This part of his argument coheres rather well with Locke's epistemology. At this point, however, Wesley introduces a point that distinguishes his epistemology from any strictly philosophical one. We possess not only natural senses, such as sight and hearing, but also "spiritual senses, exercised to discern spiritual good and evil." Thus, just "as you cannot reason concerning colours if you have no natural *sight*...so you cannot reason concerning spiritual things if you have no 'spiritual sight.'"[104]

The problem then becomes how reason will "pass from things natural to spiritual." This "immense chasm" cannot be crossed " 'till the Almighty comes in to your succour and gives you that faith you have hitherto despised."[105] It is difficult to see how this part of the argument would persuade Wesley's sick and despairing deist. The spiritual sense appears to be the product of justification by faith, which Wesley takes to be the central theme of scripture. A "reasonable" Christianity, then, really amounts to the experience of justification. This experience finds its legitimacy not only in the inward witness of the Spirit, but also in the external witness of scripture. However much this understanding of conversion and scripture may be reasonable, reason is no longer in any real sense an ally of scripture; and the spiritual senses which are God's gift eclipse those senses that are natural. No matter how hard Wesley seeks to include reason and nature in his account of scriptural Christianity, it looks to me as though he recognizes that nature and reason are at the least insufficient friends of scripture.

Conclusion

It is not possible to conclude that the latitudinarians abandon a commitment to scripture, but it is certainly arguable that for them scripture tends to resolve itself into those duties somehow taught by nature. The same sort of interpretation suggests itself with respect to their attitude toward the church. In 1716 the papers of George Hickes, a militant non-juring high churchman, were published. They revealed that clandestine episcopal consecrations had taken place in one circle of the schismatics and with at least the connivance of the exiled Stuart court at St. Germain in France. This Jacobite and seditious development horrified Benjamin Hoadly, the latitudinarian bishop of Bangor in Wales. Hoadly attacked the non-jurors in a controversial work and in March of 1717 preached a sermon on the text "My kingdom is not of this world," Christ's words to Pilate (John 18:36). He argued that Christ had left behind him no visible human authorities whatsoever. The sermon provoked a strong reaction in certain quarters. A bishop was denying that the church had no place to stand. William Law in his *Letters to the Bishop of Bangor* defended the church's ministry, but the controversy ended with a deadlock in Convocation and the virtual disappearance of that body in 1717, thus depriving the Church of England of any purely ecclesiastical forum in which theological and religious issues could be debated. To be sure,

the latitudinarian bishops of the eighteenth century committed themselves not only to their political role as members of the House of
Lords, but also to their ecclesiastical duties. Nevertheless, the church
plays a very small role in their attempts to articulate the meaning of
scripture and of Christianity.

Up to a point the same sort of judgment is possible with respect to
Wesley's stance. Of course, he repeatedly denies that he has any wish
to cause a schism in the church, and he clearly thinks of the Methodist societies as an *ecclesiola in ecclesia* — a saving remnant within the
Church of England designed to recall the church to its own profession and mission. Nevertheless, Wesley's scriptural interpretation of
Christianity emphasizes the individual's conversion and sanctification
within the context of the societies, which were in principle communities of like-minded people. What I am suggesting obviously needs
considerable qualification, but at least as a hypothesis worth considering the suggestion is that both the latitudinarians and the evangelicals
tend to neglect the church in what they say about scripture and its
meaning.

One final point seems more fully persuasive to me. The evangelical
move to restore scripture as the "one book," itself partly a reaction
to latitudinarian views, began to dominate religious opinion in the
early nineteenth century. Moreover, the hardening of their insistence
upon the Bible alone led to their acceptance of the verbal inerrancy of
scripture. As we shall see, Coleridge takes this to be the majority view
and argues against it, as well as against attempts to support Christianity by external "evidences." The evangelical view persisted, indeed
still persists. But it will founder against the impact of the emerging
historical-critical approach to the Bible, as well as of developments
in natural science associated with geology and with Darwin's theory
of evolution.

Chapter Four

Making Friends with History
The Nineteenth Century

In 1839 Thomas Arnold (1795–1842) published *Two Sermons on Prophecy, with Notes*. He had been the reforming headmaster of Rugby School for the past twelve years; and his friend and biographer, Arthur Stanley, speaks of the "calmer tone" of Arnold's last years. Yet in the same year he published the two sermons Arnold wrote, "When I think of the Church, I could sit down and pine and die." Nevertheless, he regarded his sermons as irenic, "in which it was his earnest desire to avoid as much as possible all such questions as might engender strife."[1] He apparently assumes that few people would be disturbed by his repudiation of the usual view of prophecy as the prediction of actual events and of Christ, thereby depriving them of one of the evidences for Christianity. At least he has met with few "whose faith rests much upon that evidence, or indeed who have ever really tried its validity." Instead, Arnold contrasts prophecy with history. "History, in our common sense of the term, is busy with particular nations, times, places, actions, and even persons." In contrast, "what history does not and cannot do, that Prophecy does." This is because it "fixes our attention on principles, on good and evil, on truth and falsehood, on God and on His enemy."[2]

The distinction Arnold makes is meant to be reassuring. Implicit in his argument is the recognition that when treated historically the fulfillments of prophecy at best fall short of what the prophet proclaims. But if we insist that prophecy is designed "to assure man amidst the existing evils of the world, that the cause of good would be finally and entirely triumphant," we need not fear the historians.[3] We can still claim that "Christ is the real subject of all Prophecy for good" because "All the promises of God in Him are yea, and in Him Amen" (2 Cor 1:20).[4] Arnold may well be reassuring himself as well as his readers. He saw himself as a doubting Thomas, but one who shared in his namesake's "joyful confession" — "My Lord and my God!"[5] It is possible to conclude that Arnold's message in the two sermons on prophecy is: "Do not be afraid. History and prophecy differ from one another, and history need be no threat to our faith."

There seemed much to fear and much to hope in the 1830s. People tended to see the times as an age of transition.[6] In part this was because of the French Revolution and its aftermath both in repression and in further revolutionary social and economic forces. But for my purpose the transition has to do with new attitudes toward the Bible.[7] For some, such as George Eliot, who translated David Friedrich Strauss's *Life of Jesus* (1835) into English in 1846, the critical approach to scripture was a liberation "from the wretched giant's bed of dogmas." She joined "that glorious crusade that is seeking to set truth's Holy Sepulchre free from a usurped dominion."[8] Obviously, not all agreed. The threat to the Bible from modern forms of historiography came in two forms. Hegel delivered his lectures on the philosophy of history in 1822–23. His idealist understanding built upon the insights of earlier German philosophers and contributed to the Tübingen school of New Testament criticism, whose best-known members were F. C. Baur and Strauss.[9] This sort of approach had the effect of substituting a philosophical narrative for the biblical one.[10] The more common form of history, to which Arnold alludes, owed something to positivism and was concerned with "facts."[11] And getting the supposed facts straight in order to reconstruct the past just as it was disintegrated the biblical narrative. Whether the biblical text was treated as an opportunity for larger philosophical structures or as evidence that had to be assessed and challenged, it was easy to see that much of the Bible could no longer be regarded as historically true. Developments in natural science exacerbated the problem. Geology called into question the Old Testament accounts of creation and of Noah's universal deluge long before Darwin published his evolutionary theories.

Defending the Bible from the historical-critical method on the whole took two different forms. Some simply repudiated it and resorted to a fideist position.[12] These included not only the evangelicals in the Church of England, but also some of the early Oxford apostles. Pusey himself had studied in Germany as a young man, equipping himself with the linguistic and scholarly tools he needed as Regius Professor of Hebrew at Oxford. But he came to reject the conclusions of German higher criticism and ended his life believing that fossils were either a hoax or had been created by God as a test of faith. Liddon, his disciple and biographer, regarded the welcoming stance toward criticism on the part of Charles Gore as a betrayal of the catholic movement. Other defenders of scripture, however, sought to make a friend of the new criticism; and it is this approach that gradually won the day. Consequently, my chief concern in this chapter is to examine how this attempt was made by Benjamin Jowett and William Sanday. I want to begin, however, with John Henry Newman and F. D. Maurice, both of whom understand history in what could be called a pre-scientific way, and to end with William Gladstone's rather muddled footdragging at the end of the nineteenth century. My basic conclusion will be that making friends with history, while it became largely accepted, led to a set of problems that became the preoccupation of Anglicans in the twentieth century and that cannot be said to have been resolved even now.

Newman and Maurice

In 1838 John Henry Newman published Tracts 83 and 85, which concerned "Holy Scripture in its Relation to the Catholic Creed." His aim is partly to supply "more adequate and explicit *Scripture proof*" of what he calls the church system of doctrine and partly to argue that "all those who try to form their Creed by Scripture only, fall away from the Church and her doctrine, and join one or other sect or party."[13] What Newman assumes is that any claim that a system of doctrine is what scripture explicitly says is specious. Those who appeal to the Bible alone are in fact reading the Bible with a set of presuppositions, and much of what they claim to be purely scriptural derives from the Bible by the same sort of deductive process used by Newman to prove the catholic and apostolic creed. No matter what reasons his opponents can give for their position, they are the same sort of reasons "we can give for our belief in the articles of our Creed." This means that they can escape inconsistency only "by going further either one way or the other — by adding to their creed, or by giving it up altogether."[14] Granted that scripture does not clearly teach "the Apostolical Succession of the Ministry," it is equally clear that it does not explicitly teach infant baptism, the observance of Sunday, the doctrines of the Trinity and the Holy Spirit, of the atonement and justification. Moreover, it does teach precepts about celibacy and the community of goods that Bible Christians would reject.[15] Newman obviously repudiates the idea of the perspicuity of scripture. The plain passages in scripture are no more than a factor of what Bible Christians read into the text, and Newman asks, "Whence do Protestants derive their common notion, that every one may gain his knowledge of revealed truth from Scripture for himself?" Such a view makes scripture a kind of chameleon that adapts itself to whatever presuppositions someone brings to it.[16]

These conclusions lead Newman to a lengthy discussion of difficulties to be found in scripture. We must recognize "the perplexed character of Scripture, as regards its relation of facts."[17] There are two creation narratives that are in apparent contradiction with one another. Twice scripture tells us of Abraham denying his wife, and once it has the same story about Isaac. Moses fasts for forty days twice in Deuteronomy and once in Exodus. The first three Gospels omit the raising of Lazarus. The fourth Gospel has Jesus carrying his own cross rather than Simon of Cyrene. There are two conflicting stories of the death of Judas. It is impossible to reconcile the differing accounts of the appearances of the risen Lord. While Newman is innocent of the historical-critical method, he sees the problems it sought to solve. The same sort of difficulty attaches to the doctrines most people assume that scripture teaches.[18] Moreover, scripture does not even clearly give us the knowledge that the Bible is the word of

God.[19] What compounds the problem still more is that scripture refers to knowledge that must be gained apart from scripture itself. For example, in 1 Corinthians 15 Paul refers to what he has received.[20]

Newman explains these perplexities and the fact that scripture is "unsystematic and uncertain in its communications" by his understanding of inspiration. Since the human will remains free even though God rules it, similarly inspiration is "compatible with . . . personal agency on the part of its instruments." This means that "though the Bible be inspired, it has all such characteristics as might attach to a book uninspired." We can think of different dialects, styles, times, and places, repetitions, contradictions, and hopeless obscurities. And we must remember that the Bible is not a single book but a collection of books that differ widely from one another.[21] The negative conclusion must be that scripture does not interpret itself.[22] The positive conclusion, however, is that "points of faith may be *under* the surface, points of observance need not be in Scripture *at all*."[23] Private judgment, however, is not a sufficient way of discerning these points. Newman makes his case more fully in *The Prophetical Office of the Church* (1837). He claims that the popular view gives every Christian "the right of making up his mind for himself what he is to believe, from personal and private study of the Scriptures." It may be true that we should praise "independence of mind, free inquiry, the resolution to judge for ourselves, and the enlightened and spiritual temper which these things are supposed to produce." But it is "preposterous" to claim that "every individual Christian, rich and poor, learned and unlearned, young and old" will have examined scripture and determined its meaning for himself.[24] Newman's point is not merely that not all are qualified to understand scripture but also that Christian faith is corporate in character and must exclude any individualistic reading of scripture.

The next step in the logic of Newman's argument is to pose three possible conclusions. The first is to deny that scripture contains any definite creed or system. Indeed, "the arguments which are used to prove that the Church system is not in Scripture, may as cogently be used to prove that no system is in Scripture." The second possible conclusion is that "though there really is a true creed or system in Scripture, still it is not on the surface of Scripture, but is found latent and implicit within it." The third conclusion is that "though there is a true creed or system revealed, it is not revealed in Scripture, but must be learned collaterally from other sources."[25] The three views are, respectively, the latitudinarian, Anglican, and Roman ones. Needless to say, Newman chooses the middle view. He rejects the latitudinarian conclusion on the grounds that if there are only disembodied great truths in scripture, there is bound to be no agreement as to what those truths are. Moreover, if the doctrine of the trinity is not retained, "the keystone of the mysterious system is lost," and the gospel in the course of time "will be considered scarcely more than the republication of the law of nature."[26] And obviously he rejects the Roman view since to abolish the authority of scripture altogether would be to abandon the Church of England.

What is latent in scripture includes primarily those things necessary for salvation. If asked how he knows this to be so, Newman answers "that the early Church thought so, and the early Church must have known."[27] It becomes clear that what he means is that the Catholic and apostolic system of the ancient church makes explicit what is implicit in the New Testament; what is latent becomes patent. When St. Paul "speaks of one faith, one baptism, one body" (Eph 4:5), he does indeed give "a very intelligible hint of his own view of Christianity." But the hint becomes explicit in the church, and we find "in history" what St. Paul had in mind. Newman asks, "what excuse have we for not recognizing in this system of doctrine and worship existing in history, that very system to which the Apostles refer in Scripture?"[28] History, then, is the friend that enables us to discern what lies beneath the surface of Scripture. In a sense Newman is repeating the sort of view we found in Hammond: antiquity is the essential tool for discovering in scripture what is necessary for salvation. As well, the view seems quite compatible with Irenaeus's conviction that the rule of faith is both within scripture and capable of articulation outside scripture. There is, as it were, a canon within the canon; but we can know this only by disengaging it from scripture and using it as a hermeneutical tool. On the other hand, it is possible to argue that Newman allows history to trump scripture both by giving it separate and equal status and by his theory of the development of doctrine.

However much Newman correlates scripture and the apostolic church, it occasionally becomes clear that he prefers the church system's supposed clarity to the complex muddle of scripture. It really does not matter whether this "system of doctrine and worship" is latent in scripture or not — or even whether his "hypothesis" or the "Roman view" is correct. The system is there "external to Scripture." The "further question" is whether we can find it in scripture. "Whether we adopt our Sixth Article or not, we cannot obliterate the fact that a system does substantially exist in history." Even if scripture were "lost to us, that fact, an existing Catholic system, will remain."[29] Is Newman simply overstating his case, or is he already on his way to Rome in 1838? The first possibility seems more likely, and yet the seeds of his reasons for leaving the Church of England in 1845 are there. History has the possibility of being a foe of scripture, and the Bible runs the risk of being unnecessary if not an embarrassment.

The more significant change Newman makes in his understanding of antiquity is his theory of development. For Anglicans like Hammond the appeal to antiquity functioned to establish the scriptural basis of the Church of England and to demonstrate its continuity with the apostolic tradition. Newman, however, reverses the direction of thought by shifting attention to an ongoing development. Already in his 1838 Tracts he articulates the germ of the idea he will develop seven years later in *An Essay on the Development of Christian Doctrine*. He argues that "we depend for the Canon and Creed upon the fourth and fifth centuries." What he means is that "the fifth century acts as a comment on the obscure text of the centuries before it, and brings out a meaning which, with the help of that comment, any candid person sees really belongs to them."[30] In the *Essay on the Development of Christian Doctrine* Newman applies this idea to scripture and does so in a more radical way: He sees the objection that "inspired documents" like the scriptures "determine its

[Christianity's] doctrine without further trouble." But the scriptures "were intended to create an idea, and that idea is not in the sacred text, but in the mind of the reader." The real question is whether the idea is given to him "in its completeness and minute accuracy, on its first apprehension." Newman obviously believes that the idea "expands in his heart and intellect, and comes to perfection in the course of time."[31] What he wants to show is that all appeals to scripture require interpretation and deduction, and that this is tantamount to arguing for development. Nevertheless, it is the development that counts and not its rootedness in scripture; the idea triggered by scripture in the mind of the reader takes precedence over scripture itself. Does this mean that scripture has no further role to play? Newman can give a negative answer to the question. One of his conclusions is that the "use of Scripture . . . especially its spiritual or second sense, as a medium of thought and deduction, is a characteristic principle of the developments of doctrine in the Church."[32]

The reader, however, has a right to wonder whether Newman really takes this answer seriously. At one point he refers to the "popular notion which has prevailed among us since the Reformation" that the Bible is our guide, "overthrowing the supremacy of Church and Pope." What we find, however, is that the Bible does not serve this purpose; and we are forced "to revert to that living and present guide," namely, the church as the "arbiter" of true doctrine and holy practice. People say that God has spoken in a book. "We have tried it, and it disappoints; it disappoints, that most holy and blessed gift, not from fault of its own, but because it is used for a purpose for which it was not given."[33] However much Newman preserves the Bible, he does so only to the degree that it serves the church's purposes. It is also arguable that what he means by the church is its historical development through the ages. Consider the well-known passage from his introduction:

Bold outlines, which cannot be disregarded, rise out of the records of the past, when we look to see what it will give up to us: they may be dim, they may be incomplete, but they are definite; there is that which they are not, which they cannot be. Whatever be historical Christianity, it is not Protestantism. If ever there were a safe truth, it is this.[34]

Later in life Newman writes that we can see "the beginning of the end of Protestantism, the breaking of that bubble of 'Bible-Christianity' which has been its life."[35] Not only has the church displaced the Bible, history has also become the foe rather than the friend of scripture.

The year after Newman's *Essay on the Development of Christian Doctrine* appeared F. D. Maurice published his Warburton Lectures on the Epistle to the Hebrews, including a lengthy review of Newman's work as a preface. He begins by expressing his agreement with Newman that "Christianity is to be viewed as an historical fact." But he points out that Protestants have often agreed, while medieval Catholics were indifferent to history. Newman's point, then, cannot be used to mark the difference between Catholic and Protestant.[36] He goes on to argue that there is a contradiction between Newman's rejection of the quest for a "leading idea" and his fundamental notion of development. Part of his point is that one can scarcely speak of development if there is nothing capable of it. But more significantly Maurice is concerned for a unifying idea of some kind. The painter, the scientist, and the literary critic all strive for some sense of a unity that lies behind apparent diversity.[37] Of course, for Maurice this unity lies in the universal and spiritual commonwealth he calls the Kingdom of Christ. This is where all religious principles find their unity, and it represents the true meaning both of history and of scripture. Consequently, we should really speak of revelation as the unveiling of what already exists rather than of development, which might imply the creation of something new. Moreover, "the reverent reader of Scripture" surely supposes that "the idea which he receives from Scripture is not merely in his mind; that it is also in the text."[38] People cannot regard scripture as "a collection of notions and opinions about certain great subjects, which notions and opinions they must gather out, dried and dead, from its series of living records, either by their own ingenuity, or under some absolute authority."[39]

Maurice implies his first objection to Newman's view by asking "whether our divinity is the assertion of the living God and of His presence among men, or a substitute for that assertion."[40] The right answer to this question will enable us to understand miracles as the "manifestation of the Divine Power." This power "cannot break the order of nature; it can only shew that nature is not a mere machine or system, that there is One who governs it."[41] His second objection, however, is that Newman not only fails to understand the true meaning of scripture, but also substitutes the church for it. He rejects Newman's notion of a catholic system, since it implies "a church turned adrift to be the substitute for a Divine Being, instead of His organ."[42] The reason that "not a few young men … are flying to the belief in an infallible pope [is] because they have not courage to ask themselves whether they believe in an Infallible God."[43] Newman's understanding of the church betrays his failure to "learn from Scripture to feel that the centre of a universe is One Living Person, God and Man, not a Dogma or a Pope."[44] "Christ came into the world to establish a kingdom or a family, and not to set up a notion or a doctrine."[45] Newman's theory involves identifying the church with the history of its development and so "forces history into a certain shape; prevents us from looking at it as the actual record of God's dealings with the world."[46] Instead, "the history of the world requires a Bible to interpret it." This is because the Bible, if it is understood as a whole, "is a record of a regular historical method by which it pleased God that his Son should be manifested to man."[47] Scripture, then, points beyond itself to the prime reality of the Kingdom of Christ and in this way reveals to us the true meaning of history.

Maurice's basic perspective appears clearly toward the end of his discussion. He argues that if Protestants had taken more seriously "their own principle of studying the Bible as a guide to the plan and purpose of God," they would have attended more fully to history. Failure to see how both the Bible and history point beyond themselves to God has meant that "one party among us has raised the standard of The Bible, and the other of The Church, as if there were no relation between the two; as if the one did not expound the other;

as if the one merely meant a book of opinions delivered centuries ago, and the other a system of opinions existing now."[48] Newman, then, is wrong because he substitutes the church for scripture. And since by the church he really means the history of its development, history becomes the enemy of the Bible. On the other hand, Maurice is equally clear that the Bible must not become an end in itself. Instead, it is the medium by which the Kingdom of Christ reveals itself to us; and we must remember that it is the church's book. Maurice, then, in a sense dethrones both the church and scripture. But in another sense he places both on their proper thrones as pointing beyond themselves to the Kingdom of Christ.

The view implied by Maurice's review of Newman's book is essentially the same one he expounds in *The Kingdom of Christ,* where scripture is one of the signs of that spiritual society.[49] The books of the Bible "profess to reveal a constitution, which is declared to be the Divine constitution for man."[50] The revelation progresses from a particular family to a particular nation and finally to mankind. It is "a history," and what it records is "the discovery" of the universal and spiritual society. All the signs of the Kingdom of Christ have a double character — the religious principles that find their unity in that kingdom and their embodiment in history. In the same way the "mystical" meaning of scripture is bound to its letter. Maurice's schema is basically one of revelation and response, though we might more accurately describe it as pedagogical. Education, of course, involves both teaching and learning; and Maurice's emphasis is upon the first. In scripture "we find God proclaiming Himself as the Educator, and marking out those through whom He will educate."[51] There are difficulties with Maurice's assertion of progress in the revelation and its apprehension. He is clearly more concerned with the meaning of history than with history as a narrative. Like Origen he often seems to swallow up time in eternity, and the stages of revelation all appear to reveal the same thing, namely, the Kingdom of Christ. Moreover, his conviction is that a proper apprehension of the revelation will automatically lead to the actualization of the universal and spiritual society. Putting the difficulties aside, however, he clearly thinks that

criticism of the Bible is necessary for an apprehension of its significance as a sign of the kingdom. He recognizes that "the critical spirit
and knowledge of modern Europe" as applied to scripture has called
into question the Bible's authority. Many people suppose that the
detection of even a single error in scripture is "sufficient to shake
the credit of the whole scheme."[52] This reaction depends upon a
false understanding of inspiration as requiring verbal inerrancy. This
idea really represents an idolatry because it substitutes the words of
scripture for the living God; and as we have seen, Maurice strongly
repudiates any worship of the Bible.[53]

Maurice, then, argues that we should not reject this critical spirit,
nor should we suppose we need to "take better care of His book than
He has taken of it."[54] Indeed, we can begin by taking the Bible for
granted the way we do any other book; and we need not fear the
consequences of exposing it to the tests we apply to ordinary literature. At the same time, he strongly faults the criticism "of the last
one hundred and fifty years." It is obvious that he has more in mind
than the beginnings of historical criticism of scripture in Germany.
But it is likely enough that he is thinking partly of the Germans.[55] In
any case, he opposes what he regards as two errors. The "analysts"
disintegrate scripture and by pulling it to pieces lose sight of its uni-
tary meaning and any sense of the Bible as a whole. The "idealists"
dissolve the history into ideas and by separating the idea from the
events in which it is embodied they turn "living ideas into mere notions and apprehensions of our minds."[56] Maurice sees the proper
criticism of scripture as a middle way between skepticism and Bibliolatry. Central to his discussion is the question of inspiration, but we
must begin with a more important question. We must ask whether
the writers of scripture were "in a certain position and appointed
to a certain work." This will drive us from what we read to that
of which we read. We shall ask whether there was "such a society
as that which this book speaks of," whether there was a Jewish nation with a history, and "was there a meaning in that history." Does
scripture "explain to us their history and its meaning? The question
of inspiration belongs to these questions — cannot be viewed apart

from them."[57] The clear implication is that we cannot think of inspiration apart from the community that claims the Bible. Scripture and the church belong together, and both are inspired because they both apprehend the revelation of the Kingdom of Christ. Though it is true that apprehensions of the revelation must clothe themselves in words, Maurice finds himself obliged to "reject as monstrous and heretical the notion of a *dictation*."[58] If we reject verbal inerrancy, which is really an idolatry of scripture, we need not be surprised at mistakes and inconsistencies in the Bible. What we have is "the testimony of different witnesses," all of whom lead us from their diversity to the unity of the society that binds together the religious principles we find embodied in the churches, however much those principles are crippled by the various systems involved. By uniting scripture and the church Maurice also rules out private judgment. In scripture "God is speaking to you; be silent and listen."[59]

Miracles are another concern for Maurice. The analysts interpret them by what they regard as natural causes. The idealists treat them as myths or inventions. Both false critics end by denying miracles. The common and popular view treats the miracles as an interruption of the laws of nature. None of these views suffice, since true miracles reflect the power of the Lord of nature.[60] Maurice, however, rejects the Roman insistence upon the miracles of the saints; in doing so, he explains why and makes his position clear. He allies himself with those who believe that miracles "are for the assertion of order, and not for the violation of it." They are designed to prove "the constant presence of a spiritual power" and not to show "that it interferes occasionally with the affairs of the world." These people do not expect "the frequent repetition" of the scriptural miracles, since they treat the facts recorded "in the former ages of the world" as "laws in ours." What Maurice means is that we are to acknowledge "Him who healed the sick of the palsy in every cure which is wrought by the ordinary physician, Him who stilled the storm on the Lake of Gennesareth, in the guidance and preservation of every ship which crosses the ocean; and that this effect would be lost, if we were led to put any contempt upon that which is daily and habitual."[61] Perhaps Maurice thinks that miracles no longer happen, but certainly he accepts the biblical miracles as God's ordering of nature.

Maurice summarizes his discussion of scripture by insisting upon a number of points. He cannot conceive of "a Bible without a Church," and the ministers of the church are "the appointed instruments for guiding men into a knowledge of the Bible." He rejects as false "the notion of private judgment," since inspiration attaches to the church as a whole, as well as to the writers of scripture. The miracles recorded in the New Testament introduced "a new dispensation, and were not merely a set of strange acts belonging to a particular time." The "Gospel narratives must be received as parts of the necessary furniture of the Church."[62] He argues that these views, while they might appear to be heading toward Rome, are not Roman. He insists upon the mutuality of Bible and church instead of exalting the church over the Bible. Ministers must communicate the Bible to the laity rather than concealing it from them. The Bible and the church must draw people out of their private judgment, whereas the Roman system is really a sort of collective private judgment. The work of the Spirit pervades the whole body of the church. Miracles represent God's ordering of nature, and we must prefer the Gospel narratives to the lives of the saints.[63] Even though we should probably regard Maurice's views as pre-critical, however much he is in touch with German thought, what he says is in many ways congenial with the critical view that will develop. We can read scripture like any other book. We must repudiate the idea of verbal inerrancy in order to distinguish the text of scripture from its meaning. By understanding the biblical writers as those who apprehend God's revelation we can leave room for the partial and imperfect character of their apprehensions. Equally, by distinguishing history from the meaning faith can find revealed in it, Maurice tries to make history the friend of scripture. There is, however, in Maurice's thought a tendency simply to identify history with the biblical narrative. The new criticism will call such an assumption into question. But it will also tend to omit the concern with the church that we find in differing ways in what both Newman and Maurice say.

Benjamin Jowett (1817–1893)

Only gradually did the historical-critical approach to scripture that had begun in Germany become known in Britain, and it was as much as anything the publication of *Essays and Reviews* in 1860 that first sent shock waves throughout the Church of England. As Dean Hook was reading the book, he looked out of his study window only to see the spire of Chichester Cathedral collapse to the ground. He pronounced the event God's judgment upon the Church of England for the heresy he discovered in what he read. It was Benjamin Jowett's essay "On the Interpretation of Scripture" that first established some of the conventions of the historical-critical method for the English speaking world. He begins by describing what he regards as the central problem: "It is a strange, though familiar fact, that great differences of opinion exist respecting the Interpretation of Scripture."[64] There are several explanations for the fact. The different sorts of Christians all have their own readings of the Bible. For example, some Anglicans assume that the meaning of scripture "is to be defined by that of the Prayer-book." Others adopt the slogan " 'the Bible and the Bible only' with a silent reference to the traditions of the Reformation." Another cause lies in "the growth or progress of the human mind itself." We can speak of different methods of interpretation — mystical, logical, rhetorical. People seem able to make the Bible mean whatever they please. The preacher does not always have the meaning of his text as his object, but rather "some moral or religious lesson which he has found it necessary to append to it; some cause which he is pleading, some error of the day which he has to combat." The Bible, then, tends to become the mouthpiece of whatever hobbyhorse people want to read into it.[65]

We are so used to this that we are not always troubled by the multitude of ideas that are fathered on scripture. We fail to see immediately "the absurdity of the same words having many senses," and it is difficult to "free our minds from the illusion that the Apostle or Evangelist must have written with a reference to the creeds or controversies or circumstances of other times."[66] It is this illusion that we must first dispel in order to interpret scripture, and Jowett thinks first of the false notion of inspiration that equates it with verbal inerrancy. Inspiration can mean a great many different things, but in its relation to scripture we must begin by examining the Bible itself. What we first notice is that the Bible includes writings of quite different kinds and from many different times. Nevertheless, a "principle of progressive revelation admits them all."[67] Thus, to speak of inspiration is really to make a claim about the revelatory character of scripture. But this claim and "any true doctrine of inspiration must conform to all well-ascertained facts of history or of science." It may be true that "as the idea of nature enlarges, the idea of revelation also enlarges."[68] But this by no means undermines the point just made, nor can we deny that "the idea of inspiration must expand" and take account of historical inquiries.[69] In short, we must put to one side the question of inspiration. Though important, it "is to the interpreter as though it were not important; he is in no way called upon to determine a matter with which he has nothing to do, and which was not determined by fathers of the Church."[70]

Jowett: "It is a strange, though familiar fact, that great differences of opinion exist respecting the Interpretation of Scripture."

In any case, the idea that inspiration requires verbal inerrancy is one we must not only set aside but reject absolutely. There are, of course, many who presuppose that "there can be no error in the Word of God," and who explain discrepancies as merely apparent and possibly "attributed to differences in the copies." They are foolish to claim that it is "a thousand times more likely that the interpreter should err than the inspired writer."[71] We must presume that the writers of the New Testament as well as of the Old were human and, consequently, fallible. There is no basis in the New Testament "for any of the higher supernatural views of inspiration." Their writings do not suggest "that the Evangelists or Apostles had any inward gift, or were subject to any power external to them different from that of preaching or teaching which they daily exercised, nor do they anywhere lead us to suppose that they were free from error or infirmity."[72] Jowett's denial of verbal inerrancy is in one sense no different from that found in Maurice's writings. And yet what Jowett omits is any reference to the writers of scripture as witnesses to a revelation. Since we have already seen that he supposes the idea of a progressive revelation represents the unity of the different books of the Bible, the omission cannot be a denial. Instead, he wants to set revelation aside for later consideration. We should not treat it as a presupposition of interpretation; rather we must regard it as its product.

Clearing the ground and dispelling illusions about scripture also requires the interpreter to disavow an apologetic temper. "The tone of apology is always a tone of weakness and does injury to a good cause. It is the reverse of 'ye shall know the truth, and the truth shall make you free.' "[73] It is obvious that the proofs from miracle and prophecy have become bankrupt. More broadly, however, an apologetic approach to scripture shows itself either "in the attempt to adapt the truths of Scripture to the doctrines of the creeds" or "in the adaptation of the precepts and maxims of Scripture to the language of our own age." The first alternative, attributing Catholic truth to Paul or the Twelve, is as anachronistic as treating them like systematic philosophers. It represents the same sort of error as attributing the ideas of Thales or Heraclitus to Homer or "the principles of Aristotle and Plato" to Thales.[74] The second sort of apologetic use of scripture neglects its time-bound character by tying its meaning to our contemporary ideas and concerns. "The attempt to force politics and law into the framework of religion is apt to drive us into a corner, in which the great principles of truth and justice have no longer room to make themselves felt."[75] Forcing scripture to address our own controversies about issues like divorce, marriage with a deceased wife's sister, inspiration, the personality of the Holy Spirit, infant baptism, episcopacy, the divine right of kings, and original sin leads "to an unfair appropriation of some portions of Scripture and an undue neglect of others." "What men have brought to the text they have also found there."[76]

What Jowett wishes to exclude is the tendency of interpreters to read into scripture their own beliefs, concerns, and prejudices. When we use scripture "to prove our own opinions," we notice "one class of facts" and close our eyes to another. "The favourite verses shine like stars, while the rest of the page is thrown into the shade."[77] Many people single out and detach words from scripture for incorporation into their own systems "like stones taken out of an old building and put into a new one."[78] It is obvious that what Jowett requires is an "objective" approach to interpretation. This means setting aside all our subjective notions, including our religious commitments. It is arguable that this remains today the ideal of the historical-critical method. But, of course, few people would any longer suppose such a stance possible. Historians no longer hold that reconstructing the past exactly as it was, as Ranke said, is at all possible. The role of the imagination inevitably informs our reconstructions. As Bultmann pointed out, exegesis without presuppositions is impossible. The interpreter's task, then, is to recognize and to articulate his presuppositions, not to dispel them altogether, since that is impossible. This is why Jowett's approach, while in many ways it is still embedded in New Testament studies, seems quite dated to us.

Having cleared the ground, Jowett continues by seeking to articulate his positive understanding of interpretation. What he has said in his preliminary discussion should not be regarded as merely "a wanton exposure of the difficulties of Scripture."[79] The dispelling of our illusions will enable us to approach the Bible fairly. If we use "the same rules of evidence, and the same canons of criticism" we employ for any other book to interpret scripture, "the Bible will still remain unlike any other book." Indeed, like "a picture which is restored after many years to its original state" the Bible will take on a fresh look and "will create a new interest and make for itself a new kind of authority by the life which is in it." It will become "a spirit and not a letter" (cf. 2 Cor 3:6). Its original influence will return "like that of the spoken word, or the book newly found."[80]

Historical criticism is a friend of scripture because it will restore the meaning and authority of the Bible. The "few precepts" that attach to criticism are no more than "the expansion of a single one. *Interpret the Scripture like any other book.*"[81] Its unique character will appear as the result of "such an interpretation," but the first step must be to discover its meaning in the same way "we ascertain the meaning of Sophocles or of Plato." To be sure, Jowett cannot demonstrate his claim; it is really something like a leap of faith.

Jowett continues with a disclaimer regarding method. The method "creates itself as we go on" and is really no more than using "the rules of common sense." Attempting to systematize the method risks creating "an impression that the meaning of Scripture is out of our reach, or is to be attained in some other way than by the exercise of manly sense and industry." The first rule, however, is that "Scripture has one meaning — the meaning which it had to the mind of the prophet or evangelist who first uttered or wrote, to the hearers or readers who first received it."[82] The single meaning, of course, attaches to the individual books or writers and not to scripture taken as a whole. Jowett assumes, too readily, that this single meaning will be the same both for the writer or speaker and for the reader or hearer. He neglects a whole range of difficult questions. Should we equate the meaning with the intention of the author? If so, how can we know that intention? Or, if we equate the meaning with how the text is read, are we not opening the door to a multitude of different readings? Jowett appears not to see these problems, but he does see the difficulty of coming to terms with the meaning of a specific text without considering its literary context. Consequently, his second rule, deduced from his general principle, is that we should "interpret Scripture from itself."[83] Presumably, this means that we can use easy and clear passages to explain obscure ones. But the "illustration of one part of Scripture by another should be confined to writings of the same age and the same authors, except where the writings of different ages or persons offer obvious similarities."[84] While this means that we must begin by examining scripture book by book and author by author, we shall soon find that there is "a sort of continuity."

"Such continuity or design is best explained under some notion of progress or growth, not regular, however, but with broken and imperfect stages which the want of knowledge prevents our minutely defining."[85] This continuity "is a kind of progress from childhood to manhood," and the interpreter will come to feel "that the continuous growth of revelation which he traces in the Old and New Testament, is a part of a larger whole extending over the earth and reaching to another world."[86]

After a fairly lengthy discussion of the language of the New Testament in which he emphasizes the "distorting influence of classical Greek" upon our understanding of the text, Jowett summarizes his conclusions regarding interpretation: "Scripture, like other books, has one meaning, which is to be gathered from itself without reference to the adaptations of Fathers or Divines, and without regard to *a priori* notions about its nature and origin." We must interpret scripture the way we do other books, but "not without a sense that as we read there grows upon us the witness of God in the world, anticipating in a rude and primitive age the truth that was to be, shining more and more unto the perfect day in the life of Christ, which again is reflected from different points of view in the teaching of His Apostles."[87] Jowett obviously embraces principles that commonly inform the historical-critical method to this day — the single meaning, the attempt to recover the original setting in history, the supposed elimination of a priori notions. But what is striking is that he ends by treating scripture as much more than historical evidence for reconstructing the history of Israel, the early Christian communities, or even the historical Jesus. Interpretation yields a conviction of God's progressive revelation, culminating in Christ. In this way history for Jowett is the friend not only of truth but also of scripture.

The last part of Jowett's essay turns from the interpretation of scripture to its application or adaptation. Even if we can assume that interpretation ends by giving us the idea of a progressive and divine revelation, what does that have to do with us? "In the hour of death we do not want critical explanations."[88] The application of scripture to our own conditions and concerns finds its context in the dialectic between scripture and theology, the Bible and the church, where "either has tended to correct the abuse of the other."[89] And it finds its warrant in the use of the Old Testament by the New. Two points are necessary. First, these New Testament applications are not the original meaning of the Old Testament texts. But, second, what the New Testament does "gives authority and precedent for the use of similar applications in our own day." We must, however, be cautious, since the application of scripture is "liable to error and perversion."[90] This means defining "the limits and manner of a just adaptation," and the key consideration is making a sharp distinction between interpretation and adaptation.[91] It is impossible not to think of the definitions in the *Interpreter's Dictionary of the Bible* that treat "exegesis" as descriptive and historical, and define "hermeneutics" as normative and theological. Jowett adds some "other simple cautions." The application must be in harmony with "the spirit of the Gospel, the whole of which should be in every part."[92] The implication is that we cannot apply the Bible to our concerns simply by choosing the proof texts that correlate with them. The other caution is that we must find "the real unity of Scripture" in "the common element in human nature," which is a perennial reality. "This element is two-fold, partly divine and partly human; the revelation of the truth and righteousness of God, and the cry of the human heart towards Him."[93] Jowett gives pride of place to the moral meaning of scripture. He is convinced that theological distinctions and controversies are fading away and that doctrines are now "connected more closely with our moral nature."[94] In what amounts to his peroration he argues that his platform has the possibility of healing divisions in Christianity, assisting Christian missions, reviving liberal education, and improving preaching.[95]

William Sanday (1843–1920)

In 1893, a generation after *Essays and Reviews*, William Sanday, who became Lady Margaret Professor of Divinity at Oxford two years later, delivered his eight Bampton Lectures on inspiration.[96] Much had happened in the interval. Whereas Jowett's essay broke

new ground in England by introducing a critical approach to scripture, Sanday was able to assume a somewhat wider acceptance of
that approach.[97]

One of the reasons he could do so was that a group of second generation Oxford apostles had published a collection of essays entitled
Lux Mundi in 1889. In effect the authors committed the Anglo-
Catholic movement to new "intellectual and social" developments
and to the conviction that this would "involve great changes in the
outlying departments of theology, where it is linked on to other
sciences" and would "necessitate some general restatement" of the
Catholic faith. They presented themselves in conscious opposition to
the writers of *Essays and Reviews* not only because they had arrived
through long discussion at an agreed and unified perspective, but
also because they wrote "not as 'guessers at truth,' but as servants
of the Catholic Creed and Church, aiming only at interpreting the
faith we have received."[98] Of course, they did not persuade everyone, even many like Liddon who were the educated leaders of the
Catholic party in the Church of England. Nevertheless, they added
to the Broad Church support of the new criticism their own significant
endorsement, and did so in a reassuring way.

Sanday was not an Anglo-Catholic and can be seen as following in
the steps of Lightfoot, Westcott, and Hort. But his Bampton Lectures
took the same reassuring approach found in *Lux Mundi*. The destructive character of "naturalistic" or scientific criticism has reached its
"utmost limit." The reaction that has set in ushers in the time for
"a certain reconstruction of the old edifice upon newer lines." Sanday's plea is "to let the Bible tell its own story" and to "give a fair
and patient hearing to the facts as they come before us, whether they
be old or whether they are new."[99] In his conclusion he argues that
the "mistakes" his critical approach uncovers in scripture itself "do
not touch any of the essential features of Revelation." Moreover, the
mistaken view taken of scripture before the acceptance of the new
criticism "does not need any great modification to bring it into accordance with the facts."[100] Sanday has convinced himself that the
new approach poses no threat to Christian belief and can actually

revitalize it. And because of this his lectures are calming and not at all startling.

While the structure of Sanday's lectures is a tour of the Bible prefaced by a discussion of the canon and how it came to be, his argument revolves around a movement from the critical assessment of the facts to broader interpretive conclusions that focus upon inspiration. Let me start as he does with what he regards as the "facts" and his critical approach to them. He assumes, as do the nineteenth-century historians, that getting the facts straight is the first order of business. In speaking of the "professional failings" of some of the Old Testament prophets, he does not mean to disparage them. "I only want to look the facts full in the face."[101] When Paul says that he has no commandment of the Lord (1 Cor 7:25), we "must take the facts as we find them, and give them the best name we can."[102] This, of course, does not mean that we can take the scriptural texts at face value. As "facts" they are evidence that must be critically assessed. To do so means that we must relinquish our prejudices, which include not only a bias toward "Supernaturalism," but also one toward "Naturalism." Far from abandoning "critical inquiry," the true cure for a one-sided presentation of the facts is not to be sought "in less of science but in more, not in laxer methods but in stricter."[103] Though he recognizes the provisional and hypothetical character of some critical conclusions, Sanday in several places expresses an optimism that criticism will ultimately make everything clear.[104]

Despite this kind of disclaimer Sanday is convinced that a good many results of the critical assessment of the facts found in the biblical evidence are assured. The development of Hebrew prophecy from its roots in ecstatic seers and in professional guilds is an example.[105] We can also accept the main lines of Wellhausen's hypothesis concerning the documentary sources of the Pentateuch. We can confidently date Daniel in the Maccabaean period.[106] The date of Luke is about the year 80 CE, while the synoptic tradition takes us back before the destruction of the Temple ten years earlier.[107]

It would be easy to multiply examples of this kind. One further point, however, is that Sanday in cases like these refuses to allow the conclusions of scientific history to be infected by larger interpretive conclusions. He repudiates the Hegelian interpretation of Acts by the Tübingen school that would see the development of earliest Christianity as the synthesis of Petrine Jewish Christianity and Pauline Gentile Christianity in "early catholicism." The book of Acts cannot be used to illustrate such an idealist interpretation, but must be regarded "as a sober unsophisticated historical record, from which we, as well as the generation for which it was first written, may 'learn the certainty' of the things wherein we have been instructed."[108]

In one of its aspects, then, Sanday's argument treats scripture as evidence for reconstructing bits and pieces of the historical contexts of the biblical writers. To be sure, the Gospels do give evidence for the life, work, and fate of Jesus. But we have not yet left the area in which the chief task of the critic is historical reconstruction. The opening verses of Luke's Gospel make no claim of "supernatural aid" for his record, which is based upon his own research and his appeal "to those who were eyewitnesses of the facts or who helped in the early preaching of them."[109] Sanday's aim here, as in his attempt to take the synoptic tradition back to a time before the destruction of the Temple, is to find a solid historical basis for what scripture says about Christ. Insofar as they are histories the Gospels are not inspired. But we do "seek the inspiration of the Gospels elsewhere." And this "elsewhere" is found in the inspired "sayings of the Lord Jesus" and "the deeds of mercy and love by which they were accompanied."[110] Similarly, inspiration attaches to the historical books of the Old Testament "rather as conveying a religious lesson than as histories."[111] The historical dimension of scripture, then, appears to be uninspired or, at best, only indirectly inspired. Despite his concern for the facts and their use as evidence for historical reconstructions, Sanday does not regard this part of his work as a solution to the problem of the religious meaning and authority of scripture.

Inspiration, obviously, is the solution of this problem; and so far as the Old Testament is concerned the focal point of inspiration is located in the claim of the prophets to speak God's word. Sanday recognizes the difficulty of accepting that claim. "What guarantee have we that they were not mistaken?" Are they merely "projecting their own thoughts," and so deluded in supposing that God has spoken to them? This is "the heart of the matter," but the only way we can accept the claim of the prophets and "the one point on which we must firmly take our stand is the belief that in this contention of theirs the prophets were not mistaken, that their utterances had a cause outside themselves, a real objective cause, not to be confused with any mental process of their own."[112] This faith is based upon "the still larger belief in an active Providence... 'the living God.'" This is what leads to "the further assumption of some such thing as Revelation and its correlative Inspiration."[113]

The same leap of faith enabling us to accept the prophets' claim of inspiration attaches to accepting apostolic inspiration.[114] Thus, the focal instances of inspiration are represented by the prophets and the apostles. Sanday, however, has no wish to understand these figures as merely "passive instruments." The prophets "are not a mere flute or lyre for the Spirit to blow through.... The impulse is given, and all the faculties and powers of the man are stirred to unwonted energy, in which however... there mingles something of his weakness as well as of his strength." If inspiration is a way of describing "communication of any kind between God and man," then the human attempts to convey that communication to others is what we can mean by revelation.[115] Such a view implies that we can never make a simple identification of revelation and what is revealed. Instead, revelation observes what Sanday suggests we can call "the Law of Parsimony." What he means is that "revelation is suited to the condition of those who are to receive it, that it starts from the actual circumstances in which they are placed, and that it tells them what is essential for them to know and not really more." The same rule applies to the incarnation. When God chose to reveal himself to humans, he made this "culmination of all revelation" to take its origin "from a certain well-defined historical situation."[116] Thus, revelation always occurs by accommodating itself to the capacities of those who receive it. The clear implication is that we must repudiate any notion of verbal inerrancy. The role of history is not to supply a basis for claims about inspiration and revelation; equally it is not capable of disproving such claims. But history becomes a true friend of scripture by explaining the circumstances that condition revelation as it is accommodated to its recipients.

While Sanday wants to treat the prophets and apostles as the focal recipients of inspiration, he also understands inspiration as something that admits of degrees and that somehow spreads from the prophets and apostles to much if not all the rest of scripture. Revelation in the Old Testament "is like an inland lake which receives indeed a certain amount of surface drainage, but is fed mainly by springs which penetrate deep down into the earth." These springs are "the law-makers and prophets."[117] Prophetic inspiration somehow includes the Law, and by *the Principle of Extensions* the term "the Law and the Prophets" came to include the whole of the Old Testament. The "attributes" of the Law and the prophets "were extended to all the books, and to all the parts of all the books, included in the Canon."[118] Apparently, however, we are not to take this idea with utter seriousness, since it is difficult to speak of the inspiration of books like Song of Songs, Ecclesiastes, and Esther.[119] Sanday makes the same point concerning the New Testament. St. Paul is the focus of inspiration, and he regards "all the manifestations" of divine activity that he perceives as radiating "from a single centre," which is to be identified as "the Incarnation, and the forces which the Incarnation had set in motion." It is in Paul's letters that we find the "tidal wave of God-given energy" and the "kernel of the New Testament." The Gospels, while they "enshrine" this kernel, "in a sense . . . stand outside it."[120]

The obvious question to be raised is that of the relation of the two testaments. In treating the incarnation as the "culmination" of revelation, Sanday implies what we might call a "salvation history" perspective. Granted a belief in inspiration and revelation, and a willingness "to find the finger of God traceable in human affairs," how are we to understand God's method? Ephesians 1:11 suggests that one feature of God's "purpose or design" is that it unfolds "according to election (or selection)." The "vast Divine plan . . . takes a more definite shape as our gaze lingers upon it. We observe in it a progression." The progress, however, does not seem to be a steady one. Rather, "this broadening light has not been diffused uniformly over all mankind." It finds its focus "in particular races, families, and individuals." And then it spreads "from these smaller centres," and there is "an apportionment of parts in the mighty drama."[121] Sanday is more attentive to these disparate centers and to a hierarchical notion of revelation than to the temporal continuity of the drama that reaches its climax in the incarnate Lord. Indeed, he often seems more concerned with a "vast ascending scale" of inspiration than with the unfolding of its revelation in history.

Sanday's last lecture is a summary of his conclusions and a comparison of what he takes to be the traditional view of inspiration with his own "inductive" or critical understanding. The two views need not collide; but when they do, "the more scientific statement is to be accepted." Nevertheless, "the inductive or critical theory needs to be supplemented"; and in this way the gap between the two views can be "in a manner bridged over." The discussion begins with a brief account of the traditional acceptance of the Bible as uniformly inspired, "exempt from error," and "infallible."[122] It is important to note that Sanday does not regard the traditionalists as willing to make a distinction between passages in scripture that teach what is necessary for salvation and passages that do not. Sanday's own view, however, distinguishes the "nucleus" of "primary inspiration" from "a sort of secondary inspiration." The inductive view assumes that "inspiration is not inherent in the Bible as such, but is present in different books and parts of books in different degrees." With this in mind how are we to supplement the inductive theory? "We call the theory 'inductive' because it starts by examining the consciousness of the Biblical writers." Sanday recognizes that this by itself would have the effect of fragmenting the scriptural record. The supplement is to regard individual cases of inspiration as "no longer detached units but articulated members in a connected and coherent scheme." We can begin to speak of "a common goal" and "a larger scheme."[123]

It is by no means an easy task to assess Sanday's position. Part of the difficulty revolves around the recognition that much of what he says became common currency in the way the Bible has been presented and taught in the academy and the seminary. There is much to be said for his conviction that he has found a new way of making the old truths come to life by embracing the historical-critical approach to scripture as a friend. On the other hand, the structure of thought he has elaborated poses a number of questions that have been pursued throughout the following century and have not disappeared. The first and, perhaps, most important question is how we are to relate historical reconstructions to religious claims. Sanday, of course, sees the problem and argues that we must accept the inspiration of the prophets and apostles on faith and with the conviction that God exercises the kind of providence that means he seeks to communicate his purpose and will to humans. But if this is so, have we not abandoned an inductive approach and found ourselves obliged to deduce the focal instances of inspiration from a priori ideas about God? At any rate Sanday is unwilling to say that historical reconstructions generate revelation. They do not, however, preclude it; and they do enable us to discern the attendant circumstances that accommodate revelation to those receiving it.

If the relation of history to revelation is problematic, another difficulty arises by locating inspiration and its consequent revelation in the consciousness of the prophets and apostles. Here the problem of what William Temple will call "the Cartesian faux pas" intrudes itself. Sanday wants to balance his observation about consciousness with an insistence upon the objective character of inspiration, but it is not entirely clear that he has succeeded in building the rainbow bridge from the knower to what is known. Perhaps we must start with the recognition that the larger scheme or plan of which Sanday speaks is something we must posit a priori and by faith, always acknowledging that since we are not in a position to grasp that scheme completely, we can only discern it from our own limited perspective. Finally, how are we to understand the larger scheme? Are we to think of an ascending scale of spiritual insights leading to the fullest possible communion with God? Or is the scheme really a drama that unfolds in time? Sanday does not answer these questions with any clarity. Moreover, the rungs in the ladder or the stages in the drama often seem to be critical reconstructions based upon using scripture as evidence. The biblical narrative, then, suffers an eclipse. I raise these questions not so much to find fault with Sanday's work as to suggest that his solution also poses the problems to be addressed by those who come after him.

William Gladstone (1809–1898)

There would be any number of ways to show how people reacted negatively to views like those of Jowett and Sanday by regarding historical criticism as the foe of the Bible. But one example will suffice. William Gladstone seems at first an unlikely one. Early in his political career he argued for the establishment of the Church of England, not because it was the national church, but because it was the catholic church in England. Once he was prime minister, however, he saw the necessity of disentangling the Church of England from its complicated relationships with the state. And he succeeded not only in disestablishing the Church of Ireland but also in abolishing church rates. Throughout his life he was an earnest Christian, and his reaction to the new criticism sprang from this rather than from any party loyalty to the evangelical wing of the Church of England. In 1890 he published a series of essays concerned primarily with the Old Testament that he entitled *The Impregnable Rock of Holy Scripture*.[124] He seems to know that new views in science and historiography require a change in common and popular ideas about the Bible and its authority, and he tries to make some adjustments. In the long run, however, what Jowett and Sanday regarded as a friend to scripture Gladstone regards as a foe. Gladstone's reaction is interesting because it comes from a layman who is highly educated and yet in many ways reflects popular attitudes toward scripture.

In his introductory essay Gladstone professes respect for the scientist and the historian. The same attitude also appears from time to time in the following essays, which treat the creation story, the Old Testament in outline, the Psalms, the Mosaic legislation, and "recent corroborations of scripture from the region of history and natural science." In general he makes two points that stand in tension if not contradiction with one another. The Christian religion and, specifically, scripture have as their object moral and spiritual concerns. In contrast, the historians and scientists have aims that do not affect these concerns. The second point, however, is that history and science, at least in the hands of the "reconcilers" rather than the "contradictionists," actually confirm the Bible. He makes the first of these points by saying that the scientist aims "simply to state the facts of nature in the cosmogony as and so far as he can find them." In contrast "the Mosaic writer" is concerned "to convey moral and spiritual training."[125] The same approach deals with "the negative and destructive specialist in the field of the ancient Scriptures." Everything such specialists can discover "respecting the age, text, and authorship of the books" must be accepted. But these conclusions in no way affect the moral and spiritual substance of scripture or its historicity.[126] Gladstone accepts and embraces "one of the great canons of modern criticism, which teaches us that the Scriptures are to be treated like any other book in the trial of their title."[127] He does so, however, because this approach will not affect his own understanding of scripture, an understanding that includes accepting the Bible and its miracles as history.

Gladstone's other argument abandons the idea of two tracks and attempts to show that science and history actually confirm scripture and do so not merely in its moral and spiritual senses. He says that "science and research have done much to sustain the historical credit of the Old Testament." By doing so they have strengthened the argument for "a Divine revelation." A rational view of the evidence and the conclusions drawn from it "bids us to stand where our forefathers have stood, upon the impregnable rock of Holy Scripture."[128] His discussion of the creation narrative in Genesis is one of his chief examples of how science and religion are reconcilable. We need not argue that every detail of the biblical account has "an accurately scientific form." But we can affirm that taken as a whole it stands "in such a relation to the facts of natural science, so far as they have been ascertained, as to warrant or require our concluding that the statements have proceeded, in a manner above the ordinary manner, from the Author of the creation itself."[129] The long discussion that follows revolves in large part around the "nebular theory," which basically supposes that the universe gradually resulted from the consolidation of an original "seething mass" of gases.[130] The "days" of creation, then, become chapters or stages in the development of the universe. There are some loose ends. On the whole, the sequence followed by Genesis conforms to evolutionary theories; but it is strange that the "creeping things" appear only on the sixth day, especially if we suppose that they are reptiles rather than small mammals. They ought to have come earlier in the account, but perhaps we can explain this peculiarity by arguing that Moses did not think the creeping things very important. After all he makes no mention whatsoever of insects. Another example of Gladstone's argumentation is his conviction that archaeology has demonstrated the truth of the Bible regarding the sins of Israel's neighbors. The Old Testament veils "the vicious practices of these nations...for decency's sake"; but they "are too sadly attested by the character of the remains...archaeology has recovered from their hiding places."[131] I cannot help being reminded of the aphorism attributed to Dean Fosbrook — that if Albright found a silver dollar on the shore of the Potomoc, he would say it proved that George Washington threw it across.

It is not entirely clear that Gladstone's heart is really in these two arguments. They seem more like a reluctant and grudging admission that Christians do need to reckon with the advances made by historical criticism and science. He can even say that these waves which beat upon the rock of scripture are providential and designed by God "to dispel the lethargy and stimulate the zeal of believers...to admonish their faith to keep terms with reason by testing it in all points."[132] But in the long run his hostility to historical criticism becomes clear. He dismisses Wellhausen's conclusions about the Old

Testament by saying that they are "as disputable as they are confident."[133] Huxley's reference to "the old-fashioned artillery of the Churches" and the new "weapons of precision" acquired by the critics strikes a raw nerve and triggers a long discussion of the Flood and of the miracle of the Gadarene swine. Huxley's claim that the Flood would have receded far more quickly than the Bible says drives Gladstone to consult a hydraulic engineer, who proves that Huxley's "weapons of precision" are no such thing. As to Huxley's claim that the story of the Gadarene swine shows Christ wantonly destroying other people's property, Gladstone tries to prove that the Gadarenes were subject to the Mosaic law and that the prohibition of eating swine was designed not only for ceremonial purposes but also as a sanitary measure — to avoid trichinosis.[134] Gladstone identifies himself with "the minds of many" who feel "that they have passed from a ground old and familiar to one new and strange...that if they have been wrong once, they may, perhaps, be wrong again."[135] Historical criticism and science have created doubt, but it is doubt that ought to be on the defensive.[136] The "Paean of Victory" sung by those who suppose that the "intellectual battle" against supernaturalism has been fought and won is premature.[137] Toward the end of his conclusion Gladstone comes clean regarding his basic hostility toward historical criticism:[138]

> I must, however, in drawing these observations to a close, for a moment change my tone. In their nature apologetic, they themselves require an apology; and an apology, too, which is also in the nature of a protest. They are intended to meet, so far as they go, a state of things peculiar and perhaps without example, in which multitudes of men call into question the foundations of our religion and the prerogatives of our sacred books, without any reference to either their capacity or their opportunities for so grave an undertaking.

Gladstone, of course, is fighting a losing battle, one surely already lost by 1890 in the minds of most thoughtful people.

Conclusion

It may be largely a factor of Gladstone's particular concerns, but it is astonishing that he has less to say about the unity of the Bible than either Jowett or Sanday. The fragmentation of scripture that worried Maurice seems to be as much a mark of Gladstone's view as of the biblical critics. Yet even though Jowett can speak of progressive revelation and Sanday of a divine plan and scheme, it is not clear how we are to relate these views of the unity of scripture to their understandings of history and the critical study of scripture. Is it really true that anyone who reads the Bible like any other book will end by finding it unique and unlike all other books? Jowett's implicit leap of faith becomes explicit by Sanday's recognition that only faith and our convictions about God enable us to affirm the inspiration of the prophets and apostles. Consequently, there remains on the agenda the problematic relationship of history and faith, however much we choose to regard history as friend rather than foe. A second question revolves around what we might mean by religious experience. Is its object subsumed within the consciousness of those who have it? Is the biblical text the revelation, or is it merely the apprehension of revelation? Do we find the "essence" of Christianity in religious experience? And is this essence somehow correlative with what is necessary for salvation? A third question is whether by supposing that what is known pre-exists the knower we can construct a theory of revelation and response that somehow takes account of historical questions. Finally, what would happen were we to seek for a restoration of the biblical narrative? Would this leave room for a friendly view of history? All these questions and others are an agenda for the twentieth century and for our own time. In the next chapter I want to turn to a range of responses to this agenda and to argue that Anglican thinkers — and indeed all who seek to come to terms with scripture — have by no means managed to find a way through all the puzzles and difficulties trying to make a friend of history have created.

Chapter Five

Keeping History as a Friend of Faith
The Last Century

In the introduction to his biography of George Washington, Douglas Southall Freeman describes his problem of "how to deal with traditions and myths of Washington's boyhood and youth," such as Parson Weems's tales. His solution is "applying tests of historical probability and then of classifying the traditions as valid, probable or manifestly untrue."[1] The myths and legends, however, even when untrue historically, conform to Freeman's assessment of Washington's character. In the final volume, which was published posthumously, his assistant sums up Freeman's work by saying, "The pinnacle the hero had occupied, obscured by the mist of tradition, already could be seen to rest on the firm rock of fact." And she cites a letter of Freeman in which he says, "What more could I ask for myself than to make the rediscovery that in Washington this nation and the western hemisphere have a man, 'greater than the world knew, living and dying.' "[2] In much the same way the advocates of the historical-critical approach to scripture argued that by dispelling the mists that conceal the historicity of the Bible and particularly the historical Jesus they were able to rescue scripture by placing it "on the firm rock of fact." Historical reconstructions, then, have the possibility of saving the Bible by discerning the historical truths that undergird it. Strauss, Renan, and Seeley in his *Ecce Homo* all have this positive aim in writing their lives of Jesus. Moreover, throughout the twentieth century the same stance is evident, even though critics increasingly see the problems and difficulties partly because of the gradual erosion of an Enlightenment understanding of historiography and partly because of a recognition that historical reconstructions do not necessarily solve the problem of the religious significance of scripture. Moreover, these reconstructions must be based upon evidence quite different from what Freeman had at his disposal for the quest of the historical Washington. The problem is not only the paucity of the evidence, even if we include extra-canonical writings, but also the fact that much of it makes claims about Jesus' significance that go beyond assessments historians are capable of making. Consequently, "history" can be reconstructed to refer to the Bible record of religious experience or still more to a theological schema of revelation and response. In what follows I wish to focus upon the important collections of essays published in the twentieth century. These are all conscious descendants of *Essays and Reviews* and of *Lux Mundi*. As well, there are three reports of Church Doctrine Commissions to be examined. Obviously, these sources represent neither official statements of faith nor popular understandings of scripture. But they do give us some insight into the way scholars and church leaders tried for the most part to forge an alliance between a religious reading of scripture and the new critical method.

History as the Facts

In 1902 a collection of seven essays by six Oxford tutors, including Hastings Rashdall and W. R. Inge, appeared. Its title is *Contentio Veritatis: Essays in Constructive Theology*. The preface begins by noting that the Ritualist controversy has eclipsed the "acrimonious dispute between Natural Science and the old Orthodoxy." The "facts of geology" and Darwin's theory no longer are enemies of Christian faith. Moreover, a "great many of the clergy have accepted the principle of criticism, and are prepared to apply it with some boldness at least to the Old Testament."[3] This new critical attitude to the Bible, however, "has as yet very imperfectly permeated the bulk of the clergy, or even the instructed religious laity." There is "a widespread unsettlement and uneasiness." Especially young people vaguely suspect that "the old Orthodoxy is impossible," but they do not see

what must replace it. The essayists do not pretend to have given a
full reconstruction, but they claim to be alerting people to the need
of one and to "indicate some of the lines on which they believe it
ought to take place."[4] They do not pretend to agree with one another in all respects, nor do they wish their essays to be regarded
as "a party manifesto." They do, however, have a common perspective. They are not only "lovers of truth," but also "Christians and
Churchmen." On both grounds "we have cause to be thankful for
the new light which science and criticism have within the last half-
century thrown upon religious problems." They agree that "scientific
and critical methods" should be used in approaching such questions,
and that authority should not "crush or stifle inquiry."[5] Their aim,
then is "to build up, not to pull down"; and they hope to be of use
to all who seek to bind together "an openminded pursuit of truth
with a heartfelt loyalty to Christ and to the fundamental ideas of
Christianity."[6]

Two of the essays are of particular interest since they are in part
attempts to acquaint a larger audience with the results of criticism.
C. F. Burney treats "The Permanent Religious Value of the Old Testament." His basic contention is that the new approach to the Old
Testament gives its religious value "a far more permanent and satisfactory basis than before." Treating these writings "scientifically,
i.e. in accordance with ordinary historical methods" means that we
must repudiate the idea of "verbal inspiration" and see in the Old
Testament "a large human element."[7] We can now understand much
of the Old Testament as ancient documents that often tally "with the
contemporary records of other nations, notably with the Assyrian in-
scriptions."[8] The results of historical study overturn a great many of
the usual ways of understanding the Old Testament, but they also
supply a firm basis in history that will recommend it to those committed to modern methods and attitudes. The obvious question is
whether this approach undermines the religious value of the Old
Testament. Burney's claim is that this "stands quite untouched by
such questions as can be raised by historical criticism."[9] The spiritual and moral meaning of scripture remains in place, and we can

explain the miraculous element by arguing that the biblical writers acted as teachers "of religious truth, not of natural science." For example, we can conclude that "purely natural causes" overthrew Pharaoh and his army without denying "that God used these forces to effect His purpose."[10] The fact that much of the Old Testament falls short of our moral standards finds an easy explanation in its history as one that progresses in moral and spiritual understanding. Israel's extermination of the foreign nations in the promised land rests upon their understanding God's commands while they were still "a semi-barbarous race."[11]

> The problem really revolves around what we mean by history. Are we thinking of facts and their establishment or of the explanations and interpretations we give of those facts?

Problems in the Old Testament, then, find convincing solutions in historical reconstructions. Burney emphasizes the constructive dimension of criticism, which leaves the religious value of the Old Testament untouched by "presenting us with a theory of the growth of the Old Testament literature and the development of Old Testament religion." Criticism has done this by carefully examining the sources and by "a scientific employment of the means of inquiry which lie at the disposal of students at the present day." It has also attempted "to bring the Old Testament history of the religion of Israel into line with other fields of learning" by applying *"the comparative method."*[12] This method, which is evolutionary in character, owes much to Darwin; and it supplies a historical account of religious progress that represents "an orderly process of development, leading up to the full manifestation of our Lord."[13] We can even find "the possibility and the promise of a *progressive* Revelation." We can observe that God's name "seems to mean *He who will become*," and we may infer that God's revelations will continue "up till the fulness of time when He is revealed in His Son, the effulgence of His glory and the impress of His substance."[14] While it is true that "particular prophecies should be studied primarily in relationship to the circumstances of the times at which they were produced,"[15] nevertheless when taken as a whole the prophets "point forward in a truly wonderful way to a supernatural King-Messiah ruling over a spiritually constituted kingdom — a conception which is only satisfied by our Lord Jesus Christ, the God-man, and the divine society, which He came to found."[16] Burney may be moving rather too quickly from a view of religious development that is historical in character to the idea of progressive revelation.

W. C. Allen, to begin with, takes a similar approach in his essay on "Modern Criticism and the New Testament." He begins by outlining three reactions to "biblical criticism." There are those who regard the critics as "relentless foes of Christianity." Others regard them as liberators from "outworn creeds" and "antiquated and exploded beliefs." Allen, of course, places himself in a third class for which "literary criticism of the Bible presents itself neither as a foe of Christianity nor as its conqueror, but rather as its ally."[17] After a discussion of the Gospels that recognizes the synoptic problem and the priority of Mark, he continues by insisting that criticism is necessary, that it is coherent with the attitude of the early church even though it did not possess modern resources, and that it is essential for Christian apologetics. He argues that "no tradition is of any value until and unless it has stood the test of an historical examination of its claim to be accurate and reliable."[18] The writings of the New Testament "need fear no criticism. Criticism has reasserted their value, and has shown that when subjected to the severest tests of modern science they are found to be historical documents of first-rate importance."[19] Though Allen does not say so, his remarks may imply that the solution to the synoptic problem allows us to land upon *terra firma* with Mark's Gospel. The chief value of the critical approach is to establish historical conclusions about Christ and the earliest church. We can add "an acquired value" because of the church's use of the New Testament as "the standard of belief and the test of false doctrine." Indeed, for most people "the main value" of the whole of the scriptures is "that they claim to be an authoritative expression of the Divine Character and the Divine Will."[20]

It is not entirely clear how we are to bring the "acquired" dogmatic and religious values into their proper relationship with history. It begins to look as though Allen is uncomfortable with the easy connection between history and revelation that informs Burney's discussion of the Old Testament. He implies that inspiration, which obviously cannot mean verbal dictation, is to be equated in some sense with the claim that scripture is revelatory. But he insists that "the question of the inspiration of the Bible, *i.e.* whether or no it contains a revelation of God, is really independent of criticism."[21] Asking whether scripture is revelatory is similar to the same question posed of nature or of the historical Jesus. More to the point, "Is there a Revelation in History?" It depends. Some people answer the question affirmatively because of their daily experience. "To others such an assumption is wholly superfluous and misleading."[22] At the very least there seems to be no necessary connection between historical reconstructions and the claim that they are revelatory. The problem really revolves around what we mean by history. Are we thinking of facts and their establishment or of the explanations and interpretations we give of those facts? Indeed, can we even distinguish the one from the other? It is no longer possible to suppose such a thing as an uninterpreted fact. Perhaps inadvertently, Allen has put his finger on a central problem that will become clearer as people reflect more fully on the historian's task. For example, New Testament critics often assume that by reconstructing the historical Jesus they have settled the question of his significance. Such a view may have its roots in German idealism. If we can only describe something with full accuracy, we can understand its normative significance. Common sense allows us to doubt that this is so. It begins to look as though history is a problematic ally of faith.

Let me elaborate the point by examining some of the essays published some seventy-five years after *Contentio Veritatis* in *The Myth of God Incarnate*. The preoccupation of the writers is with the uneasy relationship between the creedal doctrine of the incarnation and the historical Jesus. The essays understand the problem in differing ways and supply us with differing understandings of "myth." Nevertheless, they present their common concern as one "in the interests of truth," and one with "practical implications for our relationship to the peoples of the other great world religions."[23] Their aim is a positive one, and their call is for "adjustments" to our "modern science-oriented culture" that "will help to make Christian discipleship possible for our children's children."[24] Not all the essayists are wildly liberal in their views. Michael Goulder's essay, "Jesus, the Man of Universal Destiny," takes a decidedly conservative view of the historical Jesus. Belief in Christianity requires some kind of belief "about Jesus, called Christ, and that seems to me inevitably to mean believing certain things about him as a historical person."[25] To be sure, history "is a matter of probabilities"; but Goulder states his criteria. The "hard" ones are coherence, accidental information, and material told to the church's embarrassment; the "soft" ones, material which Paul says was handed on to him, Aramaic and Hebrew words, and very widespread tradition. "These six criteria are such as a disinterested historian would bring to the task; and if we are seeking historical probabilities, they must suffice us." By employing them Goulder makes twelve statements about Jesus that represent "historical probabilities." These conclusions include the claims that Jesus' message concerned the inauguration of God's reign through himself, that Jesus performed healings, that he probably saw himself as the Messiah and as the Son of Man, that he saw the kingdom as one of love, that he foresaw his death and interpreted its significance, and that his disciples had experiences of seeing him after his death.[26] These historical conclusions lead to a definition of Jesus as *the* man of *universal* destiny, a phrase meant "to safeguard the divine initiative in Jesus" as the deliverer.[27] The next step would be to write a "christology of agency rather than of substance," though it is not entirely clear whether this would be a replacement or a reinterpretation of the Chalcedonian Definition.

Maurice Wiles's two essays suggest he would be happier with the first alternative. He presents the first one as a question, "Christianity without Incarnation?" The question is proper, necessary, and constructive. He recognizes that Jesus can stand as "a model for human life." But such an assessment is insufficient, since "the primary importance of Jesus for Christians has never been as a model for human living." Instead, his true significance "has resided rather in the conviction that he is the one in whom we meet God, the one through whom God has acted decisively for the salvation of the world."[28]

This way of putting the significance of the historical Jesus is obviously a claim of faith rather than a historical conclusion. Yet it need not be made by employing the traditional doctrine of the incarnation. An alternative might be a change "towards a less exclusive insistence on Jesus as *the* way for all peoples and all cultures." Nevertheless, to abandon the incarnation "as a metaphysical claim about the person of Jesus (for which there is a strong case) would not involve the abandonment of all the religious claims normally associated with it." Indeed, Wiles is willing to accept much of the traditional language and imagery "as a pictorial way" of expressing these religious claims, which correlate with what he regards as the primary importance of Jesus for Christians.[29] In his second essay ("Myth in Theology") Wiles is first concerned with various ways in which theologians have used the term "myth." He approves of the idea that to make a distinction between the historical and the mythological need not deny some sort of relation between the two. "The Christian myth does not consist of super-historical events; it is a way of conveying the meaning of historical events."[30] We could argue that the historical Jesus emerges as someone open to God and "that his life depicted not only a profound human response to God, but that in his attitude towards other men his life was a parable of the loving outreach of God to the world."[31] If we accept this assessment of Jesus' character as historical and add to it the experience believers have of grace, then we have a way of linking the myth of the incarnation to the historical Jesus. The weaker form of this link "would simply state as a matter of contingent historical fact that this truth about man's relation to God came alive in our particular tradition through the figure of Jesus." The stronger form "would give to Jesus a more indispensable role."[32]

So far we have discovered that the historical Jesus, reconstructed almost entirely on the basis of the New Testament texts, is necessary but not sufficient for faith claims about him. In other words the myth is not the same thing as the history, but it must have some footing in the history. Don Cupitt's essay, "The Christ of Christendom," seems to drive in the same direction. Discovering "that the ecclesiastical Christ is not to be found in a critical reading of the records of Jesus led to scepticism about the historicity of the gospels." The scepticism, however, "served to protect the ecclesiastical Christ from historical refutation." But we need not abandon an attempt to discover the historical Jesus; "the figure behind the gospels is not quite unreachable."[33] Cupitt's plea is for a shift from the dogmatic faith to the "critical faith which is to succeed it." This will be difficult, "but it will not take us further from Jesus: it will bring us closer to him." It is not entirely clear what this means, and Cupitt continues by completing his essay with the suspicion that his readers may still fear that he leaves no room "for a religiously-adequate christology — one, that is, which does full justice to the conviction that 'God was in Christ, reconciling the world to himself,' committing himself in the midst of the human to redeem the human." He feels the objection but insists that a doctrine of Christ must strengthen our understanding of divine transcendence and demands "that christology be not any kind of man-cult: it must be theocentric, not christocentric."[34] The key to understanding Jesus appears to be his recognition of the transcendence of God. But it may be that this key neither solves the problem of the historical Jesus nor allows us to make any unique claim about him.

That what I have read between the lines of Cupitt's essay is not entirely unfair finds support in an essay he wrote several years earlier in *Christ, Faith and History*. His title, "One Jesus, Many Christs?" suggests his thesis. It is obvious that "the figure of Jesus himself has remained enigmatic, and capable of very diverse interpretations. He has been seen as moralist, prophet, apocalyptist, hero, redeemer, priest and king."[35] Cupitt rings the changes on various iconographical, literary, and religious Christs. This diversity within Christianity "is partly the result of its having flourished in so many different cultures."[36] The New Testament itself has at least four ways of interpreting Jesus. These considerations lead to a preliminary conclusion. Cupitt's argument has explained why it is so difficult to come to terms with Jesus. "Christ" has been understood many different ways, "and being Christ-like has meant so very many different ways of life, that talk of Christ must either break away from any exclusive association with Jesus of Nazareth or be severely pruned back."[37] Both alternatives have been tried but without much success. Cupitt suggests we may be moving in the direction of Hinduism and that Christianity is now "rather a family of monotheistic faiths which in various ways find in Jesus a key to the relation of man with God."[38] The pruning which he recommends yields the simple and minimal conclusion that "Jesus' legacy to mankind is...an urgent appeal to each of us to acknowledge above all else the reality of God." Such a claim need not be made about Jesus alone, but for Christians this minimal understanding of the historical Jesus is for them the point of departure. As well, we can make many different Christs of the one Jesus so understood. We can, however, understand this positively. Cupitt's final conclusion is that for the Christian tradition "Jesus is the paradigm of faith, but that paradigm may be re-enacted in a great variety of ways, and we need not labour to reduce their number."[39] The link between Jesus and Christ, then, is one thought to bind together a highly pruned understanding of the historical Jesus with many different Christs.

To return to *The Myth of God Incarnate*, Dennis Nineham's "Epilogue" reflects in a somewhat bemused fashion on the essays. The question he raises has to do with assessments of the historical Jesus that make some kind of unique claim about him. "Is it, however, possible to validate claims of the kind in question on the basis of historical evidence?"[40] The answer appears to be quite doubtful, and later in the essay Nineham points out a tendency in many modern theologians to dismiss the metaphysical claims for Jesus' uniqueness, while retaining the moral uniqueness those claims implied.[41] What he appears to mean is that it is difficult to understand such a claim as historical. It inevitably raises the christological problem of how

Christ can be fully human and yet somehow unique and distinct from other humans. Nineham introduces Norman Perrin's threefold distinction regarding knowledge of Jesus. "Historical knowledge" is a supposedly objective account of Jesus, while "historic knowledge" treats that account as having an impact and practical consequences for those who accept it. The difference, of course, is that between the two German adjectives *historisch* and *geschichtlich*. The third kind of knowledge is faith-knowledge, and by this time we have moved away from the historical Jesus. Perrin's schema, however, is so "highly sophisticated" that it is "small wonder that many preachers fall back on the implicit assumption that the preached Christ and the historical Jesus are identical." Scholars and theologians seek some "empirical anchorage" in the historical Jesus, but "even the degree of anchorage they seek is incapable of historical validation."[42]

Nineham's conclusion is in part negative, and it implies the insufficiency of the historical Jesus as a basis for faith claims about Jesus, though he admits that what we can say about the historical Jesus should not contradict our preached Christ. He puts this part of his conclusion by arguing that the essayists have "given reasons for doubting" that the link between the Jesus of history and the Christ of faith can be forged "by way of the idea that Jesus was God incarnate, as that idea has traditionally been understood." His own view and the "aim of the present postscript has been to put a 'No thoroughfare' against any alternative routes which may be suggested by way of claiming uniqueness of some sort for Jesus on historical grounds."[43] While we cannot dismiss the quest for the historical Jesus and must retain its capacity to call into question our faith claims, it is those claims that matter. What people need most is "a story, a picture, a myth, that will capture their imagination, while meshing in with the rest of their sensibility in the way that messianic terms linked with the sensibility of first-century Jews, or Nicene symbolism with the sensibility of philosophically-minded fourth-century Greeks."[44] History as the facts, then, becomes a treacherous friend of scripture for at least two reasons. First, it dissolves scripture into no more than evidence for the facts it hopes to recover. And we can even doubt that there can be such a thing as a brute or uninterpreted fact. Second, it discounts scripture's evaluation of the history it recounts and substitutes for that evaluation our own modern ones. To use an analogy, we might study the plays and poems of Shakespeare from a purely historical perspective — as evidence for Shakespeare's life and times. Doing so is obviously important since we can seek to establish the text of the plays, the meaning of words and topical allusions in the plays and poems, and the sources for Shakespeare's work. But this would fail to take that work seriously as an object of criticism and reflection.

History as Religious Experience

One way of seeking to get beyond the impasse I have described is to treat scripture as the history of religious experience, since this will enable us to include the more interpretive aspect of the scriptural evidence. Such an approach finds expression in *Foundations,* published in 1912 by seven Oxford dons who were friends and who in preparing the volume of essays found themselves in "a far greater measure of agreement than we had originally anticipated."[45] Consequently, the nine essays are "in the main, the expression of a corporate mind." Their aim resembles that of the *Lux Mundi* writers in that they seek to reexamine and "if need be" restate the foundations of Christian belief to bring them into harmony with "science, philosophy, and scholarship."[46] Nevertheless, the twenty-three years that had passed after the publication of *Lux Mundi* had seen a considerable advance in critical study, and *Foundations* does seem more concerned with accommodating its statement of the faith to that development. For example, the young William Temple goes so far as to describe the Definition of Chalcedon as "a confession of the bankruptcy of Greek Patristic Theology."[47] He will, of course, take a kindlier view of the tradition in his later writings.

The essay that is the most interesting from the point of view of my argument is Brook's "The Bible." He begins by stating flatly that "the plain man" no longer regards the Bible as "the Book of Books." He has learned that scripture "is not infallible in its statements of fact, in its ethical teaching or even in its theology."[48] But even though people no longer read the Bible, they retain some sort of vestigial recognition of its significance. We may remember Coleridge's "fine passage" in which he says that "men of all ranks, conditions, and states of mind, have found in this volume a correspondent for every movement towards the better felt in their own hearts, the needy soul has found supply, the feeble a help, the sorrowful a comfort." Heine says much the same thing, and we could scarcely find anyone who "reads the Bible in a devotional spirit, who could not add something from his own experience to give further confirmation to what is, after all, a fact of almost universal experience."[49] The religious experience that can result from reading scripture gives us a true understanding of the Bible. Modern scholarship has allowed us to discern the full significance of scripture and to realize "that the Bible is God's book because it is in a unique and universal sense Man's book." It has recorded and passed on to us "a great human experience — an experience of God, of human need, and of God's response to that need." Those who wrote, edited, or compiled the books of the Bible, as well as "their literary sources," are now revealed to us as "men of flesh and blood, linked to us by the possession of a common humanity."[50] Thus, the inherent quality of the Bible in no way depends upon verbal inerrancy; its writers are not "like the dolls of a ventriloquist."

In this way we discover "the real secret of the religious power of the Bible." Carlyle observed that we learn religion by finding people who have religion, and so the Bible leads people to God "because its writers were men who 'had religion.' The more we emphasise their real humanity, the greater will be the power of their appeal."[51] Brook continues by describing the content of the religious experience of the biblical writers. This includes "communion with God" and his love, an experience that brings us "an inner security and an absolute repose." We also discover a "passion for righteousness" and a corresponding "consciousness of sin." The experience of God's forgiveness carries with it a sense of vocation. These elements "are united in a single progressive movement," and so the Bible becomes a record of religious experience that "is expressed in a gradually developing theology."[52] What we find, then, is the claim of the biblical writers, based on their experience, that "behind the maze of history with its apparent contradictions and its apparent arbitrary occurrences, there is the hand of God guiding and controlling it all, and that in it all and through it all there is a Divine purpose slowly fulfilling itself in the ordered sequence of events."[53] Thus, experience takes scripture beyond history to its meaning, and we must think of it in evolutionary terms.

This is possible, however, only because of faith and the genius of a religious sense that is "mysterious in its origin."[54] Brook posits three conclusions to be drawn provided we assume that the experience of communion with God claimed by the biblical writers is "real and not illusory." First, their knowledge of God must be "revealed knowledge." Second, it requires "a special faculty for apprehending His self-revelation." Finally, the condition for both points must be "an essential kinship between the Divine and human nature." Brook quotes Hegel's conclusion: "The spirit of man whereby he knows God . . . is the spirit of God Himself." We can, therefore, think of revelation "as an act of God within" rather than an outward communication of "information about God."[55] What this seems to mean is that we can identify the revelation with the experience, the object within the apprehension of the subject. It is certainly possible to ask whether this is a sufficient understanding of revelation. Is Brook's conclusion flawed by German idealism and its attempt to construct a rainbow bridge to ultimate reality by locating that reality in the human mind? Brook concludes his essay by making some observations, two of which are worth noting. The church has authority for the Christian because the *consensus sanctorum* "represents the living and abiding voice of a corporate experience."[56] It is not entirely clear how we should think this through. The second observation relates to Brook's central point. Granted that "the primary purpose of the writers is religious and not strictly historical, and that, in many cases, they idealise and freely adapt their material in accordance with this purpose," we should not draw the conclusion "that their writings have little or no value for the historian."[57] Brook appears to recognize that there is a problematic relationship between historical reconstructions and their interpretation. Once again, however, he does not attempt to come to any full conclusion.

The writers of *Essays Catholic and Critical,* published in 1926, are more in line with *Lux Mundi* than those of *Foundations.* Their basic conviction is that "the two terms Catholic and critical represent principles, habits, and tempers of the religious mind which only reach their maturity in combination."[58] The only person with essays in both collections is A. E. J. Rawlinson. His two essays differ from one another in detail, but both of them seek to identify authority with religious experience. The synopsis of his earlier essay summarizes the main lines of his argument. Authority finds a correlation with inspiration, but only if we reject any notion of the infallibility of inspiration or of its requiring verbal inerrancy. Restating the meaning of authority requires us to begin with the classical meaning of *auctoritas* as "primarily a statement or an opinion for the truth of which somebody is prepared to vouch: more particularly an expression of responsible and competent opinion."[59] Augustine thinks of the authority of the Catholic Church as its corporate witness rather than its infallible voice.[60] Moreover, we must employ this understanding as a way of illuminating our study "of actual religious psychology." We may think of three "phases in the life of the educated Christian" — tutelage, abstract freedom, and concrete freedom. The last stage, which would abolish the distinction between authority and freedom, "represents an ideal progressively realised but never completely attained." The second stage is the important one, since it represents a dialectic between authority and freedom. But we must understand the authority of the church as *"the corporate witness of the saints to the validity of the spiritual experience on which their lives are based."* What this consensus of the saints guarantees "is rather a life than a theology."[61] The same perspective dominates Rawlinson's contribution to *Essays Catholic and Critical.*

Rawlinson's title, however, "Authority as a Ground of Belief," represents a certain shift of emphasis. He begins by asserting that the gospel "came originally into the world in a particular context, and as the result of a particular historical process." No one could have discovered or invented it by himself "in independence of historical tradition." This means that a person "must be content to derive his knowledge of it from authority, whether the authority in question be primarily that of a living teacher, or of past tradition."[62] Moreover, Christianity claims to be "a religion of revelation," and:

> The Church is not primarily a society for spiritual or intellectual research, but a society of which it belongs to the very essence to put forward the emphatic claim to be the bearer of revelation, to have been put in trust with the Gospel as God's revealed message to mankind, and to have been divinely commissioned with prophetic authority to proclaim it as God's truth to all the world.[63]

As opposed to Catholics, Protestants affirm that while the gospel reaches people "through the instrumentality and mediation of the Church," it does not create the church but is "entrusted to the Church."[64] The claim, then, is that both the revelation of the gospel and the authority of the church are presuppositions we must make before we can speak of belief in either.

It is at this point in Rawlinson's argument that the themes from the earlier essay enter the picture. Even when people say that their beliefs are grounded in the authority of the church and its claim to mediate revelation, "it is probable that the real grounds on which the beliefs in question are held are not exhausted by such a statement."[65] They are "at least to some extent verified in the experience of life." Part of what this means is that the beliefs "have mediated to those who entertain them a spiritual experience."[66] The intellectual and theological dimensions of the Christian faith are ways of articulating this experience and represent "a reason of the hope and of the faith" that have been accepted. It follows that we must reject the "oracular" authority of the pope, and by doing so we also reject "the oracular conception of the authority of the Bible" and "that of the authority of the ecumenical Councils and Creeds." This need not mean a rejection of the Bible or of the church and its dogmas and creeds, "only that such authority is no longer to be taken in an oracular sense, and that the final authority is not anything which is either mechanical or merely external, but is rather the intrinsic and self-evidencing authority of truth." In the long run we must appeal "to the spiritual, intellectual, and historical content of divine revelation, *as verifiable at the three-fold bar of history, reason and spiritual experience.*"[67] In the discussion that immediately follows history drops out of the picture; the doctrines of the church have authority to the degree that they express "truths which are capable of being verified — spiritually verified, in some sense, in the experience of all her members; verified intellectually, as well as spiritually, in the reason and experience of her theologians and thinkers and men of learning."[68] Rawlinson, then, focuses upon authority as experience; but he makes it clear that experience does not create the revelation it discovers, and he also places experience in the corporate context of the church.[69]

Granted that the Bible is a record of progressive religious experience, we still encounter a number of problems. What is the object of that experience, and how are the experience and its object related to historical events? What is the relation of the experiences described in scripture to our own religious experience, and how are we to relate the individual's experience to the corporate experience of the church? G. W. H. Lampe's essay in the Church Doctrine Commission Report *Christian Believing* suggests ways of solving these questions. He begins his answer to the first set of problems by arguing that "if divine revelation is given anywhere it is communicated in human experience." This means that we must "analyse the sequence: revelation, faith, and theological reflection." And we may assume that "Faith is a response to some occurrence, in the broadest sense of that word, which has been experienced as revelatory."[70] The older view treated scripture, the creeds, conciliar definitions, and sometimes the writings of the church fathers as containing revealed doctrines. Such a view is no longer possible. "Theological propositions and systems of belief are not revealed. Theology is a process of reflection on faith that arises from revelatory experience; it is not itself the locus of revelation."[71] Doctrine, then, becomes the articulation of religious experience.

Lampe equates the "locus of revelation" with the "realm of experience." And he recognizes that it "has often been asserted that divine revelation is given in the events of history." Such a view sees God disclosing himself and declaring "his nature and his purposes in human history." It does not treat the Bible as "a source-book for revealed doctrine, but [as] a record of paradigmatic acts of God which serve as a norm and reference-point by which we are enabled to discern God's love and justice and demands elsewhere in the whole course of human history."[72] But it is obvious that events themselves, "even if uninterpreted events were ever accessible to us, would not be revelatory." The same event in history can be revelatory to some but not to others. Consequently, we find that "it is the interpreted event which is the locus of revelation."[73] The external fact and its interpretation are in a highly problematic relationship. Faith apparently "both results from revelatory experience and also at the same time determines in some measure the revelatory character of the experience by interpreting it as an act of God."[74] The circle, however, is not a vicious one. The person who has a revelatory experience is quite convinced that the revelation was "not generated from his own consciousness." But at the same time his response and his sense of the compelling character of the experience are what make the occasion revelatory.[75] Lampe uses the example of meeting a friend, but we might think of the experience of love in the broadest possible sense as something that always combines what might be called an impact upon us from outside with a subjective response to that impact. The historical event, then, does not necessarily cause a revelatory experience; and that experience mysteriously combines objective and subjective elements.

The next set of questions has to do with how the individual's revelatory experience finds a relationship with scripture and the church. Lampe begins his essay with this problem and points out that the very fact of being a Christian believer puts a person "within a theological tradition embodied and mediated through the Bible, creeds, liturgy, preaching, the distinctive ethos and outlook of the particular Christian group to which he adheres." However personal and individual our faith may be, none of us "can entirely extricate himself from the complex tradition to which he belongs."[76] The Bible, of course, is central to that tradition. It "consists basically of records of, and reflections on, a series of human experiences which were believed by those who narrated the experiences and those who reflected on them to be revelatory of God." To become part of a Christian community involves accepting scripture in this sense and making it our own:

> It is within this stream of experience, faith, and theology, now re-focused around Jesus as presented to us in the New Testament, that we take our place as Christian believers. We belong to the community whose faith is based on broadly this kind of experience and awareness of God. In this sense our faith is biblically based and biblically orientated.[77]

This does not mean we should ignore the question of the historical Jesus, "but the 'Christ' who is the central reference-point of our faith in God is more than the historical Jesus, and 'Christ' belongs to the present more than to the past, and most of all to the future."[78] The church has a role to play in helping us to appropriate this Christ for our own lives. Lampe suggests that "to perceive revelation is rather like appreciating music or painting." Our individual likes and dislikes may be a point of departure, but "a wise person will pay attention to the *communis sensus* which has established certain reference-points and recognized some revelatory experiences as 'classical.' This does not mean that one will always be bound by this general opinion; but one will by no means ignore it."[79] The corporate belief of the church, then, will guide us to the "classics," to the New Testament witness to Christ in particular and to the whole of the Bible in general. History remains necessary for Lampe's understanding of revelatory experience, but it is by no means sufficient.

History as the Record of Revelation and Response

Treating scripture as a progressive record of revelatory experience may easily be transformed into a schema of revelation and response. Such a schema is central to Charles Gore's work in the first quarter of the twentieth century. He became the first principal of Pusey House at Oxford in 1883 and was the editor of *Lux Mundi* six years later. When he resigned the see of Oxford in 1919, he turned his attention to theological writing, and the volumes known as *The Reconstruction of Belief* appeared from 1921 to 1924. The theological structure he elaborates is meant to be not so much a system as the prolegomenon to one. He begins with human reason as our disposition to demand "sequence, regularity, and order in things." It represents "faith in a universal order" and is the basis of science and philosophy as well as religion. Human reason, then, discovers a universal Reason that we must identify with God.[80] "Discover" is the operative word, since Gore assumes that knowledge presupposes its object and does not create it out of experience. In his second volume, *Belief in Christ,* he builds on the conclusions he reached in *Belief in God.* "I shall take for granted not only that there is a God in some sense, but that He has really disclosed Himself to men, especially in a historical process through the prophets of Israel and through Jesus of Nazareth."[81] He recognizes that this is a claim only faith can make, but argues that it cannot be disproved by those critics who dogmatically deny the miraculous and supernatural. In examining the claims of "the first disciples of Jesus" he describes "the gradual growth of their faith in their Master, first as the promised Messiah, then as the Lord of all, then as the incarnate Son of God."[82]

In one way Gore begins with religious experience and with faith as reason in the making.[83] But his conviction that faith is a gradual discovery of its object gives that object an a priori status. Moreover, he identifies the progressive discovery of Christ's identity with the development of christologies not only in the New Testament but in the ancient church and beyond. He places the correlation of human reason with Reason as God in what we can call an evolutionary framework that can easily be applied to scripture. We are obliged "to search for God with all the energy of our reason, and in a measure we find Him; but at the same time He baffles our search." Our discovery is "*that* God is, but not *what* He is." The search and discovery, together with "the disappointment and the failure" come to be understood as "parts of a movement of God in us which is to be met by a corresponding movement of God, if I may so speak, from without or from above, to reveal Himself in much more satisfying fullness."[84] Despite his emphasis upon experience this evolutionary framework leads Gore to understand the Old Testament as revelation. Its "central claim" is that it is "the record of a real self-disclosure made by the living God to the people of Israel through the prophets." The Old Testament presents us with "a progressive and continuous doctrine about God and man," and it anticipates the "climax and fulfilment" of God's "self-revelation" in Christ.[85] The incarnation, then, is the intensification and completion of the interaction of revelation and response. At the same time, there remains a progress in the understanding of that climactic revelation. St. Paul completes the apostolic interpretation of Christ.[86] Gore goes on to ask "whether the ancient Church was right in elevating the written books of the New Testament to a throne of solitary supremacy."[87] He gives a positive answer to the question but qualifies it by arguing that "the science of history" has demonstrated that we must reject the traditional notion of inspiration as requiring verbal inerrancy and infallibility.[88] Such a rejection ought to imply that to speak of the Bible as history refers to human responses to divine revelation. But Gore does not always make the point clearly and can sometimes appear to equate the history of scripture with the revelation. For example, he accepts the priority of Mark because it enables us to find solid ground for the historical Jesus. And he insists that the clauses in the creeds regarding the virgin birth and the resurrection must be accepted as historical statements. In this way Gore's framework of revelation and response fails to deal adequately with the problem of history.

Let me make two final points. Granted that the Bible is the record of God's progressive revelation and its culmination in the incarnation, we cannot suppose that the Bible stands alone. Gore insists that "just as long experience has made it evident that the tradition needs the open Bible to keep it pure, so certainly it has made it evident that the Bible needs the guidance of the Church to introduce it to its readers."[89] We must never forget that the Bible is the church's book. The second point to make is that the roots of Gore's framework of revelation and response in the idea of scripture as the progressive record of religious experience sometimes appear. He says that "the Christian religion is first of all based on a teaching accepted as the word of God, and constantly verified in an agelong and nearly worldwide experience." Its "message and claim" must be tested not only by "moral and spiritual experience" but also "intellectually and in the field of critical history." Nevertheless, the scholar will be better equipped for inquiry if he approaches his work "with the sort of understanding that only faith, and the experience based on faith" can give him.[90] In other words the only experience that counts is one that discerns the truth of the revelation, which Gore identifies with the catholic faith. It remains somewhat unclear how his schema of revelation and response remains rooted in history.

> Granted that the Bible is the record of God's progressive revelation and its culmination in the incarnation, we cannot suppose that the Bible stands alone.

Describing scripture as revelation and response also informs the report of the Commission on Christian Doctrine that was appointed by the two archbishops in 1922. That report appeared in 1938 with the title *Doctrine in the Church of England*. In his "Chairman's Introduction" William Temple describes how the commission did its work and what it tried to do. Its members sought "to reach real agreement" through discussion, and the report sets out "divergent views" only when such agreement proved impossible. In accordance with Archbishop Davidson's original instructions the commission "considered that our function is to elucidate doctrine and doctrinal tendencies, not to declare principles of discipline except so far as these are themselves doctrinal." In other words, the report is primarily descriptive and was not designed to be in any sense an authoritative statement of "what varieties of doctrine or of interpretation are to be regarded as permissible in the Church of England."[91] The report itself is organized into three parts (the doctrines of God and redemption, the church and sacraments, eschatology) with prolegomena that consider the sources and authority of Christian doctrine. This preliminary discussion concerns itself with scripture, the church, and Anglican formularies. Temple's introduction anticipates the report by giving the following summary of its conclusions regarding scripture:

> We fully acknowledge the supremacy of Scripture as supplying the standard of doctrine; and we try to indicate how Scripture should be regarded in this connexion: everyone knows that it is possible to quote texts which, torn from their context, may be presented as supporting entirely un-Christian opinions. Short of that, everyone knows that most heretics have been convinced that they were conscientiously following and interpreting Scripture. Our attention must be fastened on the trend of Scripture as a whole and upon its climax in the record of the Word made flesh, by the light of which all the rest is to be interpreted; in that concentration of attention and in that interpretation, our best guide is the continuous stream of universal Christian tradition.[92]

There is nothing unusual about regarding scripture as the supreme authority with tradition as the best guide to its meaning. The Vincentian canon may lie in the background of this conclusion. But it is important to note that the emphasis is upon the Bible as a whole. We cannot simply pick and choose what agrees with our opinions and prejudices.

The discussion of scripture in the main body of the report begins with the question of inspiration. "Belief that the Bible is the inspired record of God's self-revelation to man and of man's response to that revelation is . . . a conclusion drawn from the character of their [the books in scripture] contents and the spiritual insight displayed in them."[93] The Bible is "more than a collection of utterances" and partly makes its appeal "in virtue of its unity as a whole." And that unity is defined as "the presentation of a self-revelation of God through history and experience — a self-revelation which develops in relation both to the response and to the resistance of man to the Divine initiative, and which culminates in the Incarnation."[94] Thus, the schema of revelation and response is rooted in the idea of scripture as a progressive record of religious experience, but that idea is transformed in such a way as to give priority to revelation — "the Divine initiative." Moreover, history enters the picture, but only as the arena in which revelation takes place. Christian faith treats the revelation as finding its focus uniquely in Christ. In this way inspiration is virtually identified with the apprehension of revelation and, consequently, with the authority of scripture. This obviously means we must reject any notion of inerrancy in scripture.[95] At the same time, inspiration attaches to the "living and worshipping society" that accepted scripture as canonical and that has continuously interpreted that canon. Inspiration in relation to the Bible, whether we mean all of scripture or "any particular book within it," includes not only "the inspiration of individual authors," but also "the inspiration of those who selected, interpreted, and used already existing material."[96] This may even include the idea that inspiration attaches to the apprehensions of revelation by the readers as well as the writers of scripture; and it is to be understood as the guidance of the Holy Spirit.

The second part of the report's discussion treats the authority of scripture as a factor of the points already established. The basic standard is "the Mind of Christ as unfolded in the experience of the Church and appropriated by the individual Christian through His Spirit. That is to say, the stages of the Biblical revelation are to be judged in relation to its historical climax." Nevertheless, in applying this standard we must not prejudge "the conclusions of historical, critical, and scientific investigation in any field" including that of biblical criticism. Nor must Christian thinkers bind themselves "to the thought-forms employed by the Biblical writers." Finally, we must remember that the scriptures "display a wide variety of literary type." Not all the books have "supreme spiritual value."[97] The report adds a number of cautions with respect to Christ's teaching. It often addressed particular occasions and was "conditioned by the thought-forms and circumstances of the time." We cannot suppose that we always have the very words of Jesus. These considerations by no means undermine the fact that "the religious and moral teaching of the Gospel conveys faithfully the impress made upon the Apostolic Church by the mind and personality of Jesus, and thus possesses supreme authority." Nevertheless, "direct appeal to isolated texts in our Lord's teaching . . . is liable to error."[98] The report clearly captures the dominant understanding of scripture and its role. Accepting the rejection of verbal inerrancy because of the impact of the historical-critical method implies the necessity of making a distinction between revelation and its apprehension as well as a distinction between both and the historical reconstructions that are possible. These distinctions leave room for explaining the discrepancies and errors of scripture. They are precisely what we should expect of witnesses to a revelation. Moreover, the focus upon the apprehension of revelation rightly implies that the revelation itself transcends its partial apprehensions. Thus, the entire framework reflected in the report accords with what I should regard as the chief characteristic of Anglicanism — a horror of absolutes and of infallibility.

In 1963 a group of scholars, largely Cambridge dons, published the collection of essays called *Soundings*. They regard their situation as a time "for making soundings, not charts or maps."[99] The theological era dominated by the incarnation had ended if not at the time of William Temple's death in 1944 then certainly in the post-war period. *Soundings* appeared at a time of great perplexity, a time that probably extends to our own day. The essayists think of themselves more like the writers of *Essays and Reviews* than those of *Lux Mundi*. Vidler ends his introduction on what he regards as a positive note. He recognizes that metaphors "can be treacherous" when we insist upon them too strongly. But, speaking for all the writers, he claims that in line with the metaphor of the title "we are thankful all to be in the same ship; whatever we do not know, we know that the ship is afloat, and the fact that we make these soundings is evidence of our conviction that there is a bottom to the sea."[100] To shift the metaphor, they may not be able to discern the foundations; but they are convinced they must exist. Vidler concludes by citing Romans 11:33–36, Paul's reflection on the unsearchable judgments and untraceable ways of God. One measure of the perplexity finds expression in Ninian Smart's essay, "The Relation between Christianity and the Other Great Religions." He questions whether the schema of revelation and response can be restricted to Christianity. We cannot equate revelation with scripture, and we must ask "what experiences? what history?"[101] Can we any longer accept the Christian revelation as unique?

J. N. Sanders's essay, "The Meaning and Authority of the New Testament," avoids these questions and focuses upon understanding the New Testament as responses to the revelation in Christ. The first part of the essay is a discussion oriented toward the history of interpretation. Differing "dogmatic presuppositions," including the failed attempt of the liberals to disavow such presuppositions, are all weighed in the balance and found wanting. The second part of the essay begins by arguing that we are no better off. "Today most Christians, even theologians, acquiesce in either a renovated dogmatism or in a compromise between that and a modified Liberalism."[102] Nor is "the fashionable biblical theology" a solution. Sanders's positive argument begins by making a distinction between the external authority for one class of documents and the intrinsic authority belonging to another class. Documents in this second class "do not depend for their authority upon any external guarantee, verifiable independently of the documents themselves. Their authority is inherent and intrinsic, and recognition of its existence is wholly dependent upon the proper understanding of their meaning."[103] We must think not of acts of Parliament implemented by judges, but of the writings of philosophers like Plato and of mystics. The authority of such documents is "quite independent of all external support or sanction." Presumably "recognition" of this sort of authority presupposes the faith and commitment of the disciple.

Sanders goes on to point out that the Hebrew prophets do not "exactly" fit into this second class, since they claim that they are "the recipients of a revelation." Thus, they are different from the philosophers and mystics:

> To this distinction between the philosopher Plato and the prophet Isaiah or Jeremiah corresponds the distinction between the Platonic love, *eros,* which expresses man's upward aspirations towards God, and the characteristically Christian love, *agape,* God's condescending towards man. Now there is no absolute antithesis between either element in the two pairs, discovery and revelation, *eros* and *agape.* There is rather a necessary element of both in the whole relationship of God and man.[104]

Sanders tries to explain revelation and response by treating it as a love relationship between God and the recipients of revelation. And he continues by speaking of the human experience of falling in love as including both revelation and discovery. But he also wants to retain the priority of revelation, and his analogy may break down at this point since the love between God and human beings scarcely involves the parity of the two parties.

The authority of the prophetic apprehensions of revelation, like the authority of the New Testament apprehensions of Christ, is "never coercive." It depends entirely upon the persuasive compulsion of faith. This is why the authority of the New Testament is intrinsic and must be accepted by faith. "Its authority can be recognized only when its meaning is understood, and there is no external power with authority to enforce obedience to it or to dictate a particular interpretation of it, though Christians have often succumbed to the temptation of trying to establish such an authority."[105] Sanders's view is reminiscent of earlier ones that saw scripture as self-evident in the sense that those who are guided by the Holy Spirit rightly see it as scripture. At the same time, Sanders thinks of scripture as the apprehension of revelation rather than as revelation unmediated by human apprehension. The next question he asks is what is left "if we reject both an infallible Church and an infallible Scripture."[106] His answer is that we must examine the New Testament critically. We shall discover discrepancies that lead us to conclude that its writers are far from inerrant. But this will in fact make the New Testament more credible. Though it is "the work of many hands, yet there is in it a remarkable unanimity in the picture which it gives of the faith of the first Christians."[107] In some tension with his view of the intrinsic authority of scripture Sanders recognizes that the authority of the New Testament "is to some extent dependent on that of the Church," since the church established the canon. Of course, we are not speaking of an inerrant authority. While it is true that we cannot locate infallibility in the church or scripture or in the conscience, "we have *in Christ himself an infallible authority,* and can trust him to use the fallible, mediated authorities of Church, Scripture, and conscience, to keep us from error."[108]

Sanders raises more questions than he solves, but it is at least clear that in 1963 the pattern of revelation and response still finds expression.

Scripture as Story

Both the idea of scripture as a record of progressive religious experience and that of it as revelation and response tend to free the Bible from history without denying that history remains the context for the experience and the apprehensions of revelation. At the same time, these structures betray presuppositions that are really theological in character. In the Church Doctrine Commission report of 1981 called *Believing in the Church* we find another way of characterizing the Bible and its religious significance. This report turns what its predecessor, *Christian Believing,* had presented as a difficulty into an advantage. The earlier report had admitted that in the Church of England there were views of the creed that were quite contradictory. Stephen Sykes's book, *The Integrity of Anglicanism,* published in 1978, lamented this fact and argued that the Church of England needed to find a way of standing for something. *Believing in the Church* responds to the problem in rather a different way. Within the church there are some who find their chief commitment to the past and to tradition, while others are more concerned with the present and future and with the ways Christians should address issues confronting them in their own time. Yet despite contradictory beliefs both the boundary-marking people and the sign-post people hold their beliefs in the community of the church. They do their believing in the church, and both those concerned with preserving the past and those concerned with moving toward the future are necessary for the life of the church. Believing, then, is "corporate believing"; and it is also "belonging."[109] The idea of Christianity as a "story" informs many of the essays in the volume. The church is a story-formed community that continues the story in its own life. Anthony Harvey's essay, "Attending to Scripture," applies the idea to the Bible in a powerful and persuasive way.

Harvey begins by arguing that to say "the church believes" or "the church teaches" makes us uneasy "because we sense that it is difficult to fill in the object." He concludes that the "Church, like the individual, discovers what it believes only by interpreting the faith which it has received in the light of its present experience."[110] Christian belief, then, is really an activity rather than a set of perennial propositions. The question we must ask is where to find the "points of reference" for this activity. The creeds represent one possibility. But even if we grant that they are summaries of the essentials of the Christian faith, "we must now ask whether the 'essentials' of the faith are in fact those areas of Christian doctrine in which the Church's contemporary believing most needs guidance. To put the question somewhat crudely: quite apart from the question of their truth, do the creeds have the right Christian priorities?"[111] Discovering the "essence" of Christianity is as problematic as defining what points are necessary for salvation. The creeds of themselves are not sufficient as a point of reference for our believing. For example, for Lutherans justification by faith is central to their understanding of Christianity, and yet this doctrine "is not present, even by implication, in the creeds." As well, "the doctrinal questions which agitate the churches today are not necessarily — indeed are not often — the ones which fall within the range of topics covered by the creeds."[112] Consequently, we must go beyond the creeds to the source of their authority in scripture.[113]

Locating final doctrinal authority in scripture obliges us to ask "how it is that Scripture possesses this overriding authority in the Church and how it is exercised." Its books do not lend themselves as a basis from which doctrinal propositions may be deduced, and this is because scripture's "most characteristic mode of writing is that of narrative."[114] We can take a step further by asking whether believing is really best understood as accepting doctrinal propositions. Worship, daily living, and evangelism are all ways of believing; but all three depend more upon "story" than upon propositions. The liturgy reenacts the biblical story so that we can participate in it. Our daily living models itself on the story of Jesus. Evangelism involves "telling the Christian story."[115] Granted this conclusion, we must ask whether the story is true. We must begin by insisting that "the Christian story is historically true." This need not mean accepting scripture at face value. But it does mean that "we shall claim that the story of Jesus, as related in the gospels, is a true story in the sense that the principal events comprised in it really happened. We shall be ready, of course, to admit certain qualifications to this claim."[116] But the distortions, uncertainties, and legendary aspects of our sources are no different from those that attach to sources for other ancient figures. We can be sure that "Jesus lived and died much as the gospels say he did." But there is a second sense in which the story is true. "*War and Peace* is a 'true' novel" because as a whole it "is true to experience, true to human nature." Moreover, the New Testament narrative includes the hero's teaching, "and the truth of this teaching will contribute to the general truth of the story." There would be other ways of claiming the story is true, but it will be evident that its historical truth, while necessary in the sense that it cannot contradict our interpretations, is not sufficient for discerning the full truth of the story.

The next question is why we should regard *this* story as authoritative for us. It is tempting to answer the question by appealing to doctrines of inspiration and revelation. We need not rule out such attempts, but they involve great theoretical difficulties. Part of the problem is that the terms are too broad. Harvey implies that we need not restrict inspiration and revelation to the Bible. He suggests that "it is possible to answer the question why Scripture is authoritative in a simpler and more pragmatic way."[117] His analogy is the U.S. Constitution, a written document that "won the assent of the American people," an assent the nation has never repudiated. What he seems to imply is that the Constitution establishes the conditions that make the American "story" possible. It is, then, the assent of Christians to scripture that makes it the authoritative point of reference for Christian believing. The prime authority of scripture springs from the fact that "all other sources of authority in the Church are ultimately dependent upon it." Any attempt to deny the authority of scripture "would end up denying the possibility of any authority in the Church whatever, indeed, it is hard to see how the Church could continue to exist as an identifiable community."[118] Though Harvey does not pursue his analogy of the U.S. Constitution, his conclusion is clearly that our nation continues to exist only by attending to the Constitution and that in the same way the church continues only by attending to scripture. In both cases the "attending" requires interpretation and adaptation.

In part attending to scripture means making doctrinal affirmations, but the question to ask in this context is not whether a doctrine is true, but what it means. To use an example of my own, the issue is not whether we claim that Christ is divine but what we should mean by saying so. At another level many Christians are concerned with attending to scripture in order to discover "authoritative statements" concerning "some of the questions which are being most keenly debated at the present time." That is, while the basic function of scripture is to create a story-formed community, it inevitably is obliged to take on the role of an arbiter of religious controversy. For example, discussions about "the ethics of homosexual behavior" or "the alleged 'politicizing' of the gospel" imply that "there must surely be some standard of what is and is not 'Christian' by which different opinions can be assessed." It is easy to understand why people might suppose that this standard is a doctrinal one or at least could be articulated in the form of some doctrinal statement. "But again, any such statement will prove elusive."[119] Different "parties to the discussion, though they all recognize the authority of Scripture and (often to a lesser extent) the tradition of the Church, nevertheless each regard a different passage of Scripture or aspect of the tradition as carrying decisive weight with regard to the question at issue."[120]

Harvey does not want to regard this conclusion as a negative one, even though he realizes that it raises the question of the authority and relevance of scripture. But he argues that what counts for Christians is "the earnestness and integrity with which they seek the truth rather than their ability to agree on a series of doctrinal propositions." What matters is a corporate wrestling with the meaning of the Christian story as found in scripture. Harvey might have pursued his analogy of the Constitution a little further. We could say that the Supreme Court interprets the Constitution not primarily as a historical document but as a basic point of reference for deciding points of law. Their decisions have not always been correct. For example, in the last half of the nineteenth century Supreme Court decisions basically undermined the amendments to the Constitution that guaranteed rights for former slaves after the Civil War. Yet in the second half of the twentieth century the Court corrected itself. It looks as though the mysterious mind of the American people is the final arbiter. Similarly, one could argue that judgments made by bishops and church synods are genuine attempts to apply scripture to our contemporary concerns, but that the final word rests with the mind of the church, which sometimes overturns those judgments.

Conclusion

It is easy enough to see that these discussions in the twentieth century represent a tension between two sets of convictions. On the one hand, no one wants to abandon the idea that Christianity is somehow a historical religion. The doctrine of the incarnation, and even the views proposed as a substitute for it, insist upon the full humanity of Christ together with what most would regard as a unique claim about him. We cannot sever the Christ of faith from the Jesus of history. On the other hand, few of the writers I have examined want to reduce Christian faith to merely historical reconstructions. What I find attractive about Harvey's view is its concern to reestablish the biblical narrative and to see it as capable of examination in two rather different ways. His position has a way of taking quite seriously the historical-critical method but at the same time putting it in its proper place. If we are to think of "story" or narrative, we can think, as I have suggested, of the analogy of interpreting Shakespeare's plays. There was a time when literary criticism concerned itself with establishing the text, the sources, and the topical allusions found in the plays. All this remains important, and some of the conclusions can actually help us to understand the plays. But surely interpreting Shakespeare is more than a historical enterprise. So, too, the truth of scripture must involve its grounding in historical events but clearly must be understood in terms of what those events mean to believing Christians. Next, thinking of scripture and of the Christian life in narrative terms is true to our experience. If scripture is to live it must be constantly reinterpreted and adapted to our changing experience. Finally, I am attracted to his reluctance to close debate on the meaning of scripture. Doing so runs the risk of turning scripture into a mouthpiece for our own ideologies. Fortunately, scripture is, as Sir Thomas Browne said, "too hard for the teeth of time." It has a way of overruling our best efforts to master it.

Chapter Six

An Inconclusive Conclusion

It is difficult to draw any firm conclusion from the samples of Anglican attitudes toward the Bible that have been discussed, and I have sought to present a highly confused picture not out of sheer perversity, but because I have become increasingly convinced that it is difficult to speak of a single Anglican view of scripture or of a single Anglican theological perspective. Those writers who are Anglicans in terms of Anglicanism's origin in the sixteenth century tend to emphasize its Protestant character, especially as that is reflected in the Articles of Religion and the Homilies. Bishop Hall is probably closest to the Puritan construal of the Elizabethan settlement, though even Hooker, despite his emphasis upon the church and its sacraments, needs in my view to be seen as an Elizabethan Protestant. Wesley and the other evangelicals of the eighteenth century seek to revive in a modified form a sixteenth-century Anglicanism with its emphasis upon justification by faith. And they do so in reaction to the latitudinarian views of their time, views that have some rooting in Chillingworth's safe Protestant way to salvation. On the other hand, in quite differing ways writers like Maurice, Newman, and Gore shift attention to Christ and the church. Looked at more narrowly, the Oxford Movement quite consciously appeals to the seventeenth century and Restoration Anglicanism. There would be other ways of describing the diversity. Paul Avis speaks of the transition from an Erastian paradigm to an apostolic one. And we could trace tendencies that lead to the description of parties within Anglicanism in the twentieth century as low, broad, and high.

No matter how we describe this theological diversity, in one way or another it represents differing understandings of scripture. Sometimes the Bible occupies a central and primary place, while in other quarters it functions in relation to nature or history. And I have suggested that many of the concepts that appear repeatedly in what people say are highly ambiguous. Reason can mean a number of different things, as can inspiration, revelation, nature, and history. Yet scripture somehow remains in place throughout despite the possible necessity of qualifying this judgment in cases like that of Newman in the nineteenth and Hick in the twentieth century. At the same time there always seems to be a search for a central feature of scripture that will assist us in coming to terms with the whole. The various theologies correlate with this attempt to locate the core of scripture, whether we are to think of what is necessary for salvation or of what is the essence of Christianity and of the Bible.[1] Even those like Wesley who tend to insist upon the whole Bible are in fact giving priority to an aspect of scripture.

The paradox that all read scripture and yet do so in quite differing ways is not surprising or necessarily threatening to the integrity of Christianity in general or of Anglicanism in particular. As I have suggested in the foreword, I should wish to repudiate any notion of *the* correct doctrine or of *the* correct reading of scripture. My analogy there was that of literary criticism, where we can certainly speak of incorrect interpretations of a poem, but must also recognize a range of valid interpretations which have at least the possibility of being complementary. The question becomes, then, not how we are to find the correct reading of scripture, but how we are to determine the limits of validity. Such a view, of course, repudiates Jowett's conviction that there can be only a single original meaning in scripture. And it is of interest to note in passing that the same "one meaning" approach is also characteristic of fundamentalism. But there remains the complex question of how we are to determine the validity of multiple meanings. I do not think there is any easy answer to the question and the many issues involved in it. Nevertheless, my inconclusive suggestion is that we first need a framework in which to consider the question. One such framework that attracts me is that supplied by Coleridge in his *Confessions of an Inquiring Spirit*.

Samuel Taylor Coleridge (1772–1834) comes to much the same view as found in F. D. Maurice's writings, and it is certainly possible to trace Coleridge's influence on Maurice. Both of them reject the idea of verbal inerrancy that dominated their time, and both seek to place scripture in dialogue with the church. Moreover, both are concerned with seeing the Bible as the revelation of a living God rather than as a set of propositions and rules. Coleridge, however, gives us a basic pattern or framework in which to think about scripture and its place in Christian belief and practice. In 1825 he published his *Aids to Reflection* and at the same time planned six "Disquisitions Supplemental of the Aids to Reflection."[2] Only one of these was eventually published — in 1840 six years after Coleridge's death. *Confessions of an Inquiring Spirit* is entirely concerned with the Bible; and even though Coleridge depends in many respects upon German thinkers, especially Lessing, his own views dominate and transform German idealism.

Coleridge toyed with the possibility of becoming a Unitarian minister early in his career, and he does not seem to have become an Anglican in any official way. But when he turned his attention from poetry to philosophy, he became increasingly preoccupied with religious questions. He is not easy to read because he is far from systematic and comes across to the reader as someone talking in a stream of consciousness fashion. He describes his *Confessions* as seven letters to a friend "concerning the bounds between the right, and the superstitious use and estimation of the Sacred Canon." The letters represent Coleridge's "own private judgment" regarding two questions. The first question is whether it is "necessary, or expedient, to insist on the belief of the divine origin and authority of all, and every part of the Canonical Books as the condition, or first principle, of Christian Faith." The second question implies an answer, since Coleridge says, "May not the due appreciation of the Scriptures collectively be more safely relied on as the result and consequence of the belief in Christ, the gradual increase — in respect of particular passages — of our spiritual discernment of their truth and authority supplying a test and measure of our own growth and progress as individual believers, without the servile fear that prevents or over-clouds the free honour which cometh from love?"[3] The last phrase is an allusion to 1 John 4:18. Let me begin with the view he opposes and then turn to the positive pattern he advocates in his "Pentad of Operative Christianity."

Put as simply as possible, Coleridge repudiates the notion that the scriptures are verbally inerrant. He sees this idea as "the Doctrine which the generality of our popular Divines receive as orthodox."[4] It treats the biblical writers as "divinely informed as well as inspired," reproducing God's oracles without contributing anything of their own to the task. Scripture is thought to be "dictated by an Infal-lible Intelligence."[5] Thinking of Deborah and the heroes of the Old Testament, Coleridge puts his objection in purple prose:

> But let me once be persuaded that all these heart-awakening ut-terances of human hearts — of men of like faculties and passions with myself, mourning, rejoicing, suffering, triumphing — are but as a *Divina Commedia* of a superhuman — Oh bear with me if I say — Ventriloquist; — that the royal Harper, to whom I have so often submitted myself as a *many-stringed instrument* for his fire-tipt fingers to traverse... that this *sweet Psalmist of Israel* was himself as mere an instrument as his harp, an *automaton* poet, mourner, and supplicant; — all is gone, — all sympathy, at least, and all example. I listen in awe and fear, but likewise in perplexity and confusion of spirit.[6]

Coleridge's reason for rejecting verbal inerrancy has little if anything to do with historical considerations, however much it makes room for them.[7] Instead, his chief motive lies in his conviction that the "or-thodox" understanding removes the human element from scripture and stifles the various voices. It "petrifies" scripture and turns the Bible's "glorious *panharmonicon*" into "a colossal Memnon's head, a hollow passage for a voice, a voice that mocks the voices of many men, and speaks in their names."[8]

The error of verbal inerrancy is its failure to distinguish the re-vealing Word from the inspiring Spirit, that is, revelation from its apprehension. The first is infallible, but not the second. "For how can absolute infallibility be blended with fallibility? Where is the infallible criterion? How can infallible truth be infallibly conveyed in defective and fallible expressions?"[9] Coleridge can call the failure to make this distinction "Bibliolatry."[10] The idea that an infallible revelation takes place through the fallible writers of scripture correlates with Coleridge's treatment of miracles. He argues that his "orthodox" opponents are following "the Hebrew Doctors" by attributing "all excellent or extraordinary things to the great First Cause, without mention of the proximate and instrumental causes." In doing so, they fail to make a distinction between the providential and the miraculous.[11] Such a distinction "between the divine Will working with the agency of natural causes, and the same Will supplying their place by a special *fiat*" may have a use in "speculative divinity." But Coleridge is not happy with it and supposes that the "weightiest practical application" of the distinction is "to free the souls of the unwary and weak in faith from the nets and snares...of the Infidel by calming the flutter of their spirits."[12]

> Put as simply as possible, Coleridge repudiates the notion that the scriptures are verbally inerrant.

Coleridge sees quite clearly the counterargument Protestants might make against his view. What about discrepancies and contradictions in scripture? Their doctrine explains them by harmonization of one kind or another. Coleridge dismisses the objection by pointing out that the problem is "so analogous to what is found in all other known and trusted histories by contemporary historians...as to form in the eyes of all competent judges a characteristic mark of the genuineness, independency, and...the veraciousness of each several document." No one wise would "care a straw" whether the discrepancies were "real or apparent, reconciled or left in harmless and friendly variance."[13] At a deeper level the usual motives for insisting upon verbal inerrancy revolve around the Bible as the single unifying agent in Protestantism. People argue from "the anticipated loss and damage" that would be the result of abandoning the conviction of verbal inerrancy. Doing so "would deprive the Christian world of its only infallible arbiter in questions of Faith and Duty, suppress the only common and inappellable tribunal." As well, it would eliminate the Bible as "the only religious bond of union and ground of unity among Protestants." Coleridge confutes "this whole reasoning" by asking a simple question that he thinks is sufficient. "Has it [the Bible] produced these effects?"[14] The Protestant view assumes that scripture contains all things necessary to salvation and that the simplest reader will be able to discern them. Coleridge is willing to agree with the first part of this assumption, but also wants to assert that "besides these express oracles and immediate revelations, there are Scriptures which to the soul and conscience of every Christian man bear irresistible evidence of the Divine Spirit assisting and actuating the authors."[15] The second part of the Protestant assumption is that what is necessary to salvation is perspicuous in scripture. But Coleridge points out that this is not really so. Instead, each individual "unaided by note or comment, catechism or liturgical preparation" will find "*his* religion. For he has found it in his Bible, and the Bible is the Religion of Protestants!"[16]

To claim as the Protestants do that the Bible is verbally inerrant and infallible not only requires questionable feats of exegetical harmonization; it also means identifying Christianity with the Bible. Coleridge admits that the Bible is "the appointed conservatory, an indispensable criterion, and a continual source and support of true Belief." But he denies that the Bible is "the sole source, that it not only contains, but constitutes, the Christian Religion." Moreover, the Bible is not a Creed, "consisting wholly of articles of Faith" so that "we need no rule, help, or guide, spiritual or historical, to teach us what parts are and what are not articles of Faith." This reading of the creed into the Bible "differs widely from the preceding [scheme], though its adherents often make use of the same words in expressing their belief."[17] What Coleridge means is that even those Protestants who argue for the creed as a key to what is necessary for salvation in scripture actually end up in the same position as those that insist upon the Bible and only the Bible. In contrast, Coleridge wants to insist that the Bible must be "taken in connection with the institution and perpetuity of a visible Church."[18] Christ himself "in the establishment of a visible Church" provided "oral and catechismal instruction" as a preparation for reading the Bible. As St. Paul says, faith comes by hearing (Rom 10:8, 17) and not by "a barren acquiescence in the letter." The written word "preserved in the armoury of the Church" is meant to be "the sword of faith *out of the mouth* of the preacher, as Christ's ambassador and representative (Rev. 1.16), and out of the heart of the believer, from generation to generation."[19]

We can already see Coleridge's positive view emerging in his polemic against the common Protestant view. He outlines that view in "The Pentad of Operative Christianity." The Pentad is a diagram in three lines. The first line consists only of "Christ, the Word" as the *Prothesis*. The second line has three members — "The Scriptures" as the *Thesis* to the left, "The Church" as the *Antithesis* to the right, and "The Holy Spirit" as the *Mesothesis,* or the Indifference, in the middle. "The Preacher" as the *Synthesis* occupies the third line. Coleridge explains his diagram as follows:

> The Scriptures, the Spirit, and the Church are co-ordinate; the indispensable conditions and the working causes of the perpetuity, and continued renascence and spiritual life of Christ still militant. The Eternal Word, Christ from ever-lasting, is the *Prothesis,* or identity; — the Scriptures and the Church are the two poles, or *Thesis* and *Antithesis,* and the Preacher in direct line under the Spirit but likewise the point of junction of the Written Word and the Church, is the *Synthesis*. This is God's Hand in the World.[20]

The diagram, then, represents a dynamic. Christ, the Word, is the revelation mediated through scripture and the church, which are correlative and bound together by the Holy Spirit. The mediated revelation, or better, the apprehensions of the revelation find their articulation in the preacher's work.

In a sense, Coleridge's framework demystifies the Bible; at least it treats both scripture and the church as means rather than ends in themselves. For this reason he can say in several places that it is possible to read the Bible like any other book and yet find it unlike, thus anticipating Jowett's argument:

> This I believe by my own experience, — that the more tranquilly an inquirer takes up the Bible as he would any other body of ancient writings, the livelier and steadier will be his impressions of its superiority to all other books, till at length all other books and all other knowledge will be valuable in his eyes in proportion as they help him to a better understanding of his Bible.[21]

Coleridge is not thinking of finding some correct interpretation. Instead, he understands reading scripture as a journey toward the incomprehensible goal of its apprehensions. Scripture is like the sun, while his reason is like the moon. And yet "the sun endures the occasional co-presence of the unsteady orb, and leaving it visible seems to sanction the comparison." But there is "a Light higher than all, even *the Word that was in the beginning;* — the Light, of which light itself is but the *shechinah* and cloudy tabernacle." Reading scripture, then, is the gradual discovery of aspects of that true light. "I have found words for my inmost thoughts, songs for my joy, utterances for my hidden griefs, and pleadings for my shame and my feebleness." Still more, scripture discovers its reader. "In short whatever *finds* me, bears witness for itself, that it has proceeded from a Holy Spirit, even from the same Spirit, *which remains in itself, yet regenerateth all other powers, and in all ages entering into holy souls maketh them friends of God, and prophets.* (Wisd. vii)"[22] Coleridge's conviction is that it is not so much he that finds scripture, as it is scripture that finds him.

Coleridge concludes the reflections I have just cited by saying that "here, perhaps, I might have been content to rest if I had not learned that, as a Christian, I cannot — must not — stand alone." The hierarchy of the Word, scripture, and the preacher or reader of scripture includes the correlation of scripture and the community of the church, and all is under the guidance of the Holy Spirit. It is in his discussions of the church that history enters the picture. Coleridge identifies his own faith with "the creed, or system of *credenda,* common to all the Fathers of the Reformation — overlooking, as non-essential, the differences between the several Reformed Churches."[23] This "creed" has five points, the third of which looks in part like a telling of the Christian story. Creation, the Fall, and redemption are followed in Coleridge's list by the incarnation, the crucifixion and resurrection, and "the Descent of the Comforter." The rest of the list applies salvation to the believer — repentance, regeneration, faith, prayer, grace, communion with the Spirit, conflict, self-abasement, "Assurance through the righteousness of Christ," spiritual growth, love, discipline, perseverance, and hope in death. This third section is preceded by belief in the "Absolute," the "Triune God," and by "The Eternal Possibilities," which appear to be those of salvation and damnation.

The most interesting sections of the "creed" are the last two. The fourth refers to repentance and the other things concerning salvation Coleridge has listed in section three, and it treats them as "offers, gifts, and graces... offered to all." Thus, they are offered to the individual "as to one of a great Household." Indeed, the entire creation is included both in the Fall and in redemption. Christianity, which is "no less than truth," is "spiritual, yet so as to be historical; and between these two poles there must likewise be a midpoint, in which the historical and spiritual meet." Coleridge's meaning in the fifth section of the "creed" is not exactly pellucid, but he appears to suggest some correlation of the historical and corporate aspect of Christianity with the church, and of the spiritual and individual aspect with scripture. I suspect this oversimplifies what he is trying to say, but it is instructive that he places the church before scripture. He makes his point more clearly later on. "Indeed, with regard to both Testaments, I consider oral and catechismal instruction as the preparative provided by

Christ himself in the establishment of a visible Church."[24] This priority of the church, however, does not make scripture subservient to it. Joseph's dream in which his brothers' sheaves of wheat bow down to his sheaf (Gen 37:6–7) makes the point. Joseph's sheaf is the Bible, and it "had *obeisance* from all the other sheaves — (the writings, I mean, of the Fathers and Doctors of the Church)... yet sheaves of the same harvest, the sheaves of brethren."[25]

Thus, Coleridge wishes to maintain the dialectic between church and scripture, and the apparent priority of the church is meant only as a way of introducing new believers to that dialectic. "First, let their attention be fixed on the history of Christianity as learnt from universal tradition." Then they must "meditate on the universals of Christian faith," as it is indicated by the references of Irenaeus and St. Augustine, and as it is "determined and explicated, but not augmented by the Nicene Fathers." The reading of scripture then follows.[26] In the long run, however, "in the Scriptures... there is proved to us the reciprocity, or reciprocation, of the Spirit as subjective and objective." The passage in Coleridge's letter is extremely dense, but what he appears to mean, with a nod toward German idealism, is that "Religion has its objective, or historic and ecclesiastical pole, and its subjective, or spiritual and individual pole." To read scripture apart from the church, then, runs the risk of a purely subjective and individualistic reading. But to read scripture as a member of the church overcomes or synthesizes the opposition of subjective and objective; and it preserves the dialectic between the church and scripture. All this is possible by the work of the Spirit.[27]

There are certainly complexities and obscurities in Coleridge's attempt to explain his Pentad, but the basic structure of the framework is reasonably clear. Moreover, the structure need by no means be confined to Anglicanism. In the previous chapters I have said little about the links that bind Anglican divines to other Christian churches. I found this necessary in order to avoid traveling down side paths that might still more obscure the main lines of my discussion. But it will be obvious that the English Reformers owed much initially to Luther and then to the Swiss Reformers, including Bullinger and Bucer as well as Calvin. In the seventeenth century one could trace the influence of Descartes, and by the nineteenth century that of German thought. These are, of course, only a few examples among many. In what follows I want to reflect on Coleridge's Pentad without limiting my consideration to Anglicanism and by seeking to attend to the present state of affairs with respect to scripture. I shall start with the Bible in order to ask how it can be brought into dialogue with the church, and then turn to the church in order to raise the same question. My reflections will be no more than that, even though they will be designed to support Coleridge's framework. But it is obvious that there would be many other ways of reflecting within that framework. It is in this sense that my thoughts are inconclusive conclusions. My reason for beginning with the Bible rather than with the church, as Coleridge's view might suggest, has to do with focusing attention on the problematic character of historical criticism for the church.

The Bible: Historical Criticism

If, as Coleridge, Maurice, and Jowett say, we can and even should read the Bible as we would any other book, will we find in each of its passages a single meaning — as Jowett at least argues? It would seem obvious that this is not so. If the other books are histories or biographies, it is plain enough that there can be differing interpretations of the same evidence. For example, many biographies of the American Founding Fathers have appeared in recent years; but they have widely differing assessments of Washington, Adams, Jefferson, Franklin, and others. Or, if we are to think of the other books as works of literature, surely we cannot speak of single interpretations. The Olivier production of Shakespeare's *Henry V* appeared against the background of the Second World War. The "band of brothers" at Agincourt served to bolster patriotism and the cause of the right vindicated by war. Other performances of the play have treated it as a polemic against war that is designed to underline its folly. Finding a single meaning in the books we read or in the Bible is an enterprise doomed to failure. But we can also ask whether Jowett is correct to suppose that reading scripture like any other book will lead us to see that it is unlike all other books. One may be forgiven for doubting that this is so on the grounds that much of historical criticism by no means leads to Jowett's conviction.

Therefore, one of the issues raised for us is whether this sort of study of scripture can make any contribution to the church. One small example of the problem may be found in Raymond Brown's widely used *An Introduction to the New Testament*. Brown's answer seems to be "yes" for himself, but not necessarily for all his readers. In his foreword he envisages a wide audience, which would include not only people of religions other than Christianity, but also people who are merely interested in the New Testament. His introduction is meant to be useful to "readers who take New Testament beginning courses on different levels (e.g. Bible study groups, religious education, college surveys, and initial seminary classes)."[28] Preachers are conspicuous by their absence, but perhaps Brown does not suppose that his book will be of no use to them. Brown laments the fact that some scholars "argue that it is hermeneutically irrelevant whether what is narrated in the Gospels ever happened," and he insists that "Christianity is too fundamentally based on what Jesus actually said and did to be cavalier about historicity."[29] He is surely correct, and it is obvious that he regards his critical work as the contribution to the churches that it is. Nevertheless, one begins to suspect that there are at least hints of what could be regarded as the captivity of the Bible by the academy. Brown appears to leave open questions regarding inspiration and revelation, but at the end of chapter 2 he points out (or warns) that at times he will ask his readers "to reflect on issues pertinent to New Testament books that go beyond the literal sense."[30] His aim is not to decide "the disputed issues," but to "clarify the subsequent differences" and "help to defuse judgments about whose view is truly biblical." It is impossible to find fault with what Brown says, granted the audience he envisages. But it seems possible to draw the conclusion that while he himself believes that historical criticism serves the cause of Christianity and the church, he recognizes that not everyone will hold this conviction.

If we can assume that historical criticism has at least the possibility of contributing to the church's (or a church's) understanding of scripture, we need to ask how this is so. The clearest answer is that it can clarify so far as possible the text of scripture. Most people may realize that our English Bibles are translations of the original Hebrew and Greek, but few have any good idea about what this really means. Textual problems are not a major difficulty for the Old Testament because of the care with which the Masoretic (traditional) text has been preserved. Nevertheless, the discovery of the Dead Sea Scrolls has revealed that there were once other text types, and this may mean that the Septuagint's Greek translation does not always presuppose the Masoretic text. Perhaps more important, there are many passages in the Hebrew Bible that are intelligible only because of a long tradition of interpretation. The English reader can discern this by comparing several modern translations of the Psalms or of Job. The same texts are translated in significantly varying ways. The textual problems in the New Testament are complex largely because of the abundance of the manuscript tradition. The critical Greek text commonly used is not based upon any single manuscript, and the notes in the NRSV alert the reader to variant readings when they say "other ancient authorities read. . . . " Apart from anything else this lower criticism makes any notion of verbal inerrancy difficult if not impossible. The contribution, of course, is in a sense negative. It prevents Christians from easily identifying interpretive translations with the text itself, and it ought to prevent them from changing the words even of such interpretive renderings to suit their fancy.

A more positive contribution of historical criticism may be found in ways by which the biblical accounts may be correlated with external evidence. Scholars have accomplished much by using Near Eastern evidence to establish at least a rough chronology for the history of Israel and Judah in the Assyrian and Babylonian periods. The biblical narrative can be located in the wider context of the ancient Near East. For the New Testament the reference in Acts 18:12 to Gallio as proconsul of Achaia can be correlated with an inscription dating Gallio's tenure of office to 51–52 CE, thus providing a key to Pauline chronology. There are a number of other examples that might be used. Moreover, despite very real difficulties in imagining the ancient world we do know a good deal about the Roman Empire in which Christianity first emerged. Sometimes the attempts to reconstruct the early Christian communities appear to forget this. Historical criticism, then, while it can say nothing about revelation, can supply a better understanding of the contexts in which it is thought to have appeared than we might discover from the biblical text taken by itself.

The three methods commonly used by biblical critics are somewhat more problematic, but they must certainly be taken into account. Source criticism of the Old Testament, for example, has concluded that at least four traditions (if not documents) have been combined in the Pentateuch — J, E, D, and P. This helps explain why there sometimes seem to be two versions of a single story, for example, the creation narratives in Genesis 1–2 and indications of different sources in the narrative of Noah's flood. On the other hand, breaking the text into its various sources may make it difficult to interpret the text as it stands. We should not suppose that those who put our text together failed to see the difficulties or thought that the sources were incompatible. Similarly, in the New Testament the usual solution of the relation of the first three Gospels to one another in terms of literary dependence (the synoptic problem) is to regard Mark as the earliest Gospel, to argue that Matthew and Luke copied and adapted Mark independently of one another, and to treat the passages that they have in common but are not to be found in Mark as the use of a common hypothetical source that has been labeled Q. Scholars also recognize that there are materials peculiar to Matthew and Luke. Of course, this set of conclusions cannot be demonstrated in an absolute way; and not all scholars would agree with the usual reconstruction, which owes much to Sanday's seminar on the synoptic Gospels. We must remember that the only effective evidence we have is found in the first three Gospels themselves, even though we may take account of the sayings of Jesus preserved in John and outside the canon in later writings such as the Gospel of Thomas. More interesting than the solution to the synoptic problem itself is the contribution made to interpretation represented by a careful comparison of all four Gospels. Such study enables us to discern the differing emphases and interpretations of the canonical Gospels.

The second method is called form criticism, and it depends upon the observation that the Bible often uses earlier traditional material to make new points. For example, Genesis 22 tells the story of Abraham's sacrifice of Isaac, including the substitution of the ram caught in the thicket for Isaac. If the story (the "form") is taken out of its present context, it is possible to argue that it might once have had a different function. It might have represented a warrant for the substitution of animal for human sacrifice, or it might have served as a story locating the site of the Temple, Mount Moriah, in the patriarchal epoch. In the narrative as it stands, however, the story illustrates Abraham's radical obedience to God. Similarly in the New Testament scholars began to see that the discovery that Mark was the oldest Gospel by no means meant they had found the bedrock of history. One peculiarity of Mark is the so-called messianic secret. Jesus repeatedly tries to keep his identity a secret. We can put the point more clearly by noting that Mark employs the literary device of dramatic irony. Just as in Sophocles' *Oedipus Rex,* the impact of the narrative depends upon the fact that the audience knows who the hero is and what will happen, while the people in the narrative do not. Those who heard Mark's Gospel already knew the story and were aware of Jesus' identity, but the people in the story, especially the disciples, are in ignorance. Even when Jesus tells the disciples that he must die and be raised, they do not understand that this pattern must also be theirs. Only the demons know who Jesus is, but we can presume that they are not to be trusted. The identity of Jesus, pronounced in the first verse of the Gospel, is revealed only at the moment of Jesus' death, when the veil of the Temple is torn in two from top to bottom and when the Roman centurion pronounces the judgment, "Truly, this was the Son of God." It becomes obvious that Mark is an interpreter of the traditions available to him and not a biographer in our sense of the word.

The form critics, then, seek to isolate the earlier traditions from Mark's interpretive framework. A clear example of how this can be done appears in the five stories Mark tells early in the Gospel in order to display Jesus in conflict with the scribes and Pharisees (Mark 2:1– 3:6). The charges made against him by his enemies are, in order: blasphemy, violating the rules of table fellowship, refusing to fast, working on the sabbath, and healing on the sabbath. But this is a very peculiar order. Why is the most serious charge placed first and the most problematic one last? When we examine the *way* the charges are expressed, we can see how Mark has ordered the material. To begin with, the objection is no more than an unexpressed thought. Next, the objection is made as a polite question, first to the disciples and then to Jesus himself. Then the objection is made openly to Jesus himself, but it takes the form of a criticism of the disciples' plucking of grain on the sabbath. Finally, the objection becomes a plot to put Jesus to death. Mark's point has little to do with the various objections; his concern is to describe mounting opposition to Jesus and to foreshadow the end of the entire story. The form critics, then, seek to isolate the individual stories in order to understand how they might have functioned in an earlier tradition with a view to reconstructing the character of the earliest Christian communities if not the teaching of Jesus himself.

The conclusions of form criticism, however, proved less conclusive than one might have hoped and tended to fall short of their aim. Consequently, a third method began to be employed. Redaction criticism focuses not on the earlier traditional material but on the interpretive framework in which they now appear. The idea seems to be that if we can clarify our understanding of the perspectives of the four Gospels, we can more confidently distinguish the earlier traditions from their contexts in the Gospels. That is, redaction criticism on this view becomes a preliminary step designed to make form criticism more fully possible and convincing. So far the methods aim at historical reconstructions, and it is difficult to see how any of them could settle the question of Jesus' significance for the church. To be sure, Christians must take the methods seriously; and they often do illuminate the text. But their larger conclusions do not really yield the interpretations that would prove helpful to the church. To repeat an analogy I have used earlier, interpreting Shakespeare's plays requires a knowledge of the textual problems, the sources used by Shakespeare, topical allusions, the meaning of words in the early seventeenth century, and so on. But none of this does the job of interpreting the plays individually or of suggesting a larger view of Shakespeare's dominant themes.

Perhaps one example from John's Gospel will help explain what I mean. The first of his resurrection stories tells how Peter and "the other disciple," upon hearing Mary Magdalene's news, run together to Jesus' tomb. When they get there, they see the grave clothes. The other disciple follows Peter into the tomb, "and he saw and believed; for as yet they did not understand the scripture, that he must rise from the dead" (John 20:8–9). How very peculiar! Why does the text not say, "the other disciple believed because he *remembered* the scripture"? Form criticism might conclude that behind John's narrative there is an older story of Peter finding the empty tomb, but reacting not by belief in the resurrection but by perplexity at what he had seen. But this does not explain the text as we have it. Redaction criticism might conclude that the other disciple's faith in the risen Lord is based not upon scripture but upon his love of Jesus. Thus, I should want to argue, the real value of redaction criticism lies in the fact that it can supply a literary and theological interpretation of each Gospel as we find it. Such an interpretation of the individual books in scripture can then contribute to a larger interpretation of scripture as a whole. By analogy the literary interpretations of Shakespeare's individual plays point toward larger interpretations of Shakespeare's work as a whole.

As I have implied, I think the most problematic aspect of historical criticism revolves around the larger historical reconstructions the critics have supplied. I am exaggerating, but it has seemed to me that the historical reconstructions of the earliest Christian communities bear the same sort of relation to the text as the ancient gnostic systems. They cannot be demonstrated with total confidence, but they become the presupposed key to interpreting the meaning of the text. I think particularly of reconstructions based upon the Gospels and oriented toward the quest for the historical Jesus. In 1926 Sir Edwyn

Hoskyns contributed an essay to *Essays Catholic and Critical* entitled "The Christ of the Synoptic Gospels." Much of what he says seems persuasive to me almost eighty years later. His concern is not to dispense with historical criticism, but to use it in the service of the church. He begins by arguing that the questions *"What think ye of the Church?"* and *"What think ye of the Christ?"* are "the same question differently formulated." But he recognizes that equating the two questions "raises a historical problem as delicate as it is important." The problem, of course, is "Lessing's gap" between the Jesus of history and the Christ of faith. Hoskyns also points out that the sharp disagreements of the historical critics mean that there can be "little surprise if the intelligent observer grows sceptical of the ability of the historian to reach conclusions in any way satisfactory."[31] He is right to argue that we must always remember that historical reconstructions are always probable in character. To take one example, the assassination of John Kennedy in Dallas took place before hundreds of witnesses, and the evidence even includes a filming of the event. And yet we cannot be entirely sure of what exactly happened. In the ancient world the evidence is far more scanty and hard to assess, so why should we be surprised that our reconstructions must be tentative and hypothetical?

Hoskyns begins the major part of his essay by describing what he calls "the liberal Protestant solution." Jesus was a Jewish prophet, "inspired by the Spirit of God at his baptism by John, and called to reform the religion of the Jews." As a true Jew and a prophet Jesus taught that "union with God and the brotherhood of men depend upon righteousness and purity of heart." This teaching appears in the Sermon on the Mount and in his parables; and his miracles of healing "were the material expression of the power of the spiritual over the material." Admittedly, Jesus used the eschatological language common in the Judaism of his time; but his "essential Gospel is not to be found in the eschatological speeches, but in the Sermon on the Mount, and in the parables of the Sower, the Prodigal Son and the Good Samaritan." We cannot know whether he claimed to be the Messiah, but "one negative conclusion may be regarded as certain. He did not claim to possess a divine nature." The crucifixion was "the greatest of all human tragedies," but the "divinely inspired ethical humanitarianism" he taught in order to reform Judaism could not be "permanently confined." Jesus "foresaw no formal mission; he founded no Church to propagate his ideals; he left them to grow and expand in the hearts of those who had heard him, conversed with him, and lived under the influence of his personality." The resurrection experiences of the disciples unfortunately led them to preach Jesus rather than his message. "Thus, Christianity became a mystery religion which tended increasingly to express its doctrines in terms of Greek philosophy." The liberal Protestant judgment is that this historical reconstruction reflects "the skill and honesty of the historian," but its real contribution is to supply a basis "for a new reformation of the Christian religion, capable of ensuring its survival in the modern world."[32]

Needless to say, Hoskyns's aim is to call into question this reconstruction, which has also affected Catholic Modernism. In what may seem a somewhat chauvinistic fashion, he points out that English theologians, "trained in the study of the Classics, and accustomed to an exacting standard of scholarly accuracy, have looked with suspicion on such popular accounts of Christian origins." This "learned conservatism" has resulted in major contributions to the study of the text of the New Testament, to the synoptic problem, and to the exegesis of the books of the New Testament. But the English scholars "have generally refrained from attempting any comprehensive reconstruction of the development of primitive Christianity on the basis of their exhaustive preliminary studies."[33] This state of affairs represents a challenge, and Hoskyns sees his task as one of presenting in a tentative form an alternative to the Protestant "solution." Several points represent presuppositions for his alternative reconstruction. These include the common solution of the synoptic problem, the danger of using the Fourth Gospel as historical evidence, the recognition that the Pauline epistles are the earliest surviving Christian documents, and the centrality in the synoptic Gospels of the mysterious Kingdom of God, which is "both present and future."[34] Hoskyns then argues for the importance of "carefully defined canons of historical criticism." His illustration of them revolves around the idea that later sources may contain earlier traditions, that their "corrections" of earlier material are not necessarily wrongheaded, and that only "what can easily be paralleled from human experience is historical."[35] It will become clear that Hoskyns wishes to include the experience of salvation as human and historical, however much the historian is finally unable to explain that experience.

The next step in Hoskyns's argument is to use these presuppositions and canons to test "the popular reconstruction" of the developmental stages of primitive Christianity. His general conclusion is that the reconstruction in question "is found to rest upon a series of brilliant and attractive intuitive judgments rather than upon a critical and historical examination of the data supplied by the documents." What he primarily means is the selection by those espousing the liberal Protestant solution of New Testament passages that echo their commitment to "ethical humanitarianism."[36] They regard the parable of the Prodigal Son, found only in Luke, as original "because forgiveness of sin is not complicated by any reference to the atoning death of Christ."[37] They think many of Jesus' miracles are untrustworthy; and the "supernatural is transferred to the period of growth, [while] what is human and merely moral and philanthropic and anti-ecclesiastical is assumed to be primitive and original." In contrast, Hoskyns argues that we must reckon with the possibility "that the experience of salvation through Christ, or as St. Paul calls it, Justification by Faith, rather than an ethical humanitarianism, was from the beginning the essence of the Christian religion." This could mean that "the peculiarly Christian love of God and of men followed, but did not precede, the experience of salvation by faith in Christ, and the incorporation into the body of His disciples." It is possible, then, that "not only may the supernatural element have been primitive and original, but also that exclusiveness, which is so obviously a characteristic of Catholic Christianity, may have its origin in the teaching of Jesus rather than in the theology of St. Paul."[38]

Hoskyns begins his alternative reconstruction with the "governing ideas of the Gospels" — the Kingdom of God, the humiliation of the Christ, the *via crucis,* and the new righteousness and eternal life.[39] His conclusion is that what we find underlying the synoptic tradition is "a whole series of contrasts"; and they are not the contrasts envisaged by the liberal Protestant solution. The opposition is not between the Jesus of history and the Christ of faith, "but between the Christ humiliated, and the Christ returning in glory." Nor should we contrast an unreformed with a reformed Judaism. Instead, the contrast is "between Judaism and the new supernatural order by which it is at once destroyed and fulfilled." Moreover, it is "not between an ethical teaching and a dreamy eschatology, or between a generous humanitarianism and an emotional religious experience stimulated by mythological beliefs, but between a supernatural order characterised by a radical moral purification involving persistent moral conflict and the endurance of persecution, and a supernatural order in which there is no place either for moral conflict or persecution."[40]

Hoskyns's reconstruction, then, is really a "synthesis of the contradictory elements within the Synoptic Tradition." The synthesis, of course, includes the claims of faith. But this does not mean that he supposes the historian can demonstrate the truth — or the falsity — of these claims. As he says elsewhere, the historian is obliged to state these claims, but he "is driven to lay down his pen, not because he is defeated; not because his material has proved incapable of historical treatment; but because he is now forced by his own results to judge — to believe or to disbelieve."[41] One could put the point this way with respect to one issue. The historian can say nothing one way or the other about Christ's resurrection for the simple reason that it transcends the world the historian is capable of examining. But he can draw the historical conclusion that there were certain people in the ancient world who followed Jesus and who claimed that they had encountered him alive after his death and who explained this overwhelming encounter by saying that God had raised Jesus from the dead. Hoskyns does not elaborate this point in his essay, but he does suggest that his conclusions supply a way of seeing continuity between Jesus and not only primitive Christianity but also the church down through the ages. His "purely historical investigation" yields results that "have a more than purely historical importance." What he means is that "the characteristic features of Catholic piety have their origin in our Lord's interpretation of His own Person and of the significance of His disciples for the world." In this way the "religion of the New Testament" is "a standard by which the Catholicism of succeeding generations must be tested, and which it must endeavour to maintain."[42]

It would certainly be possible to disagree with aspects of Hoskyns's argument, but he is surely correct to argue that the historical study of scripture cannot afford to neglect the religious claims made by the biblical writers. Only to the degree that those claims are taken seriously can historical criticism help the Bible to inform the church. Luke Johnson's somewhat impassioned repudiation of the conclusions reached by the "Jesus seminar" makes the point at least indirectly.[43] Johnson's major polemical aim is to argue that the Jesus seminar epitomizes "the progression toward a certain kind of madness in the obsessive use of the historical critical method."[44] His second chapter has the title "History Challenging Faith"; and in it he outlines what he regards as "constant traits" in the work of the scholars prominent in the work of the Jesus seminar.[45] The first four of his points are directed toward flaws in their use of historical criticism. First, they tend to reject the canonical Gospels "as reliable sources for our knowledge of Jesus." This tendency, as Johnson says elsewhere, correlates with a reliance upon the Gospel of Thomas and upon their reconstruction of Q, including supposed stages of redaction. In all probability the Gospel of Thomas, preserved in Coptic, cannot be earlier than the canonical Gospels. It may include earlier forms of some of the sayings of Jesus preserved by the canonical Gospels; but if we assemble all the known sayings of Jesus from both canonical and extra-canonical sources, it is important to note that the sayings attributed to Jesus in the Gospel of Thomas all refer to the present and inner aspect of Jesus' teaching. Eschatological sayings find no place at all. With respect to Q it is necessary to remember that it is no more than a logical concept dependent upon noting that there are places where Matthew and Luke agree and are not dependent upon Mark. The hypothetical reconstruction of Q, to say nothing of supposed stages in its composition, is entirely dependent upon the two canonical Gospels in question; and it is no more than an inference from this evidence. It is, indeed, astonishing that such radical reconstructions of the historical Jesus advocated by the scholars of the Jesus seminar should be based primarily on evidence that is later than the New Testament and upon a purely hypothetical document. The historical criticism scarcely appears either scientific or convincing. The historical Jesus that results is, indeed, similar to the liberal Protestant view Hoskyns rejects; but at least that view made use of the canonical Gospels.

> It is obviously impossible for thinking Christians to repudiate or even to ignore historical criticism. But that is precisely what it seems to me most of them do.

Johnson's second point faults the scholars of the Jesus seminar for excluding the Pauline letters from consideration. The reason they do so relates to their rejection of his eschatological perspective. Their presupposition is that all texts referring to the end of the world must be excluded; but they make no argument for this presupposition and feel able to dismiss what are the earliest documents in the New Testament without giving any grounds for doing so. Johnson's third and fourth points help explain why the Jesus seminar makes this move. Their scholars assume that Jesus' message and his original movement must be understood as "a social or cultural critique rather than in terms of religious or spiritual realities." As well, the reconstruction consciously repudiates traditional Christianity and the institutional church as forces of repression. This second point may well build upon a common understanding of many New Testament scholars that the church's development represents an institutionalization and Hellenization of Christianity, a view that may somehow be rooted in the early Protestant repudiation of the Catholic Church and its attempt to recover the pure gospel enshrined in the New Testament. The obvious difficulty is that if we take the historical Jesus to be a Jewish leader or prophet, or a "charismatic *chasid,*" we make it extremely difficult to explain the rise of Christianity.[46]

Johnson's last two points go beyond a critique of a flawed use of historical criticism to two wider considerations. First, "the shared premise of these books is that *historical knowledge* is normative for faith, and therefore for theology." Here we may remember Lampe's "no thoroughfare" from my previous chapter, as well as the remarks of Hoskyns. It is impossible to suppose any necessary connection between historical conclusions and unique claims about Jesus. Even were we able to reconstruct the past exactly as it was, doing so would by no means settle the question of its meaning. New Testament studies appear to be the last gasp of the Enlightenment and out of step with modern historiography. Johnson's final point underlines the peculiarity that the scholars of the Jesus seminar for the most part identify themselves as Christians. "This commitment, however, is less strong than that professed toward scholarship. If there is a 'church' whose rules and rituals are home to these authors, it is that of the academy." Johnson laments the fact that the primary location of the critical study of scripture is now the secular academy rather than the church.[47]

My discussion has been comparatively lengthy largely because I regard the problematic character of historical criticism as a crucial issue for the church and especially for the training of its leaders. It is obviously impossible for thinking Christians to repudiate or even to ignore historical criticism. But that is precisely what it seems to me most of them do. And it is not hard to see why. More often than not the results of historical criticism appear to have no bearing upon contemporary issues or upon the faith of the church. The local congregation scarcely finds edification when the preacher tells them that the Old Testament lesson is the work of J or that the Epistle taken from Ephesians was not written by Paul. Moreover, certain broad interpretations meant to address contemporary social and economic concerns are seldom rooted in a careful use of historical criticism. On the other hand, the historical study of scripture can make several important contributions to the church and its faith. It acts as an umpire when it calls attention to problems in the text, to the meaning of the original words, and to allusions no longer familiar to us. Moreover, it can supply us with a deeper imaginative understanding of the contexts in which scripture claims to see "God's hand in the world," to use Coleridge's phrase. Moreover, it can articulate those claims that revelation has taken place and present them in such a way that we must decide whether to believe them or not. In an essay written twenty years ago Reginald Fuller notes that he had spoken of the "bankruptcy" of the historical-critical method. What he meant by this was to call for "a shift of emphasis to the theological exegesis of the biblical text, and for a renewed commitment on the part of the biblical scholars to seeing their task as a service to the church." The tools given us by historical criticism are "indispensable," but they should be used for "our real task — which is the theological-critical interpretation of the biblical text."[48]

The Bible: Theology

If we can assume that the conclusions of historical criticism are necessary but not sufficient for doing theology, how are we to understand "theological-critical" interpretation? In what follows I shall try to suggest some answers to the question by depending on the insights of David Kelsey in *The Uses of Scripture in Recent Theology*. His argumentation is complex but judicious, and at the risk of oversimplification I wish only to describe some of its major conclusions as a way of examining how theologians may use scripture for making their theological proposals to the church. Kelsey begins by studying manageable portions of the writings of seven modern theologians, and he is initially concerned with how they *construe* scripture. He locates three rather different ways in which theologians designate the aspect of the Bible they suppose authorizes their theology. Some see this aspect in the "doctrinal or conceptual content" of scripture; others, in "its recital or narrative"; and still others in "its mythic, symbolic, or imaginative expression of a saving event."[49] His discussion of G. Ernest Wright and Karl Barth in chapter 3 is the place where the problematic relation of history to theology appears most explicitly. Wright's book, *God Who Acts,* basically infers biblical doctrine "from the historical recital."[50] Theology, then, is an interpretation of history; but this means the "salvation history" and not necessarily the history reconstructed by secular scholars. Barth, on the other hand, expressly rejects the "identification of biblical narrative with *Heilsgeschichte.*"[51] The problem I have discussed in the previous section of this chapter has not disappeared, but at least we need not suppose that history as such is capable of generating theological proposals. And so we can observe Lampe's "no thoroughfare."

The various construals of scripture that Kelsey examines amount to the theologian's appeal "not just to some aspect of scripture, but to a *pattern* characteristically exhibited by that aspect of scripture, and in virtue of that pattern, he construes the scripture to which he appeals as some kind of *whole.*" This "whole" is not a unity, but is rather "a family of concepts sharing some similarities while remaining irreducibly different concepts." Despite these complications the theologian has a "working canon." This is not to be understood as a "canon within the canon," at least if we think of that as "a function of its doctrinal content." At any rate, the working canon need not be confined to concepts or doctrines.[52] Up to a point the idea appears to resemble claims about what in scripture is necessary for salvation or represents the essence of Christianity. Kelsey does not explain where this working canon comes from, but in terms of Coleridge's Pentad we might argue that it ought to derive somehow from the church in order to maintain the dialectic the Spirit sets in motion between the church and the Bible.

Kelsey's concern, however, is to explain how the theological proposals deriving from these various construals can claim authority. Logically speaking, in a theological argument scripture can be given as what is to be proved, or it can be used as a warrant for what is to be proved, or as a backing for the warrant. Chapters 6 and 7 explore this logic in detail. But from another perspective Kelsey sees the authority of theological proposals as a factor of their function. When a theologian affirms the authority of scripture, "he does not so much offer a descriptive claim about a set of texts and one of its peculiar *properties;* rather, he commits himself to a certain kind of activity in the course of which these texts are going to be *used* in certain ways." These ways include "establishing and preserving the community's identity" and addressing "the common life of the Christian community."[53] Of course, "one does not join the church-in-general." And so, in terms of the Pentad, Coleridge's term "Church" needs to mean something generic that will include a range of churches. Kelsey asks us to allow a parable. We are to imagine a group of boys, an empty lot, and one of the boys with "a soft rubber ball about the size of a grapefruit." The boy with the ball says, "Come on, play ball." But that could refer to any number of different games, excluding, of course, those that do not require a ball. The ball presumably represents scripture; and there is a range of functions it may have, different games in which it can be used. Thus, when "a theologian says 'Scripture is authority for this theological proposal,' he thereby commits himself to participate in one or another of a family of activities called 'doing Christian theology.' "[54]

Therefore, the theologian's authority and that of scripture function in the common life of the church; and the generalization would prove true in differing ways of any theologians and churches that accept scripture. But just as the boys know what game is to be played, so the church knows how scripture is supposed to function. It does not seem to me that Kelsey would disagree with my suggestion that the relation of theology and the church moves in both directions. The church shapes the theologian's construals and hence his proposals; the theologian's proposals are meant to shape the church. Kelsey's chief concern is with the second part of this, but at one point in the argument he worries that he may have been misunderstood to side against the Protestant position that scripture creates and rules the church. His appeal is to what he regards as the common consensus of

Protestant and Roman Catholic theologians that we need not speak of "two sources for Christian theology." Instead, scripture and at least certain definitions of the church "are dialectically related concepts."[55] Even though Kelsey is looking at the dialectic from the perspective of scripture, his argument does enable us to enter the dialogue envisaged by Coleridge's Pentad. I want now to look briefly at that dialogue or dialectic from the perspective of the church.

The Church

Let me begin with Sir Edwyn Hoskyns's book, written in collaboration with Noel Davey and entitled *The Riddle of the New Testament*. The "riddle" does not concern literary criticism, date and authorship, or historicity. It is "a theological riddle, which is insoluble apart from the solution of a historical problem. What was the relation between Jesus of Nazareth and the Primitive Christian Church?"[56] The conviction that there can be no fundamental gap between the two means that from a purely historical standpoint we cannot play Paul off against Jesus, or John against Paul, or "early catholicism" against New Testament Christianity. Granted that there are gaps and confusions in the formative period of Christianity, it is necessary to suppose some continuity that stretches from the life and fate of Jesus up to the time of Irenaeus toward the end of the second century. Hoskyns and Davey argue that "any historical reconstruction which leaves an unbridgeable gulf between the faith of the Primitive Church and the historical Jesus must be both inadequate and uncritical." Such a view is inadequate "because it leaves the origin of the Church unexplained." And it is uncritical "because a critical sifting of the evidence of the New Testament points towards the Life and Death of Jesus as the growth of Primitive Christian faith, and points in no other direction."[57]

There are in effect two claims. The first is that the history of the origin and development of the Christian Bible is inextricably tied to the history of the formative period of early Christianity, roughly 30–180 CE. The second is that from a theological perspective we ought to find a coherence between the early church's claims about Christ and the witness of the Christian Bible. Both points seem persuasive to me, though there are some obvious qualifications that need to be made. It is possible to treat the evidence of Irenaeus's writings (ca. 180 CE) as the articulation of the mainline development of Christianity and so the term of the formative period, but Irenaeus's Great Church excludes other forms of early Christianity, specifically the gnostic communities and the followers of Marcion. And we have clear evidence that an ecumenical Marcionite church survived for long years after Irenaeus. As well, it seems likely that the Christian gnostic communities allied themselves with Manichaeism in the late third century and beyond. Moreover, Justin Martyr, a generation before Irenaeus, tells of Christians in Palestine who have remained law-observant Jews.

Despite these qualifications, if we are to speak of a Christian Bible essentially the same as ours, we are obliged to recognize that it was the creation of the Great Church of which Irenaeus is the chief witness. It is also apparent that the central claim both of this church and its scripture has to do with the resurrection of Christ. At first it seems odd that Hoskyns and Davey in the passage I have cited above refer only to the life and death of Jesus. But their reason for omitting the resurrection stems from their realization that it "belongs properly outside the sphere of the historian." To be sure, the historian "must insist...that St. Peter and St. Paul and others were convinced that they had seen Him risen." But since the resurrection transcends history, only faith can affirm it. Nevertheless, the resurrection would be "meaningless and ultimately trivial" were we to sever it from "belief in the active power of the Living God and in the ultimate truth of what Jesus said and did." It is also meaningless "apart from the recognition that a particular Life and Death can have universal and ultimate significance."[58] Thus, "neither the Jesus of History nor the Primitive Church fits into the characteristic nexus of modern popular humanitarian or humanistic ideas."[59]

Both the Great Church of the late second century and its canon of scripture give pride of place to Christ's death and resurrection.

At least in Alexandria and Asia Minor the central Christian feast was the celebration of the Christian Passover. In Asia Minor this sometimes took place on the anniversary of Christ's death, but it was a celebration of the death by which death was itself slain and was designed to reflect the understanding of the cross found in John's Gospel. "And I, when I am lifted up from the earth, will draw all people to myself" (John 12:32). The "lifting up" is both the lifting up of Jesus on the cross to die and also his exaltation to the life of the new age by his resurrection. In Alexandria the Christian Passover treated Christ's death and resurrection as his passage from this world of death to the new world of eternal life, a passage described as a new Exodus from the Egypt of death to the promised land of life, and as a transition from the old creation of the fallen Adam to the new creation of the second Adam. Such an interpretation correlates with a number of Pauline passages in scripture.[60] Christ's death and his resurrection are, then, so to speak, two sides of the same coin; and this pattern represents not only the destiny prepared for Christians and even for all, but also in its spiritual meaning the characteristic pattern of their life in this world.

It is possible to discern this correlation between the early church's faith and scripture in the gradual formation of what Irenaeus already calls the New Testament and of a Christian Bible. Of course, there was considerable disagreement with respect to what writings should be regarded as authoritative. The Hebrew scriptures were problematic for gnostic Christians, to say the least; and Marcion rejected them altogether. Yet even though it does represent a retrospective and tunnel-like approach to what we can know about the earliest Christian communities, it is possible in general terms to describe the steps that led to the formation of Irenaeus's Christian Bible. It is obvious from the New Testament writings that the Bible of the earliest churches was what we call the Old Testament. Ignatius of Antioch, on his way to martyrdom in Rome early in the second century, says that he found some in Philadelphia arguing that "if I do not find it in the archives, I do not believe it to be in the gospel." The "archives" are certainly the Hebrew scriptures, probably in the Greek translation of the Septuagint. The "gospel" must refer to the Christian preaching rather than to a written Gospel. Ignatius's response to what he regards as an erroneous view is to say "for me the archives are Jesus Christ, the inviolable archives are his cross and death and his resurrection and faith through him."[61] Ignatius is not repudiating the Old Testament, but he is arguing that the key to its meaning must be found in the proclamation of Christ's death and resurrection.

The argument would have to be made at greater length and with the recognition of various complexities, but for my purposes it suffices to conclude that the "gospel" is in this sense the focus of the claims made by those Christians who foreshadowed the Great Church, and that the gospel was identified with the apostolic witness to Christ. It is possible to see this second idea already stated in John's Gospel (John 19:35; 20:30; 21:24). We may speak of the gradual attribution of authority to writings thought to be apostolic and true to the proclamation of Christ's death and resurrection. There were some obvious problems. The apostolic warrant for Mark came to be the assumption that he depended upon Peter's preaching, and that of Luke rested upon the fact that he had been Paul's companion. Other writings that circulated under the name of Peter, Thomas, and others were rejected, largely because they did not cohere with the "gospel" preached by the apostles. Granting authority to writings as well as to the living voice of the Christian proclamation led to the idea of a closed canon of authoritative writings. The impact of Marcion and the Montanists on this process would require discussion; and it is the case that uniform lists of the canonical New Testament are quite late. Nevertheless, Irenaeus's references to scripture include most of the books that are now in our canon; and there is no reason to doubt that we can speak of a Christian Bible by his time. But the important point to make is that the New Testament canon and its union with the Old Testament were the creation of the church.

To return to Irenaeus and his books *Against Heresies,* we find in his arguments a way of considering the interaction of scripture and the church's tradition. He is obliged to admit that the gnostics and

Marcion cite scripture to support their own views. And so the arguments Irenaeus makes in books three to five of his treatise employ
scripture interpreted according to what he calls the rule of faith. His
first book describes what he regards as the heretical "rule," while the
second book refutes that rule on the basis of the church's rule, which
he equates with the tradition of the apostles (3.3.1). From one point
of view this rule is to be found in scripture itself. Irenaeus uses two
analogies to make the point (1.9.4). It is possible to sever specific
verses from Homer and rearrange them so as to make a new poem
that will be false to Homer. Or, if we regard the different passages in
scripture as the gems and stones of a mosaic, it is possible to rearrange
them to make a false mosaic. The heretics have in this way turned the
mosaic of a king into that of a dog or a fox. Crucial to interpreting
scripture is the proper placement of its different passages. The rule,
then, describes this placement and so is a kind of canon within the
canon. At the same time that rule can be articulated outside scripture,
and barbarians who can neither read nor write can have "salvation
written in their hearts by the Spirit, without paper or ink." This is
because they can learn the rule, which Irenaeus can describe in words
that are not fixed but which bear a shadowy resemblance to the old
Roman baptismal creed and to its descendant, our Apostles' Creed
(3.4.2). Thus, the apostles were like rich men putting money into the
bank of the church both in the form of scripture and in that of the
rule of faith (3.4.1). There can be no opposition between scripture
and the rule; they are, as it were, formally distinct but materially
identical.

My brief sketch suggests that at least at its best the early church
preserved the dialectic between itself and scripture for which Coleridge argues. Irenaeus also points out that the faith we receive from
the church and preserve "always, by the Spirit of God, renewing its
youth, as if it were some precious deposit in an excellent vessel, causes
the vessel itself containing it to renew its youth also" (3.24.1). Shifting his point slightly, we could argue that the dynamic relationship of
the church and scripture is what by the Spirit leads us into all truth
(John 16:13). Such a view carries with it the paradoxical union of

continuity with the past and its adaptation to present and emergent concerns. Breaking the paradox runs the risk either of consigning a dead past to a museum or of losing any sense of our place in history. It would be possible to write the history of the church's theological development not only as a constant attempt to adapt its heritage to new circumstances, but also as an ongoing interpretation of scripture.

The point is particularly obvious in the church's attempts in the fourth and fifth centuries to clarify its understanding of Christ. The New Testament presents Christ as fully human; he suffers and dies. But it also claims that he is the one "in the form of God" who "did not regard equality with God as something to be exploited" (Phil 2:6). He is the Word who "was God," and through him "all things came to be" (John 1:1–3). And Thomas addresses the risen Christ as "My Lord and my God!" (John 20:28). If scripture is sacred and authoritative, it must be taken seriously even when we find puzzles that seem insoluble. And there are many more such puzzles in the New Testament's judgments about Christ. If Christ is human, how can he be divine? If Christ is in some sense divine and distinct from his Father, how can we avoid speaking of two gods and so repudiating the heritage of Jewish monotheism? The early Christian dogmas of the Trinity and Christ's person, enshrined in the Nicene Creed and the Chalcedonian Definition meant to specify its meaning, are in large part no more than attempts to solve these exegetical problems, or at least to provide a framework that will delimit various doctrinal solutions.

We could certainly continue to trace down through the ages this kind of theological development, one that involves the dialectic between scripture and the church. And we could argue that the controversial settings of such developments do not fully explain them. They also have the positive function of seeking ever deeper understandings of the church's faith and of scripture. But it is important to consider another arena in which the dialectic of church and scripture appears. What I mean is the liturgical life of the church. For Anglicans, as for many if not most other Christians, the liturgy includes elements from the Christian past, for example, the reading of scripture, the recital of creeds, and the use of traditional forms of worship. But these elements are balanced not only by the adaptation of forms of worship to contemporary concerns, but also by preaching, which is meant to do the same thing. Moreover, I should think that the point of the liturgy is not merely to affirm and support the fellowship of Christians, but also to orient them toward a worshipful communion with God through Christ and in the Holy Spirit, a communion that in principle ought to empower them for their lives. Scripture, then, appears in this ecclesial context. And, if a lectionary is used, we find it in such a way that different portions of scripture are juxtaposed in what are sometimes unlikely ways. But this can have the effect of forcing us to think more deeply of scripture's multiform meaning for us and for the church. And it can at least minimize the risk that we might attend only to those parts of scripture that attract us or that echo our own presuppositions and prejudices.

Coleridge's Pentad supposes that the preacher, inspired by the Spirit, will seek to articulate meanings that derive from the dialectic between scripture and the church. While controversial issues may be part of the preacher's task, it seems unlikely to me that preachers have the power to resolve such questions. Surely the focus of the preacher ought to be the proclamation of the gospel, and this must involve the mediation of the biblical message to the congregation. It would be possible to think more broadly, since Coleridge's "preacher" is probably anyone who seeks to interpret the interaction of the Bible and the church. Yet no matter how we define the task, it is certain that it always falls short of its goal. Our ignorance and unworthiness prevent us from ever mastering scripture. Sooner or later our vain attempts to do so by making it a mouthpiece for our own prejudices and ideologies become apparent.

Here the corporate witness of the church has a role to play. And the ambiguities of that witness contribute to one of the major conclusions I should wish to draw. Scripture, indeed, resists our own efforts to understand it; and the church's attempts to adjudicate between differing interpretations never seem entirely satisfactory. In this way scripture, even when interpreted in the church, remains "too hard for the teeth of time." Nevertheless, the task of interpreting scripture in the church remains a central one not only for the preacher, but also for all Christians. George Herbert may well have a particular understanding of that task, but he describes it in a prayerful and persuasive way in his "Prayer before Sermon."[62] The first paragraph tells the Christian story, found in scripture, in Herbert's own way. The second and very short paragraph defines him as a teller of that story, while the third paragraph asks God's blessing upon preaching to the church and to the world. Let me conclude by citing this prayer:

Oh Almighty and everliving Lord God! Majesty, and Power, and Brightness, and Glory! How shall we dare to appear before thy face, who are contrary to thee, in all we call thee? for we are darkness, and weakness, and filthiness, and shame. Misery and sin fill our days: yet art thou our Creator, and we thy work. Thy hands both made us, and also made us Lords of all thy creatures, giving us one world in ourselves, and another to serve us: then didst thou place us in Paradise, and wert proceeding still on in thy Favors, until we interrupted thy Counsels, disappointed thy Purposes, and sold our God, our glorious God for an apple. Oh write it! Oh brand it in our foreheads forever; for an apple once we lost our God, and still lose him for no more; for money, for meat, for diet: But thou Lord, art patience and pity, and sweetness, and love; therefore we sons of men are not consumed. Thou hast exalted thy mercy above all things; and hast made our salvation, not our punishment, thy glory: so that then where sin abounded, not death, but grace superabounded; accordingly, when we had sinned beyond any help in heaven or earth, then thou saidest, Lo, I come! then did the Lord of life, unable of himself to die, contrive to do it. He took flesh, he wept, he died; for his enemies he died; even for those that derided him then, and still despise him. Blessed Savior! many waters could not quench thy love! nor no pit overwhelm it. But though the streams of thy blood were current through darkness, grave, and hell; yet by these thy conflicts, and seemingly hazards, didst thou arise triumphant, and therein mad'st us victorious.

Neither doth thy love yet stay here! for, this word of thy rich peace, and reconciliation, thou hast committed, not to Thunder, or Angels, but to silly and sinful men: even to me, pardoning my sins, and bidding me go feed the people of thy love.

Blessed be the God of Heaven and Earth! who only doth wond'rous things. Awake therefore, my Lute, and my Viol! awake all my powers to glorify thee! We praise thee! we bless thee! we magnify thee forever! And now, Oh Lord! in the power of thy Victories, and in the ways of thy Ordinances, and in the truth of thy Love, Lo, we stand here, beseeching thee to bless thy word, wherever spoken this day throughout the universal Church. Oh, make it a word of power and peace, to convert those who are not yet thine, and to confirm those that are: particularly, bless it in this thy own Kingdom, which thou hast made a Land of light, a storehouse of thy treasures and mercies: Oh, let not our foolish and unworthy hearts rob us of the continuance of this thy sweet love: but pardon our sins, and perfect what thou hast begun. Ride on Lord, because of the word of truth, and meekness, and righteousness; and thy right hand shall teach thee terrible things. Especially, bless this portion here assembled together, with thy unworthy Servant speaking unto them: Lord Jesu! teach thou me, that I may teach them: Sanctify, and enable all my powers; that in their full strength they may deliver thy message reverently, readily, faithfully, and fruitfully. Oh, make thy word a swift word, passing from the ear to the heart, from the heart to the life and conversation: that as the rain returns not empty, so neither may thy word, but accomplish that for which it is given. Oh Lord hear, Oh Lord forgive! Oh Lord, hearken, and do so for thy blessed Son's sake, in whose sweet and pleasing words, we say, Our Father, &c.

Discussion Questions

A Foreword Written Afterwards

The following questions can be explored throughout the book:

1. Is there a single meaning of particular biblical texts? What are we to make of a tendency both of historical critics and of fundamentalists to answer the question in the affirmative?

2. How do different Christian denominations understand the authority of the Bible in relation to other authorities? Is it true that Anglicans have answered this question in a number of different ways?

3. What is the primary purpose of scripture?

4. Does scripture reveal everything?

5. Does scripture require interpretation? If so, what tools are available? Can we identify our interpretations with scripture itself? How helpful is it to speak of "scripture, reason, and tradition"?

6. What is the relation of the gospel's promise of salvation to its moral demand? Do changing social mores affect our understanding of its moral demand?

7. In what sense is the Bible the church's book? How do answers to this question relate to issues revolving around conversion and baptism? Does the church make Christians, or do Christians make the church?

Chapter One / The Bible Moves to Center Stage: 1529–1603

1. How do historical factors shape the place of the Bible in Tudor England? What function is implied for the Bible by the measures taken by the Tudor monarchs — articles of religion, royal injunctions, homilies, and prayer books?

2. How does scripture contain what is "necessary to salvation"? Can we accept the distinction between the necessary and the indifferent? Are the necessary points found in the "plain" passages? What are they?

3. How does Hooker treat the authority of scripture, and how does his view differ from that of Rome and from the Puritan view?

4. Can we argue that Hooker's method involves the "triple cord" of scripture, reason, and tradition?

5. Does Hooker seek to correlate an ecclesiastical and sacramental understanding of Christianity with the Protestant doctrines of predestination, justification, and sanctification?

Chapter Two / The Lively Oracles of God: 1603–1660

1. Are the views of Hall, Chillingworth, and Hammond contradictory? Are there points of agreement? Do any of them appear to follow Hooker?

2. How does Hall understand the scriptural warrant for episcopacy?

3. How does Chillingworth understand the role of the primitive church? Why does he refuse to specify what is necessary to salvation?

4. Does Hammond begin to treat apostolicity as an authority alongside scripture?

5. Does George Herbert's poem capture an attitude common to all the writers examined?

Chapter Three / The Ambiguous Alliance of Scripture and Nature

1. How are we to understand the shift of sensibility at the end of the seventeenth and in the eighteenth century? How does it affect understandings of scripture and its authority?

2. In what differing ways do "reason" and "nature" help or hinder our understanding of scripture?

3. Do "holy living" and the moral life begin to lose touch with the scriptural gospel of salvation?

4. How may we distinguish the latitudinarians from the deists?

5. The question of the salvation of those who have not read scripture or become Christians appears. How do we respond to that question in our own time?

6. What are the strengths and weaknesses of the "evidences of Christianity" (prophecy and miracles) and of the argument from design?

7. In what ways is eighteenth-century evangelicalism a protest against the dominant view in England? In what ways is it a return to Elizabethan Anglicanism?

8. What views of the church do we find in the eighteenth century?

Chapter Four / Making Friends with History: The Nineteenth Century

1. Why was "history" regarded as a threat to scripture in the earlier nineteenth century?

2. What are the differing views of "history" taken by Newman, Maurice, Jowett, and Sanday? How do they affect the authority and meaning of scripture?

3. Is the historical-critical approach to scripture compatible with an ecclesial understanding of Christianity?

4. What does Jowett mean by insisting that scripture has only one meaning?

5. How are we to understand inspiration, revelation, and religious experience in relation to history?

6. How does the nineteenth-century approach to scripture set the agenda for the questions that arise in the twentieth century and in our own time?

Chapter Five / Keeping History as a Friend of Faith: The Last Century

1. What are the possibilities — and the advantages and disadvantages — of the quest for the historical Jesus?

2. What is the relation of historical accounts of the development of religious ideas to notions of religious experience?

3. How does the problem of the relation of world religions to one another complicate the question of scriptural authority?

4. In what ways does the church occupy a place in the discussions described in this chapter?

5. How is a schema of revelation and response capable of taking account of history?

6. Do the understandings of inspiration and revelation go beyond those described in the preceding chapter?

7. What are the advantages and limitations of restoring "the biblical narrative" and so regarding scripture as a "story"?

8. What are the "essentials" of the Christian faith, and how are they related to the idea that scripture contains all things necessary to salvation?

Chapter Six / An Inconclusive Conclusion

1. Is it fair to correlate different theological views with different understandings of what is essential in scripture or of what is necessary to salvation?

2. Is it better to think of the limits of validity in interpreting scripture than to look for the correct meaning? What are the limits of validity, and what are the weaknesses of this view?

3. Can we compare Coleridge's view with Chillingworth's understanding of how the Bible contains all things necessary to salvation?

4. To what degree are the "inconclusive conclusions" applicable to Christian traditions other than Anglican ones?

5. In what ways is historical criticism problematic for the churches? In what ways is it necessary?

6. Does George Herbert's prayer correlate with Coleridge's Pentad? How convincing is Coleridge's insistence that we must deny verbal inerrancy and must treat the Bible as the church's book?

Notes

A Foreword Written Afterwards

1. See the text in the 1979 Prayer Book, p. 868.

2. Arthur Michael Ramsey, *From Gore to Temple: The Development of Anglican Theology between* Lux Mundi *and the Second World War, 1889–1939* (London: Longmans, 1960).

3. See Sydney E. Ahlstrom's discussion of "The Evangelical Mainstream" in *A Religious History of the American People* (New Haven and London: Yale University Press, 1972), pp. 469–71: American evangelical Protestantism in the nineteenth century was "Reformed in its foundations, Puritan in its outlook, fervently experiential in its faith, and tending, despite strong countervailing pressures, toward Arminianism, perfectionism, and activism. Equally basic, and almost equally religious, was its belief in the millennial potential of the United States as the bearer and protector of these values."

4. H. R. McAdoo, *The Spirit of Anglicanism: A Survey of Anglican Theological Method in the Seventeenth Century* (London: Adam & Charles Black, 1965), pp. v–vi.

5. See McAdoo, *Spirit of Anglicanism* (especially pp. 48 and 53) and ch. 6, pp. 190–97 (especially p. 193).

6. William Laud, *Conference with Fisher,* section 16 (LACT, vol. 2, pp. 70–105, especially p. 97).

7. William J. Wolf and John E. Booty, eds., *The Spirit of Anglicanism* (Wilton, Conn.: Morehouse-Barlow, 1979), p. 165.

8. See also Urban T. Holmes III, *What Is Anglicanism?* (Wilton, Conn.: Morehouse-Barlow, 1982), p. 11: "The threefold nature of authority — Scripture, tradition and reason — is not original with Hooker; but sixteenth century Anglicanism felt no compulsion to make claims of originality, since it conceived itself as the continuing Catholic Church in England." The discussion goes on to suggest that we can find the idea in Thomas Aquinas and in Augustine. I find myself doubtful.

9. A. R. Vidler, ed., *Soundings: Essays Concerning Christian Understanding* (Cambridge: Cambridge University Press, 1963), pp. 142–45. See

also Christopher R. Seitz's repudiation of the three-legged stool, "Repugnance and the Three-Legged Stool: Modern Uses of Scripture and the Baltimore Declaration" in *Reclaiming Faith: Essays on Orthodoxy in the Episcopal Church and the Baltimore Declaration*, ed. Ephraim Radner and George R. Sumner (Grand Rapids, Mich.: Eerdmans, 1993), pp. 85–101.

10. John Redwood, *Reason, Ridicule and Religion: The Age of Enlightenment in England, 1660–1752* (Cambridge, Mass.: Harvard University Press, 1971), p. 198. See the whole of ch. 9 ("The Reason of Nature and the Nature of Reason"). Redwood does recognize "some common features." Reason was the language of nature. There were "certain deducibles" from sense experience. Writers tended to dissent from Thomas Aquinas and scholastic thought, from metaphysical arguments in general, and from the notion of innate ideas. Reason often means the judge of evidence.

11. Stillingfleet's work provoked three letters from Locke in reply. These letters were printed in the fifth edition of the *Essay* (1706) and are included in the Penguin Classics edition, pp. 637–726.

12. See Bernard M. G. Reardon, *From Coleridge to Gore: A Century of Religious Thought in Britain* (London: Longman, 1971), pp. 63–72.

13. See Reardon's index under T. H. Green, Hegel, idealism.

14. Nicholas Tyacke, *Anti-Calvinists: The Rise of English Arminians c. 1590–1640*, Oxford Historical Monograph (Oxford: Clarendon Press paperback, 1990; first published 1987), p. 5.

15. See Peter B. Nockles, *The Oxford Movement in Context: Anglican High Churchmanship 1760–1857* (Cambridge: Cambridge University Press, 1994). Nockles carefully describes the disillusionment of the older high churchmen with the Oxford Movement, including their fear of tendencies toward Rome. See p. 154: "For pre-Tractarian High Churchmen the Anglican theory represented a *via media* between rival theories of unity represented by Rome and Geneva. . . . Pre-Tractarian High Churchmen were proud of the title 'Protestant.' " See also p. 311: "Newman's theory of the *via media* was not the Hanoverian ideal of 'moderation' as an end in itself nor even quite the Laudian 'middle way' between Puritanism or Geneva on the one hand and Rome on the other, but rather, a 'middle way' between Protestantism *per se* and Romanism."

16. For an excellent account of where the Episcopal Church finds itself, see Robert W. Prichard, "The Place of Doctrine in the Episcopal Church" in *Reclaiming Faith*, pp. 13–45.

17. Robert N. Bellah and associates, *Habits of the Heart* (New York: Harper & Row paperback, 1986; first published 1985), p. 227.

18. See Nockles, p. 320: "The comprehensiveness of the Church of England thereafter was strained to a new degree of doctrinal elasticity.... In short, the Oxford Movement caused the Church of England to become theologically more tolerant when, in fact, its aim had been to make it more dogmatic."

19. See the 1979 Prayer Book, p. 864.

20. Paul Avis, "What Is Anglicanism?" in *The Study of Anglicanism*, ed. Stephen Sykes and John Booty (London and Philadelphia: SPCK/Fortress Press, 1988), p. 415.

21. Mark Pattison, "Tendencies in Religious Thought in England, 1688–1750," in *Essays and Reviews* (London: John W. Parker and Son, 1860), p. 329.

Chapter One / The Bible Moves to Center Stage: 1529–1603

1. John Barth, *The Sot-Weed Factor* (Garden City, N.Y.: Doubleday, 1960), pp. 373–75.

2. See A. G. Dickens and Dorothy Carr, *The Reformation in England to the Accession of Elizabeth I*, Documents of Modern History (London: Edward Arnold, 1967), pp. 74–77.

3. Dickens and Carr, *Reformation in England*, pp. 85–89.

4. Gerald Bray, ed., *Documents of the English Reformation* (Minneapolis: Fortress, 1994), pp. 179–80.

5. Bray, *Documents*, pp. 233–43.

6. Diarmaid MacCulloch, *Thomas Cranmer: A Life* (New Haven and London: Yale University Press, 1996), p. 32, points out that Cranmer's education at Cambridge would have led him to suppose a compatibility of orthodoxy with scripture. Moreover, he points out (p. 128) that in 1535 in his injunctions for the Worcester Cathedral priory Cranmer "told the monks to organize and attend a scripture reading for an hour daily throughout the year.... The injunction was the first instance of a strategy which would characterize Cranmer's career as a reformer: he appealed to the past, in this case 'the Rule of your Religion' (that is, the Benedictine Rule) to emphasize Bible-reading as a central precept of the monastic life, but the order came with an evangelical twist."

7. The Convocation comprised a house of bishops and a lower house of clerical representatives from the entire southern province of England. For what happened see MacCulloch, *Thomas Cranmer*, pp. 290–95.

8. See Dickens and Carr, *Reformation in England*, pp. 114–18; MacCulloch, *Thomas Cranmer*, pp. 310–11.

9. See Bray, *Documents*, pp. 247–57.

10. MacCulloch, *Thomas Cranmer*, p. 326. See John N. Wall, Jr., "Godly and Fruitful Lessons: The English Bible, Erasmus' Paraphrases, and the Book of Homilies" in *The Godly Kingdom of Tudor England: Great Books of the English Reformation*, ed. John E. Booty (Wilton, Conn.: Morehouse-Barlow, 1981), pp. 47–135.

11. MacCulloch, *Thomas Cranmer*, p. 372. See Wall's discussion.

12. Bray, *Documents*, p. 287.

13. 1979 Book of Common Prayer, p. 866.

14. I have used the Oxford edition of 1822.

15. See Homilies 3 and 4, also by Cranmer: "Of the Salvation of all Mankind" and "Of the True and Lively Faith."

16. Bray, *Documents*, pp. 335–48.

17. The allusion is to Eccles 4:12, though the verse scarcely bears the weight of the view based upon it. See McAdoo, *Spirit of Anglicanism*. Also John E. Booty, "Standard Divines," in *The Study of Anglicanism*, ed. Stephen Sykes and John Booty (London and Philadelphia: SPCK/Fortress Press, 1988), p. 164: "Anglican divines on the whole regard Scripture interpreted through tradition and reason as authoritative in matters concerning salvation."

18. Thomas Browne, *Religio Medici*, 1.16, in *Sir Thomas Browne: The Major Works*, ed. C. A. Patrides (Harmondsworth: Penguin Books, 1977), p. 78).

19. Browne, *Religio Medici*, 1.5 (Penguin edition, p. 64).

20. Browne, *Religio Medici*, 1.23 (Penguin edition, p. 91).

21. Citations from Hooker are from the Folger Library Edition.

22. The citation is from *Summa Theologica*, 1.2 q. 91, art. 3. For Thomas's view see, e.g., David Knowles, *The Evolution of Medieval Thought* (New York: Random House Vintage Books, 1962), pp. 261–62. I am indebted in what follows to Lee W. Gibbs's discussion of Book I in the Folger Edition, vol. 6, pp. 91–108.

23. Hippocrates, Loeb Library 4:236–37. See the note in the Folger Edition, vol. 6, pp. 486–87.

24. Hooker claims to be citing *de trin.* 4.6, but there is no such passage in Augustine's work. See Folger Edition notes, vol. 6, p. 582, where it is noted that Hooker's mistake "may well have been a gloss on the chapter in an edition he used or even a summary comment he himself had recorded in notes on the book and later mistook for a quotation."

25. *Laws* I.12.1, I.14.4. Contrast *Westminster Confession* I.1: "Although the light of nature, and the works of creation and providence do

so far manifest the goodness, wisdom, and power of God, as to leave men inexcusable, yet are they not sufficient to give that knowledge of God and of his will which is necessary unto salvation; therefore it pleased the Lord, at sundry times and in divers manners to reveal himself and to declare that his will unto his church . . . to commit the same unto writing, which maketh the Holy Scripture to be most necessary, those former ways of God's revealing his will unto his people being now ceased."

26. For general principles of church order see III.7.1 and III.7.4, where he cites 1 Cor 10:32; 14:40, 26; 10:31; and Rom 14:6–7.

27. Hooker, *A Learned Discourse of Justification*, 14. Folger Edition, vol. 5.

28. Hooker, *A Learned Discourse of Justification*, 23.

29. This at least is one way of coming to terms with Hooker's view. He distinguishes God's general or antecedent will that all should be saved from his consequent will. The issue is quite complex, and before his death Hooker was engaged in formulating his view as part of a response to *A Christian Letter*, published in 1599 as an attack upon Hooker's supposed denial of aspects of the Thirty-Nine Articles. See vol. 4 of the Folger edition and John Booty's careful introduction to Hooker's notes and drafts for the response he was prevented from making by his death.

30. Hooker, *A Learned Discourse of Justification*, 3.

Chapter Two / The Lively Oracles of God: 1603–1660

1. Henry Gee and W. J. Hardy, *Documents Illustrative of English Church History* (London: Macmillan and Co., 1896), pp. 508–11.

2. Bray, *Documents*, pp. 413–36.

3. Bray, *Documents*, p. 420.

4. Bray, *Documents*, p. 432.

5. Bray, *Documents*, p. 428.

6. A pseudonym concocted from the initials of five Puritan divines — Stephen Marshall, Edmund Calamy, Thomas Young, Matthew Newcomen, and William Spurstowe.

7. Joseph Hall, *Works*, ed. Josiah Pratt (London: C. Whittingham, 1808), Letter 6.4 to Doctor Milburne, vol. 7, pp. 261–62. Here Hall also says "he that obtrudes a new Word, no less overthrows the Scripture; than he, that denies the old. . . . God never laid other foundation, than in the Prophets and Apostles: upon their divine writings he meant to build his Church."

8. Hall, *Select Thoughts or Choice Helps for a Pious Spirit*, VI; Pratt, vol. 6, p. 248 (1648).

9. Hall, *Christian Moderation*, Book 2, Rule 4; Pratt, vol. 7, p. 444 (1639).

10. Hall, *No Peace with Rome*, 2.4; Pratt, vol. 9, p. 61 (1609). Cf. *A Serious Dissuasive from Papacy*, 2.3; Pratt, vol. 9, pp. 8–9: "Our question is ... whether, in all essential points, it [scripture] do not interpret itself; so as, what is hard in one place, is openly laid forth in another" (1609). Also *The Old Religion*, 12.2; Pratt, vol. 9, p. 287: "It is not to be imagined, that the same Word of God, which speaks for all other truths, should not speak for itself. How fully doth it display its own sufficiency and perfection!" (1627).

11. Hall, *Select Thoughts*, XLIV; Pratt, vol. 6, pp. 270–71 (1648).

12. Hall, *The Devout Soul*, 4.2; Pratt, vol. 7, pp. 505–6 (1650).

13. Hall, *A Serious Dissuasive from Popery*, 2.3; Pratt, vol. 9, pp. 8–9: " ... what is hard in one place, is openly laid forth in another ... [as Augustine says in *De doctrina christiana* 2.4] 'The Spirit of God hath royally and wholesomely tempered the Holy Scriptures, so; as, both by the plain places he might prevent our hunger, and by the obscure he might avoid our nice slothfulness: for there is scarce any thing, that can be fetched out of those obscurities, which is not found most plainly spoken elsewhere' " (1609).

14. Hall, *Christian Moderation*, Book 2, Rule 4; Pratt, vol. 7, p. 444 (1639).

15. Hall, *The Old Religion*, 1–13; Pratt, vol. 9, pp. 238–306 (1627). The errors are justification by inherent righteousness, the doctrine of merit, transubstantiation, half-communion, the sacrifice of the mass, the worship of images, indulgences and the doctrine of purgatory, divine service in an unknown tongue, full and forced sacramental confession, the invocation of saints, seven sacraments, the Romish doctrine of traditions, the encroachments of the bishop of Rome. It is interesting that Hall does not treat prayers for the dead as an error.

16. Hall, *Satan's Fiery Darts Quenched*, Decade I, iiid; Pratt, vol. 8, p. 278 (1647).

17. Hall, *No Peace with Rome*, 1; Pratt, vol. 9, p. 37 (1609). His reference is to the preface of *imper. et princip.*

18. Hall, *No Peace with Rome*, 1; Pratt, vol. 9, p. 35 (1609). Cf. *The Old Religion*, Introduction 4; Pratt, vol. 9, pp. 237–38 (1627).

19. Hall, *Episcopacy by Divine Right Asserted*, 1.4; Pratt, vol. 9, p. 529 (1640).

20. Hall, *No Peace with Rome,* Introduction 1; Pratt, vol. 9, p. 29 (1609).

21. Hall, *A Serious Dissuasive from Popery,* 2; Pratt, vol. 9, pp. 4–5 (1609).

22. Hall, *Letters,* 4.8 to Mr. Thomas James of Oxford; Pratt, vol. 7, p. 215 (1608).

23. Hall, *The Old Religion,* 12.1; Pratt, vol. 9, p. 285 (1627).

24. Hall, *Letters,* 5.2 to the bishop of Worcester; Pratt, vol. 7, p. 230 (1610).

25. Hall, *Episcopacy by Divine Right Asserted,* 1.5; Pratt, vol. 9, p. 517 (1640).

26. Hall, *Episcopacy by Divine Right Asserted,* 1.4; Pratt, vol. 9, p. 526.

27. Hall, *Episcopacy by Divine Right Asserted,* 1.4; Pratt, vol. 9, p. 525.

28. Hall, *Episcopacy by Divine Right Asserted,* 1.5 and 1.7; Pratt, vol. 9, pp. 531 and 536.

29. Hall, *Episcopacy by Divine Right Asserted,* 1.4; Pratt, vol. 9, p. 528.

30. Hall, *Episcopacy by Divine Right Asserted,* 1.4; Pratt, vol. 9, p. 526.

31. Hall, *Episcopacy by Divine Right Asserted,* Introduction 6; Pratt, vol. 9, p. 521.

32. Hall, *Episcopacy by Divine Right Asserted,* 1.10; Pratt, vol. 9, p. 538.

33. Hall, *Episcopacy by Divine Right Asserted,* 2.1; Pratt, vol. 9, p. 547. Cf. 1.15; Pratt, vol. 9, pp. 542–43: "Episcopacy, as it presupposeth an imparity of order and superiority of government" is "a sound stake pitched in the hedge of God's Church, ever since the Apostles' times; and that Parity and Lay-Presbytery are but as new-sprung briars and brambles, lately woven into the new-plashed fence of the Church."

34. Hall, *Episcopacy by Divine Right Asserted,* 2.1; Pratt, vol. 9, pp. 548–49.

35. Hall, *Episcopacy by Divine Right Asserted,* 2.1; Pratt, vol. 9, p. 544.

36. Hall, *Episcopacy by Divine Right Asserted,* 2.1; Pratt, vol. 9, pp. 552–53. See the whole discussion, pp. 552–62.

37. Hall, *Episcopacy by Divine Right Asserted,* 2.8; Pratt, vol. 9, p. 563.

38. John Aubrey, *Brief Lives,* ed. Oliver Lawson-Dick (London: Mandarin Paperbacks, 1992), p. 64.

39. John Donne, Satire 3.79–81.

40. Cf. Robert R. Orr, *Reason and Authority: The Thought of William Chillingworth* (Oxford: Clarendon Press, 1967), p. 23, where he argues that Chillingworth's two concerns are "the search for a doctrinally comprehensive Church, and the insistence that such an institution must

respect its members' intellectual integrity. Second, to follow his changing reactions... to infallible authority."

41. Citations from *The Religion of Protestants* will be given from the text printed in London by Thomas Tegg in 1845. The motto appears on p. iii.

42. Cf. 2.34–35, 2.45, 2.88, pp. 108, 112, 136.

43. Cf. 4.76, p. 321.

44. See the passages cited by Orr and his conclusion on p. 66: "...if our understanding of God's mind and intentions is inevitably fallible, then controversy as to the content of divine revelation, far from being undesirable, is both unavoidable and an invaluable tool with which to clarify the message of God to man."

45. See Orr, *Reason and Authority,* p. 157: "...his attack on the doctrine of infallibility led him to evoke a notion of reason as primarily a critical faculty which scrutinizes and appraises evidence for propositions." But he can also appeal to "right reason, grounded on divine revelation and common notions written by God in the hearts of all men." Cf. pp. 161, 166–67, 179.

46. See John Spurr, *The Restoration Church of England 1646–1689* (New Haven and London: Yale University Press, 1991), p. 11: Hammond "was the acknowledged inspiration for the group of Anglican controversialists who responded to two separate challenges [Presbyterianism and Rome].... The Hammond circle was in close contact with the exiled royalists and Anglican go-betweens like Gilbert Sheldon or George Moreley...." Cf. p. 375: "Anglican piety can now be put into place, alongside episcopacy, the theology of holy living, the campaign against national sin, and the principle of national religious uniformity, to complete our picture of Restoration Anglicanism."

47. See John W. Parker, *The Transformation of Anglicanism 1643–1660: With Special Reference to Henry Hammond* (Manchester: Manchester University Press, 1969). On p. 88 he argues that Hammond was greatest as a biblical scholar, and on p. 95 he cites the following passage from Hammond's "Postscript" or preface to *A Paraphrase:* "The understanding of the word of God contain'd in the Scripture, is no work of extraordinary illumination, but must be attained by the same means, or the like, by which other writings of men are expounded, and no otherwise."

48. *Conference with Fisher,* 11.2; LACT, vol. 2, pp. 50–51.

49. Taylor insists upon liberty and concord, but regards piety and, especially, charity as the true instruments of peace and unity (Introduction). The foundation of faith is in Christ and in the plain passages of scripture, which

are perspicuous because "no man can be ignorant of the foundation of faith without his own apparent fault" (section 3). Liberty of prophesying attaches to scriptural places of difficulty, where there can be no certain means of interpretation, partly because we tend to impose our own prejudices on them (section 4). Since "in this world we believe in part, and prophesy in part," we must embrace "mutual toleration" (section 7). Honest error is innocent (section 12). Nevertheless, the "great mysteries" of scripture represent "trials of our understanding, and arguments of our imperfection, and incentives to the longings after heaven" (section 3). Reason is an important instrument of interpretation, and "every man may be trusted to judge for himself." Reason and authority are not "enemies" and are not "repugnant" to one another. Yet reason supposes "the assistance of God's Spirit" (section 10). Taylor differs from Chillingworth in arguing that, while the Apostles' Creed derives from scripture (sections 1, 2, 4), it separates for us what is "necessary or not necessary" in scripture (section 16). Moreover, Taylor also attempts to define toleration (sections 16–19). We must distinguish the public license of a sect and the toleration of opinions. The law, since it is public, cannot be riddled with exceptions adjusting it to tender consciences. But administering the law can admit personal dispensations, provided the opinions in question do not disturb the civil order. Thus, the Anabaptists are excluded from toleration because they repudiate civil magistrates, and the Roman Catholics because they claim the pope has power to dispense oaths of allegiance. It is easy to see why Hammond was unhappy with Taylor's book.

50. Hammond, *Practical Catechism,* 1.1; LACT, vol. 1, pp. 1–2. The citation from Clement is *Paedagogus,* 1.1.

51. Hammond, *Practical Catechism,* 1.3; LACT, vol. 1, p. 42.

52. Hammond, *Practical Catechism,* 1.3; LACT, vol. 1, pp. 43 and 51.

53. Hammond, *Practical Catechism,* 1.3; LACT, vol. 1, p. 37.

54. Hammond, *Practical Catechism,* 1.3; LACT, vol. 1, p. 39.

55. Hammond, *Practical Catechism,* 5.1; LACT, vol. 1, p. 306

56. Hammond, *Practical Catechism,* 2.1; LACT, vol. 1, pp. 89–90.

57. Hammond, *Practical Catechism,* 2.1; LACT, vol. 1, pp. 90–91.

58. Hammond, *Paraenesis,* 4.4; LACT, vol. 2, p. 330.

59. Hammond, *Paraenesis,* 5.7.6; LACT, vol. 2, pp. 343–44. Cf. 5.5.2, 5.7.1, and 5.7.5, pp. 331, 340, and 343.

60. Hammond, *Paraenesis,* 5.15; LACT, vol. 2, p. 376.

61. Hammond, *Paraenesis,* 5.14.1; LACT, vol. 2, p. 375.

62. Hammond, *Paraenesis,* 5.7.3; LACT, vol. 2, p. 342.

63. Hammond, *Of Fundamentals,* 2.2; LACT, vol. 2, p. 76.

64. Hammond, *Of Fundamentals,* 2.6; LACT, vol. 2, p. 79.

65. Hammond, *Of Fundamentals,* 3.1; LACT, vol. 2, p. 82.

66. Hammond, *Of Fundamentals,* 3.8; LACT, vol. 2, p. 84.

67. Hammond, *The Reasonableness of Christianity,* Introduction; LACT, vol. 2, p. 6.

68. Hammond, *The Reasonableness of Christianity,* 1.4; LACT, vol. 2, p. 8.

69. Hammond, *The Reasonableness of Christianity,* 1.6; LACT, vol. 2, p. 8.

70. Hammond, *The Reasonableness of Christianity,* 1.18; LACT, vol. 2, pp. 20–21.

71. Hammond, *The Reasonableness of Christianity,* 1.19 and 1.24; LACT, vol. 2, pp. 21–23.

72. Hammond, *The Reasonableness of Christianity,* 1.27; LACT, vol. 2, p. 25.

73. Hammond, *The Reasonableness of Christianity,* 2.7; LACT, vol. 2, p. 30. See the whole of 2.3–15.

74. Hammond, *The Reasonableness of Christianity,* 2.16; LACT, vol. 2, p. 32.

75. Hammond, *The Reasonableness of Christianity,* 2.19; LACT, vol. 2, p. 34.

Chapter Three / The Ambiguous Alliance of Scripture and Nature

1. Bertolt Brecht, *Das Leben des Galilei,* p. 84. "Barberin: Wie, Gott hat nicht sorgfältig genug Astronomie studiert, bevor er die Heilige Schrift verfasste? Bellarmin: Ist es nicht auch fur Sie wahrscheinlich, dass der Schopfer uber das von ihm Geschaffene besser Bescheid weiss als sein Geschöpf? Galilei: Aber, meine Herren, schliesslich kann der Mensch nicht nur die Bewegungen der Gestirne falsch auffassen, sondern auch die Bibel! Bellarmin: Aber wie die Bibel aufzufassen ist, darüber haben schliesslich die Theologen der Heiligen Kirche zu befinden, nicht? Galilei schweigt."

2. Cf. John Locke, *An Essay Concerning Human Understanding,* I.i.7 (Penguin edition, p. 58): "Thus men, extending their inquiries beyond their capacities, and letting their thoughts wander into those depths, where they can find no sure footing; 'tis no wonder, that they raise questions, and multiply disputes, which never come to any clear resolution, are proper only to continue and increase their doubts, and to confirm them at last in perfect scepticism."

3. See Spurr, *Restoration Church of England,* p. 378: "One can safely conclude that even in the early eighteenth century, fewer than one in ten

of the population attended something other than the Church of England. More significant, however, was the number of English men and women who attended no form of worship. . . . Atheism and apathy, rather than any brand of religion, appeared to be the true victors of 1689."

4. *An Address to the Royal Society*, p. a.3.3. *The Vanity of Dogmatizing: The Three "Versions" by Joseph Glanvill*, with a critical introduction by Stephen Medcalf (Hove, Sussex: Harvester Press, 1970), facsimile.

5. Glanvill, *Vanity of Dogmatizing*, ch. 24: "An Apology for Philosophy" (Medcalf, p. 248).

6. Glanvill, *Vanity of Dogmatizing*, ch. 21 (Medcalf, p. 209).

7. Glanvill, *Vanity of Dogmatizing*, ch. 24 (Medcalf, p. 245). The "greater" one is St. Paul at Rom 1:20.

8. Glanvill, *Vanity of Dogmatizing*, ch. 1 (Medcalf, pp. 4–5).

9. John Pearson, *An Exposition of the Creed*, ed. E. Burton (Oxford: Oxford University Press, 1833), Epistle Dedicatory, p. xi. See Richard A. Norris, "Doctor Pearson Construes the Apostles' Creed," in *This Sacred History*, ed. D. S. Armentrout (Cambridge, Mass.: Cowley, 1990), pp. 77–88.

10. See Powel Mills Dawley, *The Story of the General Theological Seminary* (New York: Oxford University Press, 1969), pp. 21, 68, 90, 137, 285. Pearson, in company with Butler, Paley, Hooker, Chillingworth, Burnet, and others, was in the list of the 1804 Course of Ecclesiastical Studies, probably drawn up by Bishop White. His book remained a textbook at least until the 1893 scheme of studies for General Seminary.

11. Pearson, *Exposition*, To the Reader, pp. xv and xx.

12. Pearson, *Exposition*, Article 1, p. 23.

13. Pearson, *Exposition*, To the Reader, p. xviii.

14. *The Whole Duty of Man*, edition in the Ancient and Modern Library of Theological Literature (London: Griffith, Farren, Okeden, & Welsh, n.d.), Preface 1, p. 3.

15. *Whole Duty of Man*, Preface 3, p. 3.

16. *Whole Duty of Man*, Sunday 1.2–3, 7, pp. 13–16.

17. *John Dryden: The Major Works*, ed. Keith Walker, Oxford World's Classics (Oxford: Oxford University Press, 2003; first published in 1987), p. 219.

18. Walker, *John Dryden*, p. 227. The friend is Henry Dickinson.

19. Walker, *John Dryden*, pp. 222–23.

20. Cited in C. A. Patrides, *The Cambridge Platonists* (Cambridge: Cambridge University Press, 1980; first published by Edward Arnold in 1969), pp. 29–30.

21. Whichcote, "The Use of Reason in Matters of Religion," in Patrides, *Cambridge Platonists*, p. 60.

22. Whichcote, "The Unity of the Church," in Patrides, *Cambridge Platonists*, p. 81. Cf. *Moral and Religious Aphorisms*, 981 ("Determinations, *beyond* Scripture, have indeed *enlarged* Faith; but lessened *Charity*, and multiplied Divisions.") and 1188 ("Where the Doctrine is *necessary* and *important*; the Scripture is *clear* and *full*: but, where the Scripture is not clear and full; the Doctrine is not necessary or important."); Patrides, *Cambridge Platonists*, pp. 335 and 336. These views obviously parallel those of Chillingworth.

23. Patrides, *Cambridge Platonists*, p. 88.

24. Whichcote, *Moral and Religious Aphorisms*, 109, in Patrides, *Cambridge Platonists*, p. 327.

25. Whichcote, *Moral and Religious Aphorisms*, 880, in Patrides, *Cambridge Platonists*, p. 334.

26. Cudworth, "A Sermon Preached before the House of Commons" (1647), in Patrides, *Cambridge Platonists*, p. 108. Cf. p. 109: "The Gospel, though it be a Sovereigne and Medicinall thing in it self, yet the mere knowing and believing of the history of it, will do us no good: we can receive no vertue from it, till it be inwardly digested & concocted into our souls; till it be made *Ours*, and become a *living thing* in our hearts. The Gospel, if it be onely without us, cannot save us; no more then that Physitians Bill, could cure the ignorant Patient of his disease, who, when it was commended to him, took the Paper onely, and put it up in his pocket, but never drunk the Potion that was prescribed in it." Cf. also p. 92: "Inke and Paper can never make us Christians, can never beget a new nature, a living principle in us. . . . Words and syllables which are but dead things, cannot possibly convey the living notions of heavenly truths to us."

27. John Tillotson, *The Rule of Faith*, Part 1.3, 5; Part 2.3.14–15 in *Works*, ed. Thomas Birch (London: J. F. Dove, 1820), vol. 10, pp. 238–39, 259, 297–99. In Sermon 30 (Birch, vol. 2, p. 520) he does say that the scriptures "are the great and standard revelation of God to mankind; wherein the nature of God, and his will concerning our duty, and the terms and conditions of our eternal happiness in another world are fully and plainly delivered to us."

28. Tillotson, *Rule of Faith*, 1.1.3 (Birch, vol. 10, pp. 230–31).

29. Tillotson, *Rule of Faith*, 3.1.2 (Birch, vol. 10, p. 328).

30. Tillotson, *Rule of Faith*, 3.1.2 (Birch, vol. 10, pp. 326–27).

31. Tillotson, Sermon 102 (Birch, vol. 5, pp. 305–6). Cf. Sermon 21 (Birch, vol. 2, pp. 257–58).

32. Tillotson, Sermon 101 (Birch, vol. 5, p. 292).

33. Tillotson, Sermon 21 (Birch, vol. 2, pp. 257–58).

34. Tillotson, Sermon 21 (Birch, vol. 2, p. 260 and p. 262).

35. Tillotson, Sermon 136 (Birch, vol. 6, p. 423). Tillotson cites Rom 1:20.

36. Gilbert Burnet, *An Exposition of the Thirty-Nine Articles*, ed. James R. Page (London: Scott, Webster, and Geary, 1837), p. xi.

37. Burnet, *Exposition*, Introduction, pp. 7 and 10. His reference is to the Declaration preceding the Articles in the 1662 Prayer Book.

38. Burnet, *Exposition*, Introduction, p. 11.

39. Burnet, *Exposition*, Introduction, p. 8.

40. Burnet, *Exposition*, Article VI, p. 89.

41. Burnet, *Exposition*, Article VI, pp. 91–92. Cf. pp. 94, 96, 97.

42. Burnet, *Exposition*, Introduction, p. 2; Article VIII, pp. 137–38.

43. Burnet, *Exposition*, Article VI, pp. 97–99.

44. Burnet, *Exposition*, Article XX, p. 268. Cf. pp. 269–70 and Article XIX, pp. 246–47.

45. Burnet, *Exposition*, Article VI, p. 112. Cf. p. 113: "The laying down a scheme that asserts an immediate inspiration which goes to the style, and to every tittle, and that denies any error to have crept *into any of the copies*, as it seems on the one hand to raise the honour of the scriptures very highly, so it lies open, on the other hand, to great difficulties, which seem insuperable in that hypothesis; whereas a middle way, as it settles the divine inspiration of these writings, and their being continued down genuine and unvitiated to us, as to all that for which we can only suppose that inspiration was given; so it helps us more easily out of all difficulties, by yielding that which serves to answer them, without weakening the authority of the whole."

46. Burnet, *Exposition*, Article XVIII, p. 229.

47. Burnet, *Exposition*, Article XVIII, pp. 229–32.

48. Burnet, *Exposition*, Article I, p. 27.

49. John Locke, *The Reasonableness of Christianity as Delivered in the Scriptures* (1695), Clarendon edition, ed. John C. Higgins-Biddle (Oxford: Clarendon Press, 1999), Introduction, pp. xv–cxv.

50. Locke, *The Reasonableness of Christianity*, Preface (Higgins-Biddle, p. 3).

51. Locke, *The Reasonableness of Christianity*, ch. 3 (Higgins-Biddle, p. 18).

52. Locke, *The Reasonableness of Christianity*, ch. 3 (Higgins-Biddle, pp. 20–21).

53. Locke, *The Reasonableness of Christianity*, ch. 14 (Higgins-Biddle, p. 163).

54. Locke, *The Reasonableness of Christianity*, ch. 14 (Higgins-Biddle, pp. 139–40).

55. Locke, *An Essay Concerning Human Understanding*, ed. Roger Woodhouse (London: Penguin Classics, 1997), III.ix.23, p. 436.

56. William Law, a non-juring high churchman, also wrote against Tindal's *Christianity as Old as the Creation, or the Gospel a Republication of the Religion of Nature* (1730) in his *The Case of Reason and Natural Religion Fairly and Fully Stated* (1731). And in the first of his *Three Letters to the Bishop of Bangor* (1717) he says that the deists approve of Bishop Hoadly's denial that Christ left us with any ecclesiastical authority upon earth. It is, however, the latitudinarian rebuttal of deism in Butler and Paley that has pride of place.

57. The full title is *The Analogy of Religion, Natural and Revealed, to the Constitution and Course of Nature*. I am using an edition published in Edinburgh by William Whyte & Co., n.d.

58. Butler, *Analogy*, Introduction, pp. 5–6.

59. Cf. Basil Willey, *The Eighteenth-Century Background* (first published 1940, Penguin edition 1962), p. 83: "It is probable that God intends to test and prove our capacities as much in understanding Revelation as in the practical conduct of life, or in exploring the secrets of Nature. But, one feels, if this is so, what has become of the notion of Revelation? Has it not in fact been obliterated in the effort to defend it? If there is no more certainty or clarity in Revelation than in Nature, then Revelation is *part* of Nature? To this pass has orthodoxy come in the reign of George II, that it can only defend Revelation by denying that it reveals."

60. Butler, *Analogy*, Part 2.1, p. 178.

61. Butler, *Analogy*, Part 2.1, p. 180.

62. Butler, *Analogy*, Part 2.1, p. 200.

63. Butler, *Analogy*, 2.3, pp. 214, 219, 224.

64. Butler, *Analogy*, 2.1, p. 181. Cf. 2.7, p. 295.

65. Cf. the well-known passage in *Analogy*, 1.1, pp. 37–38: "And from hence it must follow, that persons' notion of what is natural will be enlarged, in proportion to their greater knowledge of the works of God and the dispensations of his Providence. Nor is there any absurdity in supposing, that there may be beings in the universe, whose capacities, and knowledge, and views, may be so extensive, as that the whole Christian dispensation may to them appear natural, *i.e.* analogous or conformable to God's dealings with

other parts of his creation, as natural as the visible known course of things appears to us."

66. See Introduction, p. 1: "Probable evidence is essentially distinguished from demonstrative by this, that it admits of degrees, and of all variety of them, from the highest moral certainty, to the very lowest presumption." See also p. 3: "For nothing which is the possible object of knowledge...can be probable to an infinite Intelligence....But to us probability is the very guide of life."

67. M. L. Clarke, *Paley: Evidences for the Man* (London: SPCK, 1947), p. 43.

68. William Paley, *Natural Theology*, ch. 2, III (*The Works of William Paley* [Cambridge: Hilliard and Brown, 1830], vol. 1, p. 14).

69. Paley, *Natural Theology*, ch. 23 (*Works*, vol. 1, p. 212).

70. Paley, *Natural Theology*, ch. 24 (*Works*, vol. 1, p. 229).

71. Paley, *Natural Theology*, ch. 25 (*Works*, vol. 1, p. 232).

72. Paley, *Natural Theology*, ch. 26 (*Works*, vol. 1, p. 235).

73. Paley, *Natural Theology*, ch. 26 (*Works*, vol. 1, p. 236).

74. David Hume, of course, takes this approach to demolish the argument from design. See *An Enquiry Concerning Human Understanding*, Section XI; *The Natural History of Religion* III and VI; *Dialogues Concerning Natural Religion*, Part XI.

75. Paley, *Natural Theology*, ch. 26 (*Works*, vol. 1, p. 240).

76. Paley, *Natural Theology*, ch. 26 (*Works*, vol. 1, p. 270).

77. Paley, *Natural Theology*, ch. 24 (*Works*, vol. 1, p. 229).

78. Paley, *Natural Theology*, ch. 27 (*Works*, vol. 1, p. 278).

79. See Willey, *Eighteenth-Century Background*, pp. 124–27. Hume's essay "On Miracles" is section 10 of his *Enquiry Concerning Human Understanding*. Willey points out a contradiction in Hume's argument. Having proved that anything may be the "cause" of anything, Hume also, paradoxically, "disproved the possibility of miracles because they violated the invariable laws of Nature" (p. 124). This could lead to an acceptance of miracles on the basis of faith, but Hume is not willing to draw this conclusion.

80. William Paley, *A View of the Evidences of Christianity in Three Parts*. ed. Robert Potts (Cambridge: Cambridge University Press, 1850), 3.8, pp. 301–3.

81. Paley, *Evidences*, 1.8, p. 58.

82. Paley, *Evidences*, 1.7, p. 57.

83. Paley, *Evidences*, 2.9.2, pp. 244–45.

84. Paley, *Evidences*, 1.1, p. 15.

85. Paley, *Evidences*, 2.2, pp. 155–56.
86. Paley, *Evidences*, 3.8, p. 296.
87. Paley, *Evidences*, 3.8, p. 299.
88. Paley, *Evidences*, 3.8, p. 296.
89. The first schism was the organization of the American Methodists in 1784. The British schisms (in the plural) occurred in the early nineteenth century.
90. Albert C. Outler, ed., *John Wesley* (New York: Oxford University Press, 1980 paperback; first published 1964), p. 79.
91. Outler, *John Wesley*, pp. 105–7.
92. For a full account see Ted A. Campbell, *John Wesley and Christian Antiquity: Religious Vision and Cultural Change* (Nashville: Kingswood Books, Abingdon Press, 1991), pp. 26–40.
93. Outler, *John Wesley*, pp. 46–47.
94. Outler, *John Wesley*, pp. 300–301.
95. John Wesley, *An Earnest Appeal*, 5 (Outler, *John Wesley*, p. 386). Gal 5:6 is cited explicitly in section 49 (Outler, *John Wesley*, p. 401).
96. Wesley, *An Earnest Appeal*, 40 (Outler, *John Wesley*, p. 398).
97. Wesley, *An Earnest Appeal*, 41 (Outler, *John Wesley*, p. 398).
98. Wesley, *An Earnest Appeal*, 46 (Outler, *John Wesley*, p. 400).
99. Wesley, *An Earnest Appeal*, 12–37 (Outler, *John Wesley*, pp. 388–97).
100. Wesley, *An Earnest Appeal*, 18–19 (Outler, *John Wesley*, p. 390).
101. Wesley, *An Earnest Appeal*, 20–21 (Outler, *John Wesley*, p. 391).
102. Wesley, *An Earnest Appeal*, 30 (Outler, *John Wesley*, p. 394).
103. Wesley, *An Earnest Appeal*, 31 (Outler, *John Wesley*, p. 395).
104. Wesley, *An Earnest Appeal*, 32–34 (Outler, *John Wesley*, p. 395).
105. Wesley, *An Earnest Appeal*, 35 (Outler, *John Wesley*, p. 396).

Chapter Four / Making Friends with History: The Nineteenth Century

1. Arthur P. Stanley, *The Life of Thomas Arnold, D.D.* (London: Hutchinson & Co., 1903; first published 1844), pp. 270–71, 266.
2. The two sermons may be found in A. O. J. Cockshut, ed., *Religious Controversies of the Nineteenth Century: Selected Documents* (London: Methuen & Co. Ltd., 1966). The citations above are on pp. 92–93.
3. Cockshut, *Religious Controversies*, p. 96.
4. Cockshut, *Religious Controversies*, p. 98.
5. Thomas Arnold, *Christian Life: Its Hopes, Its Fears, and Its Close: Sermons, Preached Mostly in the Chapel of Rugby School*, 2nd ed. (London:

B. Fellowes, 1843), Sermon 20: "St. Thomas: Faith Triumphant in Doubt," p. 310. Cf. Stanley's *Life,* p. 28 and also p. 315, where he describes Arnold's repetition of the story on his deathbed.

6. See Walter E. Houghton, *The Victorian Frame of Mind, 1830–1870* (New Haven and London: Yale University Press, 1957), p. 1. Houghton's point is that the idea of transition from old to new could be viewed optimistically or pessimistically, depending upon the view taken of the old.

7. For a full account see Owen Chadwick, *The Victorian Church,* 2 vols. (London: Adam & Charles Black, 1971, 1972; first published 1966 and 1970), Part I, ch. 8, and Part II, chs. 1–3.

8. See Houghton, *Victorian Frame,* p. 50.

9. See R. G. Collingwood, *The Idea of History* (Oxford: Clarendon Press, 1946), pp. 113–22. Collingwood locates Hegel and other philosophers of history at the "threshold" of "scientific history."

10. See Hans W. Frei, *The Eclipse of Biblical Narrative: A Study in Eighteenth and Nineteenth Century Hermeneutics* (New Haven and London: Yale University Press, 1974), p. 322: "But most important in our general context is that the whole procedure — whether in the form that Schleiermacher and his later followers gave it or in that which Hegel and his followers gave it — simply undercuts all realistic narrative."

11. See E. H. Carr, *What Is History?* (London: Pelican Books, 1964; first published 1961), pp. 8–9.

12. See Houghton, *Victorian Frame,* pp. 125–26.

13. John Henry Newman, *Discussions and Arguments on Various Subjects* (London: Longmans, Green, and Co., 1911; first published 1872), 1.1, p. 110. Selection III republishes Tracts 83 and 85: "Holy Scripture in Its Relation to the Catholic Creed."

14. Newman, "Holy Scripture," 1.1, p. 112.

15. Newman, "Holy Scripture," 1.1–3, pp. 113, 120–23.

16. Newman, "Holy Scripture," 1.3, pp. 123, 133.

17. Newman, "Holy Scripture," 1.4, p. 153.

18. Newman, "Holy Scripture," 5.4–5, pp. 178ff.

19. Newman, "Holy Scripture," 6.1, p. 199.

20. Newman, "Holy Scripture," 4.2, p. 162. Newman also refers to 1 Cor 11:2, 16, 23 and 1 Thess 2:15.

21. Newman, "Holy Scripture," 3.2, pp. 145–46.

22. Newman, "Holy Scripture," 5.2 and 5.3, pp. 176 and 178.

23. Newman, "Holy Scripture," 4.3, p. 166.

24. Newman, *Prophetical Office of the Church,* in Owen Chadwick, *The Mind of the Oxford Movement* (London: A. and C. Black, 1960), pp. 136–37.

25. Newman, "Holy Scripture," 2.1, pp. 126–27.

26. Newman, "Holy Scripture," 2.1, pp. 127–29.

27. Newman, "Holy Scripture," 3.2, p. 149.

28. Newman, "Holy Scripture," 2.3, p. 136.

29. Newman, "Holy Scripture," 2.3, p. 137.

30. Newman, "Holy Scripture," 8.1, p. 237. Cf. p. 241: "if you do consider the fourth and fifth centuries enlightened enough to decide on the Canon, then I want to know why you call them not enlightened in point of doctrine."

31. John Henry Newman, *An Essay on the Development of Christian Doctrine* (1845), Pelican Classics, ed. J. M. Cameron (Harmondsworth: Penguin Books, 1974), 2.1.1, p. 149.

32. Newman, *Development,* 6.1.1, p. 342.

33. Newman, *Development,* 2.2.7, p. 175.

34. Newman, *Development,* Introduction, p. 72.

35. Cited from *Letters and Diaries* by Ian Ker, *John Henry Newman: A Biography* (Oxford: Oxford University Press, 1988), p. 586.

36. F. D. Maurice, *The Epistle to the Hebrews* (London: John W. Parker, 1846), pp. v–viii.

37. Maurice, *Hebrews,* pp. xiii–xv, xxi.

38. Maurice, *Hebrews,* p. xxiv.

39. Maurice, *Hebrews,* p. xxvii.

40. Maurice, *Hebrews,* p. xxxviii.

41. Maurice, *Hebrews,* p. xxxiv.

42. Maurice, *Hebrews,* p. xliii.

43. Maurice, *Hebrews,* p. xliv.

44. Maurice, *Hebrews,* p. lxix.

45. Maurice, *Hebrews,* p. xcvi.

46. Maurice, *Hebrews,* p. xxxviii.

47. Maurice, *Hebrews,* p. lxxix.

48. Maurice, *Hebrews,* p. cxxv.

49. Maurice, *The Kingdom of Christ* (1838), Part 2, chapter 4, section 6. The other signs are baptism, the creeds, forms of worship, the eucharist, and the ministry.

50. Maurice, *Kingdom of Christ,* 2.4.6, p. 179.

51. Maurice, *Kingdom of Christ,* 2.4.6, p. 183. Cf. the letter he wrote in 1842 to the Revd. A. Atwood (*Life,* vol. 1, p. 333): We should not regard the

Bible or the church as authorized dogma from the past. "On the contrary, if we receive one as well as the other in its own place and for its own purposes as the perpetual living lesson of a living teacher, we must suppose that by them He is training our reason and all our faculties to higher exercises and fuller apprehension than they at present possess. There must be perpetual growth, but a growth which does not falsify any previous stage, because it is a growth into the knowledge of Him who is the same yesterday, to-day, and for ever." See also his letter of 1844 to Kingsley (*Life*, vol. 1, pp. 372–74) where he speaks of the Bible as a "history containing the gradual discovery of God."

52. Maurice, *Kingdom of Christ*, 2.4.6, p. 184.

53. Cf. his letter of 1865 to Mr. John Hodgkin after reading his son's pamphlet on inspiration (*Life*, vol. 2, p. 501): "Yet I feel compelled often to stand with both [arraigners and critics] against those who turn it [the Bible] into a god, and so deny the living God of whom it bears witness. That idolatry is so fearful, and the numbers who are rushing into it so great and respectable, that I feel we ought to bear any reproaches and any suspicions, rather than be the instruments of promoting it."

54. Maurice, *Kingdom of Christ*, 2.4.6, p. 188.

55. In 1840 he wrote to Hare, asking him to translate a piece by Schelling because "it lays the axe to the root of that Rationalism of which Straussianism and all the kindred notions of our time are the flower" (*Life*, vol. 1, p. 289). In 1848 a letter to Canon Barry suggests that the Germans start from below, while "we" start from above; and it is clear he has idealism in mind (*Life*, vol. 1, pp. 467–68, cf. 453–54 and vol. 2, p. 253).

56. Maurice, *Kingdom of Christ*, 2.4.6, pp. 189–92

57. Maurice, *Kingdom of Christ*, 2.4.6, pp. 193–94.

58. Maurice, *Kingdom of Christ*, 2.4.6, pp. 194–95.

59. Maurice, *Kingdom of Christ*, 2.4.6, pp. 201–2.

60. Maurice, *Kingdom of Christ*, 2.4.6, pp. 203–5.

61. Maurice, *Kingdom of Christ*, 2.4.6, p. 217.

62. Maurice, *Kingdom of Christ*, 2.4.6, p. 214.

63. Maurice, *Kingdom of Christ*, 2.4.6, pp. 217ff.

64. Benjamin Jowett, "On the Interpretation of Scripture," in *Essays and Reviews* (London: John W. Parker and Son, 1860; Gregg reprint), p. 330.

65. Jowett, "Interpretation," pp. 330–33.

66. Jowett, "Interpretation," p. 334.

67. Jowett, "Interpretation," pp. 344–48.

68. Jowett, "Interpretation," p. 348.

69. Jowett, "Interpretation," p. 350.

70. Jowett, "Interpretation," p. 351.

71. Jowett, "Interpretation," pp. 342–43.

72. Jowett, "Interpretation," p. 345.

73. Jowett, "Interpretation," p. 351.

74. Jowett, "Interpretation," pp. 353–54.

75. Jowett, "Interpretation," p. 357.

76. Jowett, "Interpretation," pp. 358–59.

77. Jowett, "Interpretation," p. 366.

78. Jowett, "Interpretation," p. 367.

79. Jowett, "Interpretation," p. 372. Cf. pp. 372–73: "Doubt comes in at the window, when Inquiry is denied at the door." "It would be a strange and almost incredible thing, that the Gospel, which at first made war only on the vices of mankind, should now be opposed to one of the highest and rarest of human virtues — the love of truth."

80. Jowett, "Interpretation," p. 375. Cf. p. 377.

81. Jowett, "Interpretation," p. 377.

82. Jowett, "Interpretation," p. 378.

83. Jowett, "Interpretation," p. 382.

84. Jowett, "Interpretation," pp. 382–83. He also says, p. 383: "The indiscriminate use of parallel passages taken from one end of Scripture and applied to the other . . . is useless and uncritical."

85. Jowett, "Interpretation," pp. 384–85.

86. Jowett, "Interpretation," pp. 387 and 389.

87. Jowett, "Interpretation," p. 404.

88. Jowett, "Interpretation," p. 405.

89. Jowett, "Interpretation," p. 420.

90. Jowett, "Interpretation," p. 407.

91. Jowett, "Interpretation," pp. 408–9.

92. Jowett, "Interpretation," p. 410.

93. Jowett, "Interpretation," pp. 411–12.

94. Jowett, "Interpretation," p. 421.

95. Jowett, "Interpretation," pp. 423–29.

96. William Sanday, *Inspiration: Eight Lectures on the Early History and Origin of the Doctrine of Biblical Inspiration* (London: Longman, Green, and Co., 1901). This is a reprint of the third enlarged edition with a new preface, first published 1896. The first edition was published in 1893.

97. See Chadwick, *The Victorian Church*, Part II, pp. 97–111: "The Acceptance of Biblical Criticism by the Churches 1887–95."

98. Charles Gore, ed., *Lux Mundi: A Series of Studies in The Religion of the Incarnation* (London: John Murray, 1889), Preface, p. viii.

99. Sanday, *Inspiration,* Lecture I, p. 2.

100. Sanday, *Inspiration,* Lecture VIII, pp. 429–30.

101. Sanday, *Inspiration,* Lecture III, p. 134.

102. Sanday, *Inspiration,* Lecture VII, p. 358.

103. Sanday, *Inspiration,* Lecture II, pp. 116–19.

104. See Lecture IV, pp. 192–93: There are divergent views regarding the Psalms, "but the whole position is hopeful . . . The patient labour which is being devoted to them cannot be long without fruit." Also Lecture VI, p. 282: With respect to the synoptic problem, "It must not be thought that I despair of a solution. I greatly hope that before long a sustained and combined effort, for which the circumstances are now particularly favourable may be made to grapple at close quarters with the difficulties and wring from them a better result than has been obtained hitherto." Sanday's expectation proved true, and the main lines of his solution of the synoptic problem remain widely accepted today.

105. Sanday, *Inspiration,* Lecture III, pp. 128–44.

106. Sanday, *Inspiration,* Lecture IV, pp. 172–73 and 215–16.

107. Sanday, *Inspiration,* Lecture VI, pp. 277–79 and 283.

108. Sanday, *Inspiration,* Lecture VI, pp. 320–30.

109. Sanday, *Inspiration,* Lecture VI, p. 317.

110. Sanday, *Inspiration,* Lecture VI, p. 298.

111. Sanday, *Inspiration,* Lecture VIII, p. 400.

112. Sanday, *Inspiration,* Lecture III, pp. 145–46.

113. Sanday, *Inspiration,* Lecture III, p. 124.

114. Sanday, *Inspiration,* Lecture VII, pp. 352–54.

115. Sanday, *Inspiration,* Lecture III, p. 144 and pp. 124–25.

116. Sanday, *Inspiration,* Lecture VIII, pp. 417–18.

117. Sanday, *Inspiration,* Lecture IV, p. 189.

118. Sanday, *Inspiration,* Lecture V, pp. 264–65.

119. Sanday, *Inspiration,* Lecture IV, pp. 211–13.

120. Sanday, *Inspiration,* Lecture VII, pp. 333–34.

121. Sanday, *Inspiration,* Lecture III, p. 126. Cf. Lecture III, p. 164: "Revelation proceeds by way of growth, by development, by a gradual opening of the eyes to higher ranges of truth." Revelation "is an organism, a connected and coherent structure, fitly joined and compacted together. A continuity runs through it all, and even that which seems to be lower is necessary as a stepping-stone to the higher." Cf. also Lecture VIII, pp. 422–23, for a similar structural and spatial understanding. Here he also cites Ephesians 1:11.

122. Sanday, *Inspiration,* Lecture VIII, pp. 391–93.

123. Sanday, *Inspiration,* Lecture VIII, pp. 396, 400, and 402.

124. William E. Gladstone, *The Impregnable Rock of Holy Scripture.* London: Wm. Isbister Ltd., 1890.

125. Gladstone, *Rock,* Essay 2, p. 48.

126. Gladstone, *Rock,* Essay 1, p. 5. Cf. p. 28: "I have endeavoured to point out that the operations of criticism properly so called, affecting as they do the literary form of the books, leave the questions of substance, namely those of history, miracle, and revelation, substantially where they found them."

127. Gladstone, *Rock,* Essay 1, p. 8.

128. Gladstone, *Rock,* Essay 1, p. 28.

129. Gladstone, *Rock,* Essay 2, p. 40.

130. Gladstone, *Rock,* Essay 2, pp. 56–57, 60–63. Cf. Essay 6, pp. 226–29.

131. Gladstone, *Rock,* Essay 3, p. 113.

132. Gladstone, *Rock,* Essay 7: Conclusion, p. 259.

133. Gladstone, *Rock,* Essay 5, p. 174. See the whole of pp. 174–79 and p. 199.

134. Gladstone, *Rock,* Essay 7, pp. 260–74.

135. Gladstone, *Rock,* Essay 7, p. 277.

136. Gladstone, *Rock,* Essay 7, p. 291.

137. Gladstone, *Rock,* Essay 7, pp. 254–55.

138. Gladstone, *Rock,* Essay 7, pp. 288–89.

Chapter Five / Keeping History as a Friend of Faith: The Last Century

1. Douglas Southall Freeman, *George Washington: A Biography* (New York: Charles Scribner's Sons, 1948–1954), vol. 1, p. xx.

2. Freeman, *George Washington,* vol. 6, p. xxxviii.

3. *Contentio Veritatis: Essays in Constructive Theology* (London: John Murray, 1902), preface, p. v.

4. *Contentio Veritatis,* preface, p. vi.

5. *Contentio Veritatis,* preface, p. vii.

6. *Contentio Veritatis,* preface, pp. viii–ix. It is worth noting that they refer to Christianity rather than to the church.

7. *Contentio Veritatis,* Essay 4, p. 169.

8. *Contentio Veritatis,* Essay 4, p. 170.

9. *Contentio Veritatis,* Essay 4, p. 173.

10. *Contentio Veritatis,* Essay 4, p. 175.

11. *Contentio Veritatis,* Essay 4, p. 177.

12. *Contentio Veritatis*, Essay 4, p. 178.

13. *Contentio Veritatis*, Essay 4, p. 179.

14. *Contentio Veritatis*, Essay 4, p. 181.

15. *Contentio Veritatis*, Essay 4, p. 183.

16. *Contentio Veritatis*, Essay 4, pp. 190–91.

17. *Contentio Veritatis*, Essay 5, pp. 206–7.

18. *Contentio Veritatis*, Essay 5, pp. 227–29.

19. *Contentio Veritatis*, Essay 5, p. 230.

20. *Contentio Veritatis*, Essay 5, pp. 234–35.

21. *Contentio Veritatis*, Essay 5, p. 236.

22. *Contentio Veritatis*, Essay 5, p. 237.

23. John Hick, ed., *The Myth of God Incarnate* (London: SCM Press, 1977), Preface, p. ix.

24. Hick, *Myth*, Preface, p. x.

25. Hick, *Myth*, Essay 3, p. 49.

26. Hick, *Myth*, Essay 3, pp. 50–55.

27. Hick, *Myth*, Essay 3, p. 60.

28. Hick, *Myth*, Essay 1, p. 8.

29. Hick, *Myth*, Essay 1, p. 9.

30. Hick, *Myth*, Essay 8, p. 158.

31. Hick, *Myth*, Essay 8, p. 162.

32. Hick, *Myth*, Essay 8, p. 163.

33. Hick, *Myth*, Essay 7, p. 145.

34. Hick, *Myth*, Essay 7, p. 146.

35. *Christ, Faith and History*, Cambridge Studies in Christology, ed. S. W. Sykes and J. P. Clayton (Cambridge: Cambridge University Press, 1972), Essay 8, p. 132.

36. *Christ, Faith and History*, Essay 8, p. 135.

37. *Christ, Faith and History*, Essay 8, p. 139.

38. *Christ, Faith and History*, Essay 8, p. 142.

39. *Christ, Faith and History*, Essay 8, pp. 143–44.

40. Hick, *Myth*, Essay 10, p. 188.

41. Hick, *Myth*, Essay 10, p. 194.

42. Hick, *Myth*, Essay 10, p. 200.

43. Hick, *Myth*, Essay 10, p. 201.

44. Hick, *Myth*, Essay 10, pp. 201–2.

45. B. H. Streeter, ed., *Foundations: A Statement of Christian Belief in Terms of Modern Thought* (London: Macmillan and Co., 1912), introduction, p. viii.

46. Streeter, *Foundations*, introduction, p. vii.

47. Streeter, *Foundations*, Essay 5: "The Divinity of Christ," p. 230. Temple, however, adds a cautionary footnote that asks us to remember that Chalcedon "preserved belief in our Lord's real Humanity!"

48. Streeter, *Foundations*, Essay 2, p. 27.

49. Streeter, *Foundations*, Essay 2, p. 29.

50. Streeter, *Foundations*, Essay 2, p. 30.

51. Streeter, *Foundations*, Essay 2, p. 31.

52. Streeter, *Foundations*, Essay 2, pp. 32–46.

53. Streeter, *Foundations*, Essay 2, p. 51.

54. Streeter, *Foundations*, Essay 2, p. 52.

55. Streeter, *Foundations*, Essay 2, p. 56.

56. Streeter, *Foundations*, Essay 2, p. 66.

57. Streeter, *Foundations*, Essay 2, p. 67.

58. Edward Gordon Selwyn, ed., *Essays Catholic and Critical* (London: SPCK, 1926), preface, p. vi.

59. Streeter, *Foundations*, Essay 8, p. 366.

60. Streeter, *Foundations*, Essay 8, p. 373.

61. Streeter, *Foundations*, Essay 8: Synopsis, pp. 362–63.

62. Selwyn, *Essays Catholic and Critical*, Essay 3, pp. 85–86.

63. Selwyn, *Essays Catholic and Critical*, Essay 3, p. 87.

64. Selwyn, *Essays Catholic and Critical*, Essay 3, pp. 88–89.

65. Selwyn, *Essays Catholic and Critical*, Essay 3, p. 91.

66. Selwyn, *Essays Catholic and Critical*, Essay 3, p. 92.

67. Selwyn, *Essays Catholic and Critical*, Essay 3, p. 95, and the whole of pp. 93–95.

68. Selwyn, *Essays Catholic and Critical*, Essay 3, p. 96.

69. Cf. the second part of Essay 3, written by Wilfred Knox, pp. 98–119. The Bible cannot stand alone, but requires interpretation. Its authority cannot be oracular and instead correlates with the progressive experience discovered in scripture. This experience in turn correlates with that of those receiving it. The corporate experience of the church is the final test of the survival of doctrine. Knox appears to be suggesting an experiential understanding of the Vincentian canon.

70. G. W. H. Lampe, Essay 4 in *Christian Believing: The Nature of the Christian Faith and Its Expression in Holy Scripture and Creeds*, a report by the Doctrine Commission of the Church of England (London: SPCK, 1976), p. 101.

71. *Christian Believing*, Essay 4, p. 102.

72. *Christian Believing*, Essay 4, p. 103.

73. *Christian Believing*, Essay 4, pp. 103–4.

74. *Christian Believing*, Essay 4, p. 105.

75. *Christian Believing*, Essay 4, p. 108.

76. *Christian Believing*. Essay 4, p. 100.

77. *Christian Believing*, Essay 4, pp. 108–9.

78. *Christian Believing*, Essay 4, p. 112.

79. *Christian Believing*, Essay 4, p. 107.

80. Charles Gore, *Belief in God* (London: John Murray, 1921), p. 49.

81. Gore, *Belief in Christ* (London: John Murray, 1922), p. 3.

82. Gore, *Belief in Christ*, pp. 34–35.

83. Gore, *Belief in God*, p. 136.

84. Gore, *Belief in God*, p. 67.

85. Gore, *The Holy Spirit and the Church* (New York: Charles Scribner's Sons, 1924), p. 246. Chapter 8 (pp. 244–81) is entitled "The Authority of Holy Scripture."

86. Gore, *The Holy Spirit and the Church*, pp. 250–51.

87. Gore, *The Holy Spirit and the Church*, p. 252.

88. Gore, *The Holy Spirit and the Church*, p. 266.

89. Gore, *The Holy Spirit and the Church*, p. 273.

90. Gore, *The Holy Spirit and the Church*, p. 274.

91. William Temple, ed., *Doctrine in the Church of England* (London: SPCK, 1938), pp. 2–3. Cf. p. 19, and Davidson's letter defining the commission's task: "To consider the nature and grounds of Christian doctrine with a view to demonstrating the extent of existing agreement within the Church of England and with a view to investigating how far it is possible to remove or diminish existing differences." The letter continues by approving the idea that the report "should not be an authoritative statement" and that any action would be for the bishops to consider.

92. *Doctrine in the Church of England*, p. 8.

93. *Doctrine in the Church of England*, Prolegomena, p. 27.

94. *Doctrine in the Church of England*, Prolegomena, p. 28.

95. *Doctrine in the Church of England*, Prolegomena, p. 29.

96. *Doctrine in the Church of England*, Prolegomena, p. 30.

97. *Doctrine in the Church of England*, Prolegomena, p. 32.

98. *Doctrine in the Church of England*, Prolegomena, pp. 32–33.

99. A. R. Vidler, ed., *Soundings: Essays Concerning Christian Understanding* (Cambridge: Cambridge University Press, 1963), Introduction, p. ix.

100. Vidler, *Soundings*, Introduction, p. xii.

101. Vidler, *Soundings*, Essay 5, p. 105.

102. Vidler, *Soundings*, Essay 6, p. 130.

103. Vidler, *Soundings*, Essay 6, p. 132.

104. Vidler, *Soundings*, Essay 6, p. 132.

105. Vidler, *Soundings*, Essay 6, p. 134. Cf. p. 135: "For compulsion is incompatible with love, and all Christians are agreed that God is love." "Anyone who has ever 'fallen in love' has experienced the paradox of simultaneous constraint and freedom."

106. Vidler, *Soundings*, Essay 6, p. 135.

107. Vidler, *Soundings*, Essay 6, p. 137.

108. Vidler, *Soundings*, Essay 6, p. 138.

109. *Believing in the Church: The Corporate Nature of Faith*, a report by the Doctrine Commission of the Church of England (London: SPCK, 1981), Introduction, pp. 2 and 4.

110. *Believing in the Church*, Essay 2, p. 28.

111. *Believing in the Church*, Essay 2, p. 29.

112. *Believing in the Church*, Essay 2, p. 29.

113. *Believing in the Church*, Essay 2, p. 30.

114. *Believing in the Church*, Essay 2, p. 30.

115. *Believing in the Church*, Essay 2, pp. 31–32. Cf. Essay 4, "Story and Liturgy."

116. *Believing in the Church*, Essay 2, p. 33.

117. *Believing in the Church*, Essay 2, p. 36.

118. *Believing in the Church*, Essay 2, p. 37.

119. *Believing in the Church*, Essay 2, p. 38.

120. *Believing in the Church*, Essay 2, p. 39.

Chapter Six / An Inconclusive Conclusion

1. Cf. David H. Kelsey, *The Uses of Scripture in Recent Theology* (Philadelphia: Fortress Press, 1975), p. 102: "In every case, when a theologian appeals to scripture to help authorize a theological proposal, he appeals, not just to some aspect of scripture, but to a *pattern* characteristically exhibited by that aspect of scripture; and in virtue of that pattern, he construes the scripture to which he appeals as some kind of *whole*." I shall want to return to Kelsey later in this chapter.

2. Samuel Taylor Coleridge, *Confessions of an Inquiring Spirit*, ed. H. StJ. Hart, reprinted from the third edition, 1853, with the introduction by Joseph Henry Green and the note by Sara Coleridge. London: Adam & Charles Black, 1956), Hart's Introductory Note, p. 8.

3. Coleridge, *Confessions*, p. 38.

4. Coleridge, *Confessions*, Letter 4, p. 55. Cf. Letter 4, pp. 62–63: He has been to meetings of the British and Foreign Bible Society and heard Calvinists and Arminians, Quakers, Methodists, dissenters and dignitaries of the Established Church, "and still have I heard the same doctrine; — that the Bible was not to be regarded or reasoned about in the way that other good books are or may be; — that the Bible was different in kind . . . dictated by Omniscience, and therefore is in all its parts infallibly true and obligatory, and that [the authors] . . . were in fact but as different pens in the hand of one and the same Writer, and the words the words of God himself . . . oracles of infallibility."

5. Coleridge, *Confessions*, Letter 2, p. 43.

6. Coleridge, *Confessions*, Letter 3, pp. 53–54.

7. See, however, Letter 4, p. 58, where he speaks of "the positive harm which, both historically and spiritually, our religion sustains from this Doctrine."

8. Coleridge, *Confessions*, Letter 3, pp. 51–52.

9. Coleridge, *Confessions*, Letter 2, p. 46. Cf. Letter 6, p. 72.

10. Coleridge, *Confessions*, Letter 7, p. 77.

11. Coleridge, *Confessions*, Letter 2, p. 47.

12. Coleridge, *Confessions*, Letter 6, pp. 72–73.

13. Coleridge, *Confessions*, Letter 4, p. 55.

14. Coleridge, *Confessions*, Letter 4, p. 60.

15. Coleridge, *Confessions*, Letter 6, p. 74.

16. Coleridge, *Confessions*, Letter 6, p. 76.

17. Coleridge, *Confessions*, Letter 4, p. 60.

18. Coleridge, *Confessions*, Letter 5, p. 67.

19. Coleridge, *Confessions*, Letter 5, p. 66.

20. Coleridge, *Confessions*, p. 35. The diagram and its explanation precede the letters.

21. Coleridge, *Confessions*, Letter 6, p. 75. Cf. Letter 1, p. 41; Letter 3, p. 48; Letter 4, p. 62.

22. Coleridge, *Confessions*, Letter 1, p. 42.

23. Coleridge, *Confessions*, Letter 1, pp. 40–41.

24. Coleridge, *Confessions*, Letter 5, pp. 65–66.

25. Coleridge, *Confessions*, Letter 6, p. 72.

26. Coleridge, *Confessions*, Letter 6, p. 73.

27. Coleridge, *Confessions*, Letter 7, p. 79.

28. Raymond E. Brown, *An Introduction to the New Testament.* The Anchor Bible Reference Library (New York: Doubleday, 1997), p. vii.

29. Brown, *Introduction*, p. 26.

30. Brown, *Introduction*, pp. 29–35 and p. 46.

31. Selwyn, *Essays Catholic and Critical*, p. 154.

32. Selwyn, *Essays Catholic and Critical*, pp. 154–58.

33. Selwyn, *Essays Catholic and Critical*, p. 160.

34. Selwyn, *Essays Catholic and Critical*, pp. 261–63.

35. Selwyn, *Essays Catholic and Critical*, pp. 164–66.

36. Selwyn, *Essays Catholic and Critical*, p. 166 and p. 168.

37. Selwyn, *Essays Catholic and Critical*, p. 166.

38. Selwyn, *Essays Catholic and Critical*, pp. 168–69.

39. Selwyn, *Essays Catholic and Critical*, pp. 171–76.

40. Selwyn, *Essays Catholic and Critical*, pp. 176–77.

41. Sir Edwyn Hoskyns and Noel Davey, *The Riddle of the New Testament* (London: Faber & Faber, 1931), p. 264.

42. Selwyn, *Essays Catholic and Critical*, p. 178.

43. Luke Timothy Johnson, *The Real Jesus: The Misguided Quest for the Historical Jesus and the Truth of the Traditional Gospels* (New York: HarperCollins Paperback, 1997; first published 1996).

44. Johnson, *The Real Jesus*, p. 101.

45. Johnson, *The Real Jesus*, pp. 54–56.

46. Johnson, *The Real Jesus*, p. 42.

47. Johnson, *The Real Jesus*, pp. 71–74, 169–70.

48. Reginald H. Fuller, "Historical Criticism and the Bible," in *Anglicanism and the Bible*, ed. Frederick H. Borsch, Anglican Studies Series (Wilton, Conn.: Morehouse Barlow, 1984), p. 142.

49. David H. Kelsey, *The Uses of Scripture in Recent Theology* (Philadelphia: Fortress Press, 1975), p. 15.

50. Kelsey, *Uses of Scripture*, p. 33.

51. Kelsey, *Uses of Scripture*, p. 50.

52. Kelsey, *Uses of Scripture*, pp. 102–4.

53. Kelsey, *Uses of Scripture*, p. 89.

54. Kelsey, *Uses of Scripture*, pp. 109–10.

55. Kelsey, *Uses of Scripture*, pp. 94–98.

56. Hoskyns and Davey, *Riddle*, p. 14.

57. Hoskyns and Davey, *Riddle*, pp. 246–47.

58. Hoskyns and Davey, *Riddle*, pp. 257–58.

59. Hoskyns and Davey, *Riddle*, p. 261.

60. Some examples are Rom 5:10, 12–21; Rom 6:5; Rom 8:16–17; 1 Cor 15; 2 Cor 5:17; Eph 2:1–10; Heb 2:14–15; Heb 4:9–10.

61. Ignatius, *Philadelphians* 8.2. See the translation and notes in William R. Schoedel, *A Commentary on the Letters of Ignatius of Antioch* (Philadelphia: Fortress Press, 1985), p. 207.

62. George Herbert, *George Herbert: The Country Parson, The Temple,* ed. John N. Wall, Jr., Classics of Western Spirituality (New York: Paulist Press, 1981), pp. 113–14.

Bibliography of Works Consulted

Primary Sources

Arnold, Thomas. *Christian Life: Its Hopes, Its Fears, and Its Close: Sermons, Preached Mostly in the Chapel of Rugby School.* 2nd ed. London: B. Fellowes, 1843.

————. *Two Sermons on Prophecy* (1839). In *Religious Controversies of the Nineteenth Century: Selected Documents.* Ed. A. O. J. Cockshut. London: Methuen & Co., Ltd., 1966.

Aubrey, John. *Brief Lives.* Ed. Oliver Lawson-Dick. London: Mandarin Paperbacks, 1992.

Believing in the Church: The Corporate Nature of Faith. A Report by the Doctrine Commission of the Church of England. London: SPCK, 1981.

Bray, Gerald, ed. *Documents of the English Reformation.* Minneapolis: Fortress, 1994.

Browne, Thomas. *Religio Medici* (1642/1643). *Sir Thomas Browne: The Major Works.* Ed. C. A. Patrides. Harmondsworth: Penguin Books, 1977.

Burnet, Gilbert. *An Exposition of the Thirty-Nine Articles* (1699). Ed. James R. Page. London: Scott, Webster, and Geary, 1837.

Butler, Joseph. *The Analogy of Religion* (1736). Edition published in Edinburgh: William Whyte & Co., n.d.

Cambridge Platonists. *The Cambridge Platonists.* Ed. C. A. Patrides. Cambridge: Cambridge University Press, 1980; first published by Edward Arnold, 1969.

Chadwick, Owen. *The Mind of the Oxford Movement.* London: A. & C. Black, 1960.

————. *The Victorian Church.* 2 vols. London: Adam & Charles Black, 1971, 1972.

Chillingworth, William. *The Religion of Protestants, a Safe Way of Salvation* (1638). London: Thomas Tegg, 1845.

Christian Believing: The Nature of the Christian Faith and Its Expression in Holy Scripture and Creeds. A Report by the Doctrine Commission of the Church of England. London: SPCK, 1976.

Coleridge, Samuel Taylor. *Confessions of an Inquiring Spirit* (1840). Ed. H. StJ. Hart. Reprinted from the third edition of 1853 with the introduction by Joseph Henry Green and the note by Sara Coleridge. London: Adam & Charles Black, 1956.

Contentio Veritatis: Essays in Constructive Theology. London: John Murray, 1902.

Dickens, A. G., and Dorothy Carr. *The Reformation in England to the Accession of Elizabeth I.* Documents of Modern History. London: Edward Arnold, 1967.

Doctrine in the Church of England. Ed. William Temple. London: SPCK, 1938.

Dryden, John. *Religio Laici* (1682). *John Dryden: The Major Works.* Ed. Keith Walker. Oxford World's Classics. Oxford: Oxford University Press, 2003; first published 1987.

Essays and Reviews. London: John W. Parker and Son, 1860.

Essays Catholic and Critical. See Selwyn, Edward Gordon, ed.

Foundations: A Statement of Christian Belief in Terms of Modern Thought. See Streeter, B. H., ed.

Gee, Henry, and William John Hardy. *Documents Illustrative of English Church History.* London: Macmillan and Co., 1896.

Gladstone, William E. *The Impregnable Rock of Holy Scripture.* London: Wm. Isbister Ltd., 1890.

Glanvill, Joseph. *The Vanity of Dogmatizing* (1661). *The Vanity of Dogmatizing: The Three "Versions" by Joseph Glanvill.* With a critical introduction by Stephen Medcalf. Hove, Sussex: Harvester Press, 1970.

Gore, Charles. *Belief in God.* London: John Murray, 1921.

———. *Belief in Christ.* London: John Murray, 1922.

———. *The Holy Spirit and the Church.* New York: Charles Scribner's Sons, 1924.

Hall, Joseph. *Works.* Ed. Josiah Pratt. London: C. Whittingham, 1808.

Hammond, Henry. *A Practical Catechism* (c. 1644). Library of Anglo-Catholic Theology. Vol. 1. 3rd ed. Oxford: John Henry Parker, 1847.

———. *Miscellaneous Theological Works.* Library of Anglo-Catholic Theology. Vol. 2. 3rd ed. Oxford: John Henry Parker, 1849.

Herbert, George. *George Herbert: The Country Parson, The Temple.* Ed. John N. Wall, Jr. Classics of Western Spirituality. New York: Paulist Press, 1981.

Hick, John, ed. *The Myth of God Incarnate.* London: SCM Press, 1977.

Homilies Appointed to be Read in Churches (1547, 1562, 1571). Oxford: Clarendon Press, 1822.

Hooker, Richard. *The Folger Library Edition of the Works of Richard Hooker.* Ed. W. Speed Hill.

    Vol. 1: *Of the Laws of Ecclesiastical Polity. Preface, Books I to IV.* Cambridge, Mass., and London: Belknap Press of the Harvard University Press, 1977.

    Vol. 2: *Of the Laws of Ecclesiastical Polity, Book V.* Cambridge, Mass., and London: Belknap Press of the Harvard University Press, 1977.

    Vol. 3: *Of the Laws of Ecclesiastical Polity, Books VI, VII, VIII.* Cambridge, Mass., and London: Belknap Press of the Harvard University Press, 1981.

    Vol. 4: *Of the Laws of Ecclesiastical Polity, Attack & Response.* Cambridge, Mass., and London: Belknap Press of the Harvard University Press, 1982.

    Vol. 5: *Tractates and Sermons.* Cambridge, Mass., and London: The Belknap Press of the Harvard University Press, 1990.

    Vol. 6, Part 1: *Introductions; Commentary, Preface and Books I–IV.* Binghamton, New York: Medieval & Renaissance Texts & Studies, 1993.

    Vol. 6, Part 2: *Introductions; Commentary, Books V–VIII.* Binghamton, New York: Medieval & Renaissance Texts & Studies, 1993.

Hoskyns, Edwyn, and Noel Davey. *The Riddle of the New Testament*. London: Faber & Faber, 1931.

Laud, William. *Conference with Fisher* (1622/1639). Library of Anglo-Catholic Theology. Oxford: John Henry Parker, 1849.

Locke, John. *An Essay Concerning Human Understanding* (1690). Ed. Roger Woodhouse. London: Penguin Classics, 1997.

———. *The Reasonableness of Christianity as Delivered in the Scriptures* (1695). Clarendon edition. Ed. John C. Higgins-Biddle. Oxford: Clarendon Press, 1999.

Lux Mundi: A Series of Studies in the Religion of the Incarnation. Ed. Charles Gore. London: John Murray, 1889.

Maurice, Frederick Denison. *The Kingdom of Christ* (1838). 4th ed. London: Macmillan and Co., 1891.

———. *The Epistle to the Hebrews*. London: John W. Parker, 1846.

Maurice, Frederick. *The Life of Frederick Denison Maurice, Chiefly Told in His Own Letters*. 2 vols. London: Macmillan and Co., 1884.

The Myth of God Incarnate. See Hick, John, ed.

Newman, John Henry. *Tracts 83 and 85*. Republished in *Discussions and Arguments on Various Subjects*. London: Longmans, Green, and Co., 1911; first published 1872.

———. *An Essay on the Development of Christian Doctrine* (1845). Pelican Classics. Ed. J. M. Cameron. Harmondsworth: Penguin Books, 1974.

Outler, Albert C., ed. *John Wesley*. See Wesley, John.

Paley, William. *The Works of William Paley*. Cambridge: Hilliard and Brown, 1830.

———. *A View of the Evidences of Christianity in Three Parts* (1794). Ed. Robert Potts. Cambridge: Cambridge University Press, 1850.

Patrides, C. A., ed. *The Cambridge Platonists*. See Cambridge Platonists.

Pearson, John. *An Exposition of the Creed* (1659/1683). Ed. E. Burton. Oxford: Oxford University Press, 1833.

Sanday, William. *Inspiration: Eight Lectures on the Early History and Origin of the Doctrine of Biblical Inspiration* (1893). Reprint of the third enlarged edition of 1896. London: Longman, Green, and Co., 1901.

Selwyn, Edward Gordon, ed. *Essays Catholic and Critical*. London: SPCK, 1926.

Soundings: Essays Concerning Christian Understanding. See Vidler, A. R., ed.

Streeter, B. H., ed. *Foundations: A Statement of Christian Belief in Terms of Modern Thought*. London: Macmillan and Co., 1912.

Sykes, S. W., and J. P. Clayton, eds. *Christ, Faith and History*. Cambridge Studies in Christology. Cambridge: Cambridge University Press, 1972.

Tillotson, John, *Works*. Ed. Thomas Birch. London: J. F. Dove, 1820.

Vidler, A. R., ed. *Soundings: Essays Concerning Christian Understanding*. Cambridge: Cambridge University Press, 1963.

Wesley, John. Selections in Albert C. Outler, *John Wesley*. New York: Oxford University Press, 1980 paperback; first published 1964.

The Whole Duty of Man (1658). The edition of The Ancient and Modern Library of Theological Literature. London: Griffith, Farren, Okeden, & Welsh, n.d.

Secondary Works

Ahlstrom, Sydney E. *A Religious History of the American People*. New Haven and London: Yale University Press, 1972.

Avis, Paul. *Anglicanism and the Christian Church: Theological Resources in Historical Perspective*. Minneapolis: Fortress Press, 1989.

Bellah, Robert N., and associates. *Habits of the Heart*. New York: Harper & Row paperback, 1986; first published 1985.

Booty, John E., ed. *The Godly Kingdom of Tudor England: Great Books of the English Reformation*. Wilton, Conn.: Morehouse-Barlow, 1981.

Brown, Raymond E. *An Introduction to the New Testament*. Anchor Bible Reference Library. New York: Doubleday, 1997.

Campbell, Ted A. *John Wesley and Christian Antiquity: Religious Vision and Cultural Change*. Nashville: Kingswood Books, Abingdon Press, 1991.

Carr, E. H. *What Is History?* London: Pelican Books, 1964; first published 1961.

Chadwick, Owen, *The Victorian Church*. 2 vols. London: Adam & Charles Black, 1971 and 1972; first published 1966 and 1970.

Clarke, M. L. *Paley: Evidences for the Man*. London: SPCK, 1947.

Collingwood, R. G. *The Idea of History*. Oxford: Clarendon Press, 1946.

Dawley, Powel Mills. *The Story of the General Theological Seminary*. New York: Oxford University Press, 1969.

Frei, Hans W. *The Eclipse of Biblical Narrative: A Study in Eighteenth and Nineteenth Century Hermeneutics*. New Haven and London: Yale University Press, 1974.

Fuller, Reginald H. "Historical Criticism and the Bible." In *Anglicanism and the Bible,* ed. Frederick H. Borsch. Anglican Studies Series. Wilton, Conn.: Morehouse-Barlow, 1984.

Holmes, Urban T., III. *What Is Anglicanism?* Wilton, Conn.: Morehouse-Barlow, 1982.

Houghton, Walter E. *The Victorian Frame of Mind, 1830–1870*. New Haven and London: Yale University Press, 1957.

Johnson, Luke Timothy. *The Real Jesus: The Misguided Quest for the Historical Jesus and the Truth of the Traditional Gospels*. New York: HarperCollins Paperback, 1997; first published 1996.

Kelsey, David H. *The Uses of Scripture in Recent Theology*. Philadelphia: Fortress Press, 1975.

Ker, Ian. *John Henry Newman: A Biography*. Oxford: Oxford University Press, 1988.

Knowles, David. *The Evolution of Medieval Thought*. New York: Random House Vintage Books, 1962.

MacCulloch, Diarmaid. *Thomas Cranmer: A Life*. New Haven and London: Yale University Press, 1996.

McAdoo, H. R. *The Spirit of Anglicanism: A Survey of Anglican Theological Method in the Seventeenth Century*. London: Adam & Charles Black, 1965.

Nockles, Peter B. *The Oxford Movement in Context: Anglican High Churchmanship 1760–1857*. Cambridge: Cambridge University Press, 1994.

Norris, Richard A. "Doctor Pearson Construes the Apostles' Creed." In *This Sacred History*, ed. D. S. Armentrout. Cambridge, Mass.: Cowley, 1990.

Orr, Robert R. *Reason and Authority: The Thought of William Chillingworth.* Oxford: Clarendon Press, 1967.

Parker, John W. *The Transformation of Anglicanism 1643–1660: With Special Reference to Henry Hammond.* Manchester: Manchester University Press, 1969.

Prichard, Robert W. "The Place of Doctrine in the Episcopal Church." In *Reclaiming Faith: Essays on Orthodoxy in the Episcopal Church and the Baltimore Declaration,* ed. Ephraim Radner and George R. Sumner. Grand Rapids, Mich.: Eerdmans, 1993.

Ramsey, Arthur Michael. *From Gore to Temple: The Development of Anglican Theology between* Lux Mundi *and the Second World War, 1889–1939.* London: Longmans, 1960.

Reardon, Bernard M. G. *From Coleridge to Gore: A Century of Religious Thought in Britain.* London: Longman, 1971.

Redwood, John. *Reason, Ridicule and Religion: The Age of Enlightenment in England, 1660–1752.* Cambridge, Mass.: Harvard University Press, 1971.

Seitz, Christopher R. "Repugnance and the Three-Legged Stool: Modern Uses of Scripture and the Baltimore Declaration." In *Reclaiming Faith: Essays on Orthodoxy in the Episcopal Church and the Baltimore Declaration,* ed. Ephraim Radner and George R. Sumner. Grand Rapids, Mich.: Eerdmans, 1993.

Spurr, John. *The Restoration Church of England 1646–1689.* New Haven and London: Yale University Press, 1991.

Stanley, Arthur P. *The Life of Thomas Arnold, D.D.* London: Hutchinson & Co., 1907; first published 1844.

Sykes, Stephen, and John E. Booty, eds. *The Study of Anglicanism.* London and Philadelphia: SPCK/Fortress Press, 1988.

Tyacke, Nicholas. *Anti-Calvinists: The Rise of English Arminians c. 1590–1640.* Oxford Historical Monograph. Oxford: Clarendon Press paperback, 1990; first published 1987.

Willey, Basil. *The Eighteenth-Century Background.* Harmondsworth: Penguin Books, 1962; first published 1940.

Wolf, William J., and John E. Booty, eds. *The Spirit of Anglicanism.* Wilton, Conn.: Morehouse-Barlow, 1979.

Index

Of Related Interest

Rowan A. Greer
CHRISTIAN HOPE AND CHRISTIAN LIFE
Raids on the Inarticulate

Voted "Book of the Year"
by the Association of Theological Booksellers

Chosen as "Book of the Year" by the Association of Theological Booksellers, this is already one of the most honored works in early church spirituality in the past thirty years. What is the destiny of the human soul in this life and the next? Dare we hope to "see God face to face," or will our vision of God remain forever filtered "through a glass, darkly"? In this remarkable volume, Rowan A. Greer turns to the New Testament, the church fathers, and later writers to throw light on their own visions of the human soul.

He suggests that Augustine of Hippo and Gregory of Nyssa represent two distinct strands of Christian thinking that find expression later in writers such as John Donne and Jeremy Taylor. Greer, who has trained two generations of historians and theologians in the rich thought of the early church, has succeeded in writing a volume that is both full of original scholarly insight and, by virtue of his elegant writing, accessible to laypeople and non-specialists.

0-8245-1916-7, $24.95 paperback

Check your local bookstore for availability.
To order directly from the publisher,
please call 1-800-707-0670 for Customer Service
or visit our website at *www.cpcbooks.com*.
For catalog orders, please send your request to the address below.

THE CROSSROAD PUBLISHING COMPANY
16 Penn Plaza, Suite 1550
New York, NY 10001

All prices subject to change.

crossroad

About the Author

Herder & Herder is honored to present our second book from the Rev. Dr. Rowan A. Greer, Professor Emeritus of Yale University Divinity School. Dr. Greer, who has trained three generations of historical theologians and early church scholars, is the recipient of the Association of Theological Booksellers' Book of the Year Award for *Christian Hope and Christian Life,* also from Herder & Herder. An authority in Anglican history and patristic readings of scripture, Dr. Greer is also the author of *Broken Lights and Mended Lives* and (with James Kugel) *Early Biblical Interpretation.* He is currently working on other major works in early Christian mysticism and theology, including the works of Evagrius Ponticus.